Modern Girls on the Go

Modern Girls on the Go

GENDER, MOBILITY, AND LABOR IN JAPAN

Edited by Alisa Freedman,
Laura Miller,
and Christine R. Yano

Stanford University Press
Stanford, California

Stanford University Press
Stanford, California

Printed in the United States of America on acid-free, archival-quality paper

Library of Congress Cataloging-in-Publication Data

Modern girls on the go : gender, mobility, and labor in Japan / edited by Alisa Freedman, Laura Miller, and Christine R. Yano.
    pages cm
  Includes bibliographical references and index.
    ISBN 978-0-8047-8113-8 (cloth : alk. paper) — ISBN 978-0-8047-8114-5 (pbk. : alk. paper)
  1. Women—Employment—Japan—History—20th century. 2. Women—Employment—Japan—History—21st century. 3. Social mobility—Japan—History—20th century. 4. Social mobility—Japan—History—21st century. 5. Sex role—Japan—History—20th century. 6. Sex role—Japan—History—21st century. 7. Japan—Social conditions—20th century. 8. Japan—Social conditions—21st century. I. Freedman, Alisa, editor of compilation. II. Miller, Laura, 1953- editor of compilation. III. Yano, Christine Reiko, editor of compilation.
  HD6197.M596 2013
  331.40952—dc23
                        2012039001

ISBN 978-0-8047-8554-9 (electronic)

Typeset by Bruce Lundquist in 10/14 Minion Pro

In memory of Yoko McClain (1924–2011)

Contents

Figures

MODERN GIRLS
IN A GLOBAL WORLD

Carol A. Stabile

She's picked for her beauty from many a belle,
And placed near the window, Havanas to sell
For well her employer's aware that her face is
An advertisement certain to empty his cases.
                    —Daniel Stashower, 2006

In 1841, storeowner John Anderson hired pretty young Mary Cecilia Rogers, who had recently arrived in New York City with her widowed mother, to play the role of "butter-fly catcher" in his tobacco shop at 319 Broadway. Although the practice of using young girls to sell products to men had become more commonplace in Europe, in New York City, hiring a young woman to sell cigars in a public shop was unusual, to say the least. When Rogers's body was found in Hoboken, New Jersey, in 1842, at a popular tourist destination ironically known as Elysian Fields, her transgression of the boundaries of what was then deemed appropriate female behavior was taken by the city's mass circulation dailies to have directly caused her unfortunate demise.

During a period in which internal migrations from agricultural regions to cities and incipient processes of industrialization were causing massive social and cultural changes, girls like Mary Rogers became cautionary tales about the dangers of modernity—canaries in the coal mines of these economic, cultural, and political shifts. As vehicles for moral panics about normative gender roles, these modern girls were represented through a narrow lens that viewed their presence as workers and avid consumers of new forms of leisure and entertainment as dangerous symptoms of the ills associated with wide-scale cultural change. Critics of such changes represented young women as incipient or actual victims deprived of agency and entirely at the mercy of industrialization, patriarchy, consumerism, or capitalism.

But as the chapters in *Modern Girls on the Go* demonstrate, to focus on victimhood is to understand one part of the picture, and a part that dovetails far too neatly with broader sexist understandings of girls' and young women's lives and cultures. In these pages, the contributors are attentive to the narrow interpretive frameworks through which girls' lives and cultures have been historically understood, either as the debased and devalued consumers of mass culture or as the victims of a system over which they had no control. One central strength of *Modern Girls on the Go* lies in its authors' analyses of modern girls' labor, lives, and loves within contexts richly attentive to agency. The girls and women who populate this book are subjects in motion, girls and women attempting to take advantage of the cracks and fissures modernity created in dominant narratives of gender norms and not simply powerless pawns taken advantage of by systems beyond their control. Here we delve into the experiences of "shop girls" who moved out of homes and into public spaces, and others who traveled much farther, as young Japanese women who came to the United States to pursue educational opportunities in the years before World War II. In their own ways, each of these experiences offered both opportunities and new constraints for working women. Throughout, this book consistently draws our attention to the complexities of lives lived on the move in transformative times.

The "new woman" discourses associated with modernity figure girls themselves as standing outside of history and historical processes. As repositories for anxieties about modernity, girls are treated as figures without a history—synchronous entities thrown up by a contemporary moment. Much writing on "girl culture" in the United States at the turn of the twenty-first century thus abstracts girl culture and related terms like "girl power," constituting them as entirely new, modern, and historically unprecedented. *Modern Girls on the Go* resists this impulse and offers an important historical corrective. The contributors to this volume insist on the necessary historicity of the girls that are the subject of their essays, recognizing the presence of "premodern" girls, as well as the historical and economic contexts that gave birth to the girls of modernity. The dancehall girls profiled here, who belong to 1920s and 1930s Japanese culture, are manifestations themselves of the transnational circuits of culture that brought dancehalls—and the conditions of possibility for dancehall girls— from cities in the United States and Europe to Japan and Shanghai.

Modern Girls on the Go also reminds readers of the historical and cultural contingency of what we consider to be "modern," underscoring the processual, uneven, and incomplete nature of modernity and modernization. Rather than understanding the modernity of these women in motion as a periodizing concept, the volume helps us see how resistant patriarchal structures are to change and how modernity itself needs to be understood as an expansive, long-term global project. Elevator girls may have been going up, but their movement was historically constrained within a framework that sought to eroticize and domesticate their movements. Similarly, bus girls have performed the emotional labor of facilitating the movements of other travelers. Even now, the caring role of their predecessors, the commuter bus conductors whose job of taking tickets and ensuring safety on the bus no longer exists, lingers in the tape-recorded female voices used by bus companies. Modern girls like these—and Mary Rogers for that matter—do not fit into a neat historical schema—their presence and representations illustrate that the public/private divide conjured into existence by industrialization continues to exercise a narrative hold over how gendered lives in dynamic contexts get represented.

Modern Girls on the Go also insists on the importance of culture and context. Changes in modes of economic and cultural production may engender a familiar set of overarching narratives about gender and social change, but the very flexibility and dynamism of these processes means that they must be highly adaptive. When secretary Xi Shangzhen hanged herself in her workplace in Shanghai in 1912, for instance, her death became the vehicle for exploring what historian Bryna Goodman describes as "the fragile and contradictory nature of Shanghai's new economic formations, new cultural aspirations to gender equality, and political aspirations for popular democratic governance, a dynamic public sphere, and legal sovereignty" (Goodman 2011). However consistent narratives about girls' and women's lives in new cities and new economic formations may seem, these narratives need to be understood within their specific historical and cultural contexts. Like Mary Rogers, Xi Shangzhen symbolized the fears and hopes that accrued to social, cultural, and economic changes, but she did so in a context that shaped her life along different lines—a context that also imbued her story with dramatically different cultural meanings.

Girls and young women remain the favored laboring subjects of rapidly industrializing economies, as Leslie T. Chang points out in *Factory Girls: From Village to City in a Changing China* (2008). Studies that enhance our understanding of the similarities and differences in how they are represented, disciplined, and utilized as conductors of meaning across still ongoing processes of "modernization" make invaluable contributions to feminist scholarship in an international frame. *Modern Girls on the Go* importantly helps to internationalize our understanding of girls and girl culture, bringing perspectives and analyses overlooked by Anglophone studies of girls and girl culture that focus mainly on Britain or the United States.

As a feminist scholar who is keenly aware of the limits of her own U.S.-centric perspective, I was helped by this volume to think about girls and girl culture broadly construed in unanticipated and often surprising ways. In their own ways, each chapter in this volume reminds us that we have not escaped the strictures of the modern with which this volume critically engages. *Modern Girls on the Go* takes an interdisciplinary approach to its subjects, with contributions from scholars in anthropology, history, literature, and visual studies. Perhaps more than anything else, this book whets our appetites for accounts of girls in motion throughout the twentieth century and for similarly rich comparative accounts of how these girls marched—and continue to march—across the twenty-first century.

Modern Girls on the Go

Chapter One

YOU GO, GIRL!

Cultural Meanings of Gender, Mobility, and Labor

Alisa Freedman, Laura Miller,
and Christine R. Yano

This volume investigates the lived experiences and cultural depictions of women who worked in service industries and other jobs that were inspired by ideas of mobility in twentieth- and twenty-first-century Japan. Dignified uniformed women operating elevators and rhythmically announcing floors represented the height of luxury in twentieth-century department stores but were scorned in the global media as symbols of a regimented society. Especially in the 1920s, young women coveted employment as department store clerks, an occupation they perceived as a step toward self-cultivation. Artists and writers, both before and immediately after World War II, objectified women paid to dance with men in dancehalls as tantalizing aspects of foreign allure in the Japanese city, while providing glimpses of their real physical and emotional exhaustion. During the Jet Age, stewardesses on Pan American World Airways were paragons of glamour and the public face of Japanese economic and technological progress. Beauty queens competing in international pageants embodied new possibilities for women in the postwar era. Students and educators led the way toward cosmopolitanism as some of the first Japanese people to travel to the United States during two pivotal historical moments: the years of modernization following the 1868 Meiji Restoration and the years of recovery after the war. Female soldiers have changed the composition and image of the Japanese Self-Defense Forces, while female soccer players have promoted women's roles in competitive sports and corporate culture. Ladies League soccer in the 1990s paved the way for the victory of the national team, Nadeshiko Japan, in the 2011

World Cup Finals, an event touted by the mass media as the most hopeful in a year marred by the triple disaster of the March 11 Great East Japan Earthquake, tsunami, and nuclear meltdown. Tour and charter buses are still staffed with female guides, who turn an ordinary ride into a memorable event.

All of these modern working women, often conspicuous in their various uniforms, have influenced social roles, patterns of daily life, and Japan's global image. Some have led lives that were ordinary and routine; others enjoyed rare privileges. What binds them together as the focus of this volume are the ways in which their lives, and the modernity they circumscribe, have been defined by their mobility, both literally and figuratively.

These women have labored in new places, which they have made more inviting by their presence and have used their jobs as means to move into spaces once exclusive to men. Not only have they occupied urban spaces, but they have also defined them, both enacting the cosmopolitanism of their moment and serving as a domesticating salve. They have been featured in photographs, artworks, and stories about the growth of Japan. They have performed jobs that were considered fashionable at their inception and thereby represented ideas of modernity at different historical times. Their presence has been taken for granted by Japanese consumers: if these women were not seen working, many people would feel that something was amiss.

Crossing the traditional borders between anthropology, history, literature, and visual studies, *Modern Girls on the Go* tells the stories of these women who have affected how Japanese history has been experienced and is remembered. We discuss aspects of modern women's labor that are rarely analyzed, including hiring and recruitment, training, job performance, manners, uniforms, interpersonal communication, and physical motion. Our chapters question what employment outside the home has meant to women and how women, in turn, have changed the look and meaning of "work."

We profile these employees and use them as a framework for viewing general opinions about women in the workplace and family and to bring to light unexpected ways women have supported, even challenged, the corporate structures underpinning the Japanese economy, currently the third largest in the world. Our chapters highlight how work has been a major factor in shaping women's attitudes toward marriage, childrearing, sexuality, and self-improvement. By exploring how female laborers have been conceptualized simultaneously as model employees, erotic icons, and domesticating presences, our research exposes contradictions inherent for women in the workforce.

In fictional accounts and often in reality, working women have been young and unmarried, raised in the countryside but seeking employment in the city. Their accounts disclose differences between values associated with Tokyo and the rest of the nation. The symbolic meanings ascribed to women's laboring bodies provide insight into the relationship between gender, technology, and modernity and how mobility has been associated with sexuality in the popular imagination. Although some jobs have been phased out by technological advances or economic recessions, the employees who held them opened doors, some literally, for women in Japan today. This volume demonstrates how seemingly ordinary workers may be reconfigured as pioneers of modernity. *Modern Girls on the Go* details the symbolic places working women have led themselves and others to go. We do not attempt here to catalogue all the

Figure 1 Service in Japanese department stores. *Jiji manga* (Comic Times) no. 402, May 26, 1929, page 7. Photo courtesy of Laura Miller; photo taken at the Billy Ireland Cartoon Library and Museum, Ohio State University.

places where they have gone. Rather, by selecting a representative sampling of jobs, experiences, historical time frames, and class positions, we take gender (particularly, the image of young adulthood) as a guiding frame that binds our discussion of the constitutive ties of modernity, mobility, and labor in Japan.

The Mobile Modern Girl

Many of the jobs we analyze were created in the 1920s and 1930s, a time of unprecedented change in Japan, the effects of which are still felt today. Tokyo, more than other cities, became a construct through which to view the advances and contradictions of national modernization characterized by both capitalist growth and control of the police state. Rebuilt after the 1923 Great Kantō Earthquake into a modern metropolis, Tokyo was filled with mass transportation, new architecture, and crowds at work and play in bustling business and entertainment districts. The urban labor force grew, and new middle classes arose. Yet economic recessions were a source of social instability, and numbers of the unemployed and the homeless increased.

Women, who could be paid less than men and were believed to be better mannered and more subservient, replaced male employees in several service sector jobs. Their hire followed the expansion of employment opportunities for women in Europe and the United States and was similarly the object of both critical analysis and media curiosity.[1] Tokyo versions of American and European jobs, such as bus guide and elevator girl, spread to other parts of Asia. Women also staffed new urban entertainments where men and women mixed, including dancehalls and department stores. These workers were associated with the erotic allure of the modern metropolis, while their lives were usually far less glamorous than their images. As explained particularly in the first part of this volume, some social critics saw the women in these sites as symbolizing the threats urban culture posed to the patriarchal family, which was promoted as the backbone of the nation, especially as Japan mobilized toward war.

In the interwar period, urban modernity was experienced through the circulation of images, such as photographs in magazines, movies, and department store windows, rather than through the purchase of goods. The Japanese publishing industry flourished, though subject to strict censorship, and a variety of magazines became available for a diverse readership (see, e.g., Frederick 2006). Authors and journalists shared a prevalent desire to document and classify the material culture of daily life (see, e.g., Silverberg 2007). As we discuss in the chapters, media accounts of female workers convey the promises and failures of consumer capitalism and paradoxes underlying new gender roles. In the 1920s, social critics coined words to describe the social advances and contradictions that were visually apparent in Tokyo and to make sense of rapid historical change. For example, "*modan*," from the English "modern," was used playfully and pejoratively to denote a kind of modernity characterized by spectacles of newness and consumption.

The "modern girl" (*modan gāru*, abbreviated as *moga*) is the media figure that best represents this complex time and is the category in which women employed in new urban jobs were often placed. The neologism "modern girl" might have been used first by journalist Nii Itaru in an article published in the April 1923 issue of the highbrow journal *Central Review* (*Chūō kōron*) discussing the "Contours of the Modern Girl" (*Modan gāru no rinkaku*) (Silverberg 1991b: 241). The term has also been attributed to social critic Kitazawa Shūichi's essay titled "Modern Girl" (*Modan gāru*) in the August 1924 issue of the magazine *Woman* (*Josei*) (Silverberg 1991b: 240; Sato 2003: 57; Yonekawa 1998: 14).

Especially from the second half of the 1920s, the word "*gāru*," a loanword based on the English "girl," was included in the titles of several fashionable jobs, particularly those with Western-style uniforms, and in nicknames associated with receiving money (Yonekawa 1998: 22, 38–39). "Marx girls" (*Marukusu gāru*) and "Engels girls" (*Engerusu gāru*) were criticized for their radical fashions and politics. "Stick girls" (*sutekki gāru*) and "steak girls" (*sutēki gāru*), perhaps more imagined than real, were paid the price of a beefsteak to be fashionable accessories to men as they strolled Tokyo's entertainment districts (Onoda 2004: 79–80). "Kiss girls" (*kissu gāru*) allegedly exchanged kisses for a modest fee (Nakayama 1995). "One-star girls" (*wan sutā gāru*) played bit parts in films.

Although plastic mannequin dolls had been produced in Japan since 1925, the Takashimaya department store employed two movie actresses, Sakai Yoneko and Tsukiji Ryōko, to stand silently and model fashions in their show window in 1928, launching the job of "mannequin girl" (*manekin gāru*). Their less alluring male counterparts were sandwich men and advertising clowns. Women assisted cab drivers as "one-yen taxi girls" (*entaku gāru*). Three women were chosen from 141 applicants to be Japan's first "air girls" (*ea gāru*) and began work as attendants on an April 1, 1931, flight operated by the Tokyo Air Transport Company (Tōkyō kōkū yusōsha), one year after "sky girls" were first employed in the United States on a commercial flight between Chicago and San Francisco (Inagaki and Yoshizawa 1985: 30). The "air girls" resigned on

April 29 because of working conditions and salaries. All of these workers did new things in spaces that were new in Japan. They were seen as simultaneously attractive and dangerous because they flaunted a new agency premised on consumer culture.

Images of the modern girl at work and play filled Japanese journalism, literature, and film in the late 1920s and early 1930s. The modern girl was understood by postwar scholars, including Miriam Silverberg, to be a media construct that represented anxiety that Westernization and consumer capitalism had advanced too far in Japan. According to Silverberg (2007: 148), the modern girl "existed largely as a phantasm of the anxiety-ridden critics who clung to a seemingly established order during a period of rapid transition." The modern girl was represented by her striking physical appearance—sporting short hair and wearing either Western fashions or Japanese kimono with the *obi* sash tied high to emphasize her hips and make her legs look longer—and her perceived licentious behavior. As observed by members of the scholarly collective Modern Girls around the World (2008a: 9), which has been devoted to studying gender in the global interwar context, the modern girl projects "an up-to-date and youthful femininity, provocative and unseemly in its intimacy with foreign aesthetic and commodity influences."

Yet the modern girl, in Japan and elsewhere, was not merely a passive consumer of goods; she was also an active producer of customs. Among the many traits assigned to the modern girl, her overdetermined physical mobility, seeming autonomy from the family system, and extended sexuality most vividly illustrated her subjectivity in and subjection to this moment of rupture with the past. This notion of the modern girl was predicated on the urban act of seeing and the appearance of more young women in public places, developments made possible by increased educational and employment opportunities and mass transportation. Arguably, the few favorable and mostly derogatory assessments of the modern girl involved her ability to leave home to go to work. While many scholars have analyzed images of the leisurely modern girl, few have acknowledged the iconography of her labor.

Interwar modern girls were often shown in motion. Especially from the mid-1920s, female legs, standing or walking, symbolized a new kind of urban woman. The cover illustration of Maeda Hajime's 1929 *Story of Working Women* (*Shokugyō fujin monogatari*), a study of more than twelve progressive new jobs and problems in marriage that these employees faced, contrasts a uniformed female bus conductor (often called a "bus girl," *basu gāru*) and a passenger clothed in ornate kimono, looking as if she could be either going to work or shopping. In 1931, ethnographer Kon Wajirō (1888–1973) and his "Modernology" (kōgengaku) associates, whose work is cited in several of the following chapters, carefully diagrammed the legs of bus conductors and other working women as they walked or rode about Tokyo and sketched their sock wrinkles to see patterns of both social and physical mobility.[2] They mapped the patterns dancehall girls etched on the dance floors during their working hours (Kon and Yoshida 1931: 35–55).

Especially between 1929 and 1931, the height of modernist artistic movements depicting Tokyo life, photographic montages of women walking and getting in and out of buses and taxicabs were published in magazines to convey the rhythms and tempo of the city. These images were often given musical titles, such as the many "Symphonies of Ginza Women" (Ginza nyonin kōkyōkyoku) included in the Shiseidō geppō (Shiseidō Monthly), the publicity periodical for Shiseidō. Some of the women pictured in this periodical might have been "Shiseidō girls" (Shiseidō gāru), models who traveled around Japan to give demonstrations of new beauty techniques. In literature ranging from Natsume Sōseki's late Meiji novels like Sanshirō (1908) to Tanizaki Jun'ichirō's 1925 Naomi (Chijin no ai), a fictional character's ability to traverse the city showed his or her level of acclimation to modern practices.

We adopt the mobile modern girl as a heuristic device to show how she has been visibly present in other time periods and places. Aware that the modern girl moniker began life as a historically tethered reference, we appropriate the idea, not only for its potency, but because we wish to semantically extend its meaning and thus provide new ways of understanding the significance of women's labor. The concept of the modern girl offers the possibility of seeing in working women of many eras and locations the qualities that first led to the creation of the term. We argue that women in Japan after the 1930s have often been viewed through her image. We show that women continue to be associated with spectacles of modernity premised on the possibilities of mobility, consumption, and technological advancement. In addition, we give examples of modern girls incarnate to underscore how images of female employees often differ from their real material and social conditions and the discrimination they face on the job.

Whether they have realized it or not, stewardesses, soldiers, athletes, beauty queens, educators, and the other women we profile not only exemplify larger economic, political, intellectual, and social forces, but also have actively changed the notion of work in Japan. We recognize the importance of examining how historical terms originated and do so in our above discussion on Silverberg and the modern girl. At the same time, we view the extension of academic concepts to other domains as a productive method for stimulating new lines of research and understanding. Recognizing genealogies while extending concepts to new realms is one of our primary goals with this volume.

Another theme here is the language used by and for women to describe their jobs. Modern girl is a prime example of the Japanese historical custom of labeling women who mark a break in preconceived notions of gender, thereby making their lifestyles easier to comprehend and less threatening and turning them into symbols of social progress and problems. Jan Bardsley (2000) explores early postwar concerns about potential ruptures in gender politics in her analysis of the new types of working women who were debated in the pages of the magazine *Fujin kōron* (Women's Review). One of these new workers was the 1950s "salary girl" (*saraii gyaru*), a type described as desiring independence through work and leisure. Many denigrating labels were created in subsequent decades. For example, women who take too long for their lunch breaks, who wear sexualized clothing to the office, and who use a baby-talk register when speaking to male coworkers have all been labeled in negative ways (Miller 1998, 2004). A twenty-first-century example is "*arafō*," short for "around forty," voted the top media buzzword of 2008 in the U-Can survey (Jiyū kokuminsha 2008).[3] *Arafō* is one of a series of value-laden terms used to designate women around age forty who theoretically have more choices in family and employment than earlier generations; the word has been applied most often to single members of this demographic who have prioritized careers over marriage and are thus believed to shoulder the blame for Japan's falling fertility rate (See Freedman and Iwata-Weickgenannt 2011).

We are not suggesting that women were static until the twentieth century.[4] Instead, the extent and nature of women's mobility, its cultural definitions and critical assessments, and the way it has been publicized have changed. It is important to acknowledge the existence of "pre-modern girls on the go," who lie outside the scope of this volume. Throughout history, women have held jobs requiring travel, near and far; their occupations range from priestesses, wives of *daimyō* (feudal lords), and their ladies-in-waiting to teashop girls, midwives, and various kinds of itinerant dancers, musicians, and storytellers. As is evident from travel diaries and poetry, pilgrimages, although rare and difficult, were life-changing events for medieval women (see, e.g., Laffin 2007). Edo Period

(1600–1868) kabuki, *bunraku* puppet plays, and other popular entertainments included travel scenes (*michiyuki*). Elite female students (*jogakusei*) became a prevalent topic of literature and art from the first decade of the twentieth century, in part because they were seen commuting by rickshaw, bicycle, and train (Czarnecki 2005; Freedman 2010).

Among the factors that make our workers more modernly mobile is the presence of new public spaces and these women's ability to traverse them. These conditions create increased opportunities that make it possible, even desirable, for any woman to be employed outside the home. As our chapters explain, the notion of home itself changed as a result. In addition, the 1920s modern girl was propagated by developments in journalism. A subtheme of this volume is the role of modern media—daily newspapers, monthly magazines, advertisements, photographs, comic strips, cinema, television, websites, music videos, and more—in promoting and sometimes belittling working women. Media created and spread the word and look of these modern girls, images that then took on lives of their own. Here were dream girls as aspirational figures, made vivid by their publicized connections to new things, practices, and places. Thus the lived experiences and historical placement of these women can only be understood in juxtaposition to the mediatized images that framed them.

Aspects of Modern Girls' Labor
The notion of mobility, like the new practices it represents, is fraught with contradictions. This is especially true for women who work in jobs premised on movement. As geographer Tim Cresswell (2006: 1–2) indicates, mobility is linked to concepts of progress, freedom, opportunity, and modernity, as well as deviance, resistance, and shiftlessness—all traits ascribed to the modern girl. Both the celebratory and critical aspects of the modern girl's multiple and overlapping forms of mobility inform our research.

The workers we examine have been on the move physically, geographically, culturally, and metaphorically. They have taken occupations once reserved for men. They have moved out of the domestic space of the home and into the public sphere, a decision made sometimes at the disapproval of parents. Their desires for social mobility and self-improvement, in addition to their economic necessity, have influenced their job choices. In the workplace, women could, theoretically, advance within hierarchies through training and in turn be paid higher wages. Especially after passage of the 1985 Equal Employment Opportunity Law (Danjo kōyō kikai kintō-hō) and subsequent supporting legislation in the

1980s and 1990s, women have made inroads into jobs that require longer work-ing hours. They have established camaraderie and formed lateral bonds with coworkers and teammates. They have traveled both within Japan and abroad, experiences that have helped them to redefine their roles as wives and mothers. The movement into Japan of jobs created in Europe and the United States and the export of the Japanese versions to other parts of Asia reveal much about the political flows of culture and power. In addition, female workers ease the public's transition; they are a comforting presence in unfamiliar places, acting as an ex-tension of the home to the bus, department store, airplane, and tourist destina-tions. Women in service industries become, in a way, mother-daughter-sisters but with the professionalism that their uniforms signify.

Especially since the 1920s, women have operated and worked in vehicles in motion. We explore the different ways female employees both eroticize and domesticate technologies, making machines seem more attractive while easing their adoption into daily life. This is apparent in the second part of the volume, which analyzes transport workers. These women serve as human links between vehicles and the people who ride in them. In 1920s advertisements and art, mod-ern girls were positioned in automobiles, buses, ships, and other vehicles, asso-ciating women with desires for speed, luxury, and travel. Japanese beauty queens were the first floor models for Toyota at the Detroit auto shows of the 1950s. (In many cultures, ships and other large vehicles are named for women.) Recruit-ment posters for the Self-Defense Forces allude to the prevalence of female sol-diers bearing weapons in video games and other forms of popular culture.

Women's affective labor in this respect and others is perhaps analogous to the circulation of cute (and cutely named) characters in Japan to soften stern messages, such as Prince Pickles, the mascot of the Japanese Self-Defense Forces, and Peopo, the gender-ambiguous superhero of the Tokyo Metropolitan Police (Freedman 2011: 221). (The name "Peopo" comes from the first syllables of "People" and "Police.") Similar to how use of cute animal characters involves a degree of displacement that renders potentially dangerous topics safe (Miller 2010), having women and images of women performing work that might other-wise be unsettling suggests safety, as well as a lack of manipulation.

The 2009 appointment of three young women to serve as Japan's "Ambas-sadors of Cute" (*kawaii taishi*) is an example of the use of women to promote popular culture and to present a gentler image of Japan overseas (Miller 2011b). The selected Ambassadors of Cute wore the uniforms of three subcultures that have come to characterize Japanese youth culture in the global imagination:

the schoolgirl, the Lolita, and the Harajuku fashion queen. Although all three women had other forms of employment, these uniforms remade them into icons of an endearing and nonthreatening Japan. Kimura Yu, a singer, was promoted as the representative of "Harajuku deko cool." Aoki Misako, a nurse and part-time model, wore the frilly Sweet Lolita ensembles; and Fujioka Shizuka, a clothing coordinator for a school-uniform store, sported the sailor suit uniform of a much younger schoolgirl (Kaminishikawara 2009; Miller 2011b). These women's coded ensembles were a visual contrast to the dark-suited consular men who accompanied them during their world tour. The Ambassadors of Cute are a dramatic example of how concepts of "girlhood" influence public opinions about working women, another theme of this volume.

Like the interwar modern girl and the Ambassadors of Cute, the workers we study have all been highly visible in public spaces; most are instantly recognizable by their uniforms. The act of watching women at work has helped construct the gendered gaze that shapes and is shaped by Japanese social norms and the ways men and women have been depicted in literature and visual culture. Following gendered constructions of visuality and embedded eroticism, women as decorative objects have become an assumption of modern public space, from offices to department stores to airplane cabins. Beauty queens, athletes, and tour bus guides are, by nature of their occupations, the focal points of spectator attention. Often selling points of the job, uniforms make workers instantly recognizable, show they are doing serious labor, reflect feelings of pride and belonging, serve as signboards for companies, and promote workplaces as stylish sites.

Female students and service workers were the first women in Japan to wear Western-style clothing on a regular basis. In the prewar era, Western clothing for women's daily use received media attention, as was evident in the buzz about the "*appappa*," a loose-fitting, simple summer dress that was first marketed in Osaka for one yen in 1923 (Asahi Shinbunsha 2000: 30).[5] The sailor uniform that has come to represent Japanese schoolgirls was increasingly worn after 1925. In the 1920s, when dresses, jackets, and pants were a rare sight in Japan, bus guides, department store clerks, elevator girls, and other urban service workers looked the height of Western fashion.

Uniforms promote mobility and safety on the job, as they do for soldiers, factory laborers, and athletes. Uniforms in Japan are symbols of professionalism that imply discipline, training, standardization, and service (McVeigh 2000). Wearing special clothing helps women workers to compartmentalize work, home, and play. As described in almost every case study in this volume, uniforms mark women's positions in the highly gendered organizational hierarchy of corporations, the military, and other institutions. The beauty queen's somatic uniform of a swimsuit and tiara, an impractical combination, turns her into a living mannequin. Women working as teachers are expected to dress in ways that code their superiority over their students. At the same time, the erasure of individuality through wearing uniforms also speaks to the fungibility of workers under capitalism. The fantasy of stripping women of their uniforms is the subject of pornography. It is important to note that uniforms, once they go out of date, often become objects that represent a longing for the past. The women who wore uniforms thus have been viewed, often simultaneously, as modern girls and as figures of nostalgia.

Lessons Learned from Modern Girls
The media image of the interwar modern girl has been an object of passing reference in Japanese history and an object of art exhibits, including *Modern Boy, Modern Girl: Modernity in Japanese Art, 1910–1935* (1998, in Kamakura and Sydney) and *Taisho Chic: Japanese Modernity, Nostalgia, and Deco* (Honolulu in 2002, Berkeley in 2005, and other places worldwide). Yet the real women classified under this name have rarely been taken seriously as initiating and symbolizing changes in discourse about gender, labor, and modernity.

Prior studies by two scholars have opened up this research domain: Miriam Silverberg's writing on the café waitress (in *Erotic Grotesque Nonsense: The Mass Culture of Japanese Modern Times*) and Barbara Sato's analysis of interwar working women (in *The New Japanese Woman: Modernity, Media, and Women in Interwar Japan*). Both Silverberg and Sato have been influential in explaining how issues of gender and class structure Japanese modernity, a theme of this volume. Silverberg's 1991 article the "Modern Girl as Militant" inspired such international scholarship as the 2008 edited volume *The Modern Girl around the World: Consumption, Modernity, and Globalization* by the Modern Girl Around the World Research Group, which analyzes how images and ideas of the modern girl in diverse countries were used in the 1920s and 1930s to shore up or critique nationalist and imperial agendas. The 2010 Japanese collection *Modern Girls and Colonial Modernity: Empire, Capital, and Gender in East Asia* (*Modan gāru to shokuminchiteki kindai—higashiajia ni okeru teikoku shihon jendā*), edited by Itō Ruri, Sakamoto Hiroko, and Tani Barlow, further investigates these issues.

This volume is the first to examine representations and realities of modern girls in Japan in depth across disciplinary boundaries and spanning several decades. By presenting a spectrum of cases across time and social classes, we illustrate the critical role of women in the formation of Japanese modernity and its gendered representation. We strive to recapture a piece of forgotten Japanese women's history by showing the cultural and economic significance of service jobs often deemed mindless and minor.

Our work engages in dialogue with and builds on studies of women and employment in Japan, on research published on early postwar Japan, and on accounts of Japanese service industries. The pioneering *Recreating Japanese Women, 1600–1945* (Bernstein 1991) introduced us to women working as factory labor, agricultural workers, sake brewers, and artists. Continuing where that volume ends, *Re-Imaging Japanese Women* (Imamura 1996) analyzes women from the postwar to the 1990s who worked as bar hostesses, legislators, and department store shop girls. Another notable collection, *Japanese Women Working* (Hunter 1993) provides detailed material on the lives and working conditions of female domestic servants, textile factory workers, pieceworkers, hospital care assistants, and coal miners. Among some of the many outstanding monographs on women's working lives and conditions are studies of Meiji-era textile mill workers (Tsurumi 1992), pre-war textile mill workers (Hunter 2003; Faison 2007), and authors (Copeland; Melek 2006). Contemporary ethnographies of women workers in diverse occupations include confectionary workers (Kondo 1990), bar hostesses (Allison 1994), Office Ladies (Ogasawara 1998), and blue-collar workers (Roberts 1994).

Female service workers have been the topic of nonfiction for a diverse readership in Japan. For example, a few of the chapters here draw on a series of at least seven glossy paperback books released by Media Factory, a small publishing company headquartered in Tokyo.[6] Each book, full of photographs, profiles a different female service worker who wears a uniform, including elevator girls, tour bus guides, and *shinkansen* bullet train pursers. The first book in the series, *Shinkansen Girl* (*Shinkansen gāru*, 2007) was inspired by an August 2006 installment of a popular *Asahi* newspaper column in which readers discuss something they have achieved. Tokubuchi Mariko (2007) describes how she became the top-ranked purser on the Tōkaidō shinkansen for sales of food and drink after only one year and four months on the job. None of the Media Factory series books has been a bestseller, but *Shinkansen Girl* went through nine printings and was made into a television drama special that aired on July 4, 2007. The

Media Factory books explain in detail the training to acquire the level of politeness expected from service laborers and appearance as representatives of the company and thereby of Japan. The premise of the series is that female workers' pride gives their lives meaning, and its purpose is to provide behind-the-scenes glimpses of jobs most people in Japan have taken for granted.

Attention to the complex intertwining of modernity, gender, mobility, and labor is what distinguishes *Modern Girls on the Go*. We adopt academic approaches ranging from labor historiography to autobiography and survey an array of sources—journalism, literature, film, television, advertising and propaganda, sports programs, beauty pageant footage, university and corporate histories, government surveys, popular songs, video games, toys, and more— to ask how women's working lives and their public perceptions have changed through different phases of Japan's modernization. What has not changed in the lives, depictions, and debates about women workers over the past two centuries is as illuminating as what has.

The case studies in this volume, thematically arranged in four parts, provide answers to questions about the cultural, economic, and political impact of the circulation of images of women working in new occupations and about what the lives of these women were like. Part I, "New Female Occupations," explores the lives and experiences of women whose work in new places, such as department stores and dancehalls, defined the cityscape of modern Japan. These new "pink-collar jobs" of the service industry positioned women as intermediaries—between home and the consumer realm, newer and older ways of doing things, upper-middle and lower-middle classes, and men and women. The public looked upon these modern girls favorably as founts of knowledge because they comported themselves in new settings with professionally trained ease; at the same time, the public viewed with askance the degree to which women could inhabit such public spaces. The shop girl, elevator girl, and dancehall girl all helped usher in new forms of consumer culture in twentieth-century urban Japan.

Part II, "Models and Modes of Transportation," ties women directly to technology, examining ways in which the female presence in some of the newest modes of transportation provided important social bridges. Women were a domesticating presence, quelling fears and soothing anxieties. They did so by their very professionalism, with explicit training in both efficiency and graciousness, as exemplified by the hostess. By extending notions of "home" to technological spaces of transportation, the gendered labor of these women helped reconfigure Japanese public notions of themselves as people on the go.

Part III, "Modern Girls Overturn Gender and Class," presents two case studies of women whose movement into jobs once held only by men enabled them to pursue life courses different from that which promoted marriage and motherhood as women's main goals. This section positions women in unlikely places—the "military" setting of Japan's Self-Defense Forces and Ladies League Soccer. These case studies inspire us to analyze the highly specific codes of gender, made all the more prominent when they are overturned. Female soldiers and athletes challenge us to reconsider women's bodies in motion, not only in admiration of what they can do but also for the possibilities they raise.

In Part IV we offer evidence of Japanese women's achievements beyond the homeland. "Modern Girls Go Overseas" situates beauty queens and scholars as women who have gone beyond the bounds of Japan. In many ways, these international settings provide some of the most dizzying challenges: beauty queen

Figure 2 Yoko McClain arriving in Seattle, 1952. Photograph courtesy of Yoko McClain and her family.

matchups on a global scale and English-language learning as the key to global mobility. These Japanese women often went beyond image to long-term engagements with the foreign, and, in the process, extended the global view of and in Japan. Finally, we could find no better way to finish to this collection of modern, mobile female experiences than to celebrate a woman who embodied many of the themes from which we draw. We thus end fittingly with an essay by Yoko McClain (1923–2011), whose life of gracious privilege alongside conscientious labor quite simply inspires us.

Acknowledgments

We would like to thank Stanford University Press acquisitions editor Stacy Wagner, senior production editor Judith Hibbard, and assistant Jessica Walsh for their creative vision, enthusiasm, patience, and support.[7] Janet Mowery excelled as a copyeditor. We are grateful to colleagues who generously shared their time and knowledge, especially Rebecca Copeland, Jeffrey Hanes, Christopher Hood, Glenda Roberts, Barbara Sato, and William Tsutsui. Anonymous reviewers provided valuable feedback. Sean Casey helped with the bibliography. Generous funding for this project has come from the Northeast Asia Council, the Japan–United States Friendship Commission, the Ei'ichi Shibusawa-Seigo Arai Endowed Professorship, and the University of Oregon.

We are grateful to many individuals and organizations for permission to reproduce the images in this book, and to the people who helped us to find them. We thank Nagumo Jiro and Kawakami Hiroshi of Mitsukoshi Isetan Holdings; photographer Katō Arata and Katō Nana of Takashimaya; Imada of Century and Company; Kure Rena, Ambai Akiko, and Kikuchi Keiko of Media Factory; Yamada Ayumi and Katō Nanako of Hato Bus; Jane Euler, president of World Wings International, Inc.; former Pan Am stewardess Takahashi Fumiko; Yamamori Kentarō of Kyodo News International; Erik Ropers; Junko Kawakami; Mizutani Yuima; and Kawanishi Yūzaburō. Others were of great assistance to us as well, including Maureen Donovan and Hyejeong Choi at Ohio State University for access to the Jiji Manga collection in the Billy Ireland Cartoon Library and Museum. Lesli Larson and her staff at the Image Services Center, University of Oregon Libraries, made expert-quality scans. We made every effort to contact copyright holders for their permission to reprint images. The editors would be grateful to hear from any copyright holder who is not here acknowledged and will undertake to assign proper credit in future editions of the book.

Note

Japanese names are written with the last (family) name first. The *sen*, which equaled 1/100 of a yen, was first coined in 1871 and taken out of circulation in 1953. Unless otherwise noted, all translations are our own.

PART I

New Female Occupations

Chapter Two

MOVING UP AND OUT

The "Shop Girl" in Interwar Japan

Elise K. Tipton

[The shop girl] has become the "flower of great Western cities" today.
—Kitazawa Shūichi, 1925

As suggested by the title of this volume, the women workers we profile experienced progress and mobility in both the social and physical senses. This would seem to be the case too for female department store workers in 1920s and 1930s Japan. In fact, becoming a department store "shop girl" (*shoppu gāru*) or "department store girl" (*depāto gāru*) proved to be one of the most desirable of the new occupations that opened up for educated middle-class women after World War I because it was associated with the modernity represented by the department store. And as author and essayist Kitazawa Shūichi's declaration suggests, interwar social commentators also welcomed the appearance of the shop girl as a sign of Japan's progress toward Western-style modernity.

The job not only entailed but also defined different kinds of mobility, especially for the small but growing number of graduates of girls' higher schools in the 1920s. Becoming a shop girl in a department store was a "modern" occupation that drew young women from the countryside to the cities. Even for the much larger number of urban women who did not move geographically, taking up paid work meant moving "out" of the home and into public spaces.

This was a new phenomenon for middle-class women, who previously did not often leave the house and certainly did not do so alone. In addition, many shop girls saw their work as an opportunity for mobility in a personal sense. The vast majority entered the workforce as they prepared to move to the next stage in their lives—marriage. Until the 1910s, middle-class women had spent the few years between completing elementary school and marriage at home, learning domestic skills, such as sewing, and developing cultural and social accomplishments, such as etiquette, tea ceremony, and flower arrangement. But increasingly during the interwar decades, daughters of both the old middle class of small businessmen and rural landowners and the new middle class of salaried white-collar workers (known as "salarymen," *sarariiman*) and professionals attended secondary schools.

Upon graduation, instead of marrying immediately, many sought new experiences in order to equip themselves to fulfill their future role as "modern" housewives (*shufu*). Those who sought new experiences through employment were consciously and unconsciously redefining the ideal of "good wife, wise mother" (*ryōsai kenbo*) that since the 1890s had been propagated in girls' higher schools as the proper role for middle-class women. This ideal assumed a gendered separation of spheres between the home and workplace and regarded the nurturing and educational responsibilities of wife and mother as the way in which home-centered (and confined) women would serve the nation. World War I, however, stimulated the expansion of industrialization, urbanization, and Japan's engagement in global affairs. Educators and many social commentators encouraged girls' higher school graduates to adjust to the changing times and become knowledgeable about social and economic developments, thus reconfiguring the "good wife, wise mother" as an efficient, socially aware housewife for the modern era.

However, the consequences of modernity for working women are contradictory and ambivalent. As anthropologist Mary Beth Mills argues regarding rural women moving to urban factory work in Thailand, there is a fundamental contradiction:

> [T]he meanings of modernity in Thailand offer young women attractive models of personal autonomy and cosmopolitan citizenship; however, these same gendered meanings engage young women in practices that tend to reproduce the exploitative structures in which their own lives and those of their families are enmeshed. (Mills 2001: 31)

Mills was writing about modernity in late twentieth-century Thailand, but modernity in early twentieth-century Japan similarly offered both opportunities and constraints for women, and not all social critics welcomed the new trend of middle-class working women. The reality of department store work was not as glamorous or fulfilling as women expected. In addition, although commentators expressed fascination with the beauty and other allures of the department store shop girl, they also voiced concerns about the deleterious effect of the work on women's moral as well as physical health. Some critics saw the shop girl's mobility, along with that of other new kinds of urban working women, as a symptom and a cause of perceived sexual licentiousness that could threaten values associated with the family, the backbone of the nation.

We will see through department store hiring and management policies and from social commentary on the shop girl that Japanese society was ambivalent about women's, especially middle-class women's, mobility out of the home into the public sphere. By going out to work these women were challenging the gendered division of labor between home and workplace. Such anxiety about women working is not confined to Japan. The feminist geographer Doreen Massey has noted in relation to women factory workers in industrializing England that:

> It wasn't so much "work" as "going out to" work which was the threat to the patriarchal order. And this in two ways: it threatened the ability of women adequately to perform their domestic role as homemaker for men and children, and it gave them an entry into public life, mixed company, a life not defined by family and husband. (Massey 1994: 198)

In Japan there were similar concerns about young female workers in the textile industry (Tsurumi 1990: 165–166), which underlay both company policies and society's assumptions that work would only be temporary. Among the urban working classes, financial need meant married women had to continue working. Nevertheless, by the 1920s the ideal of the "housewife" was also spreading among industrial workers. Working-class wives increasingly took in work at home (*naishoku*) rather than working outside when their husband's earnings reached a certain level (Chimoto 1995: 53), although others continued to work outside not only in factories, but also in new low-skilled service occupations, such as café waitress and bus conductor. Given such attitudes among the lower classes, whose daughters had been going out to work in factories since the 1870s and 1880s, it must be emphasized that middle-class women's going out to work created still greater anxieties, if not outright opposition, even though certain elite modernizing reformers were encouraging it and, as will be discussed, financial conditions necessitated it.

Using government surveys, department store company histories, and contemporary social commentary in various books and journals, this chapter highlights the contradictions and tensions that modern social change entailed for working women in interwar Japan. Government surveys of working women's backgrounds, their motives for working, and their experiences in and outside work provide some access to women's perspectives as well as official views of working women, while intellectuals and social reformers articulated society's ambivalence toward the new phenomenon of middle-class women entering the workplace.

Among these working women, the shop girl constitutes a particularly appropriate focus because she embodied the modernity that blossomed in Japan during the late 1920s. That modernity held promises of a more affluent and liberated lifestyle, encapsulated in the Westernized "modern life" (*modan raifu*) visualized in the burgeoning mass media and the department store. But at the same time, modernity's challenges to existing social roles, values, and structures—the "beautiful customs of the past"—provoked intense debates during the interwar period. These debates often swirled around the "modern girl" (*modan gāru* or *moga*, for short), typically represented as a young Westernized beauty striding boldly in Western dress, hairstyle, and makeup or drinking cocktails and smoking a cigarette in a café or cabaret. Opinions differed greatly as to her political significance, but many criticized her for her independence, materialism, open sexuality, and lack of social consciousness (see Silverberg 1991b; Sato 2003).

How many modern girls actually existed is debatable, but similar modern girls aroused controversy around the world in the early decades of the twentieth century (Modern Girl Around the World Research Group 2008b). The "shop girl" could have been seen as one. So could the many other "girls" who appeared in public spaces in Japan during the interwar years—"elevator girl" (*erega*), "mannequin girl" (*manekin gāru*), "walking stick girl" (*sutekki gāru*), "Engels girl" (*engerusu gāru*), "bus girl" (*basu gāru*), and "air girl" (*ea gāru*), among others. In general, though, the shop girl was classified as one of the middle-class "professional working women" (*shokugyō fujin*) who entered the workforce after World War I. They were not always equated with the "modern girl," but they shared with her controversy and contradictory judgments about their emergence.

Moving Up and Out

Among the occupations open to middle-class women, the professions of teaching and nursing attracted the largest number during the interwar decades. By the early 1930s, around one-third of all teachers nationwide were female, and many of them were married (Newell 1997; Hunter 1990: 114). However, the total number of female teachers and nurses remained small, and women were confined to the lower, nonsupervisory levels of these professions. Office work, including typists, receptionists, and switchboard operators, also attracted growing numbers of young middle-class women, as did a few new occupations opened to women, such as magazine reporter. Most of these occupations required education beyond the minimum compulsory six years of elementary school.

In moving from rural areas to the major cities to improve their lives, young, educated Japanese women might be seen as paralleling upwardly mobile youths who since the Meiji period had "moved up" (in Japanese, the verb *noboru* was used) to the capital, Tokyo, in search of successful careers (see Kinmonth 1981). Teaching and nursing were the occupations that provided the highest salaries and status open to women, but responses to surveys of young women arriving from the countryside that were carried out by the Tokyo City government in 1922 and 1931 reveal that becoming a department store sales clerk or office worker actually topped the list of desirable jobs. The popularity of department store work is also exemplified by the close to 12,000 applications from women received by an employment agency over just three days in 1931 for positions in three Tokyo department stores (Sato 2003: 129).

Middle-class women entered the workforce voluntarily or were pushed into it by their families even before the effects of the Great Depression were felt in Japan. For example, the 1925 Tokyo City Social Bureau study showed that more than half the respondents were working to help their families' finances (Tōkyō shakaikyoku 2003). After the economic boom of World War I, a recession and stagnation in white-collar employment throughout the 1920s created difficulties for middle-class families. According to the bureau's study, it was the desire either to maintain or to raise their standard of living that led the young women to seek work after leaving school, especially if they were not needed in the home. The bureau was referring here to the rising aspirations for a "modern life" among the emerging new urban middle class. Other financial reasons included earning income for their future marriage expenses (Tōkyō shakaikyoku 2003: 1–2; other survey results in Nagy 1991: 204–206).

Nevertheless, although financial difficulties were the main reason for working, there were also social ideas and trends that motivated young middle-class women to seek employment outside the home. Growth in the number of young women with a secondary education was one development. The Girls' Higher School Law of 1899 had set the goal of at least one girls' higher school in every prefecture, which was quickly reached and exceeded. By 1910, girls' higher schools numbered 193; by 1920 their number had tripled (Newell 1997: 19). The percentage of girls who advanced to secondary levels of education remained small (about 10 percent in the mid-1920s), but was increasing rapidly (Koyama 1994: 34). The 1925 Tokyo City Social Bureau study of "professional working women" pointed to the rising levels of female education and its influence on young middle-class women entering the workforce. The study concluded that, along with historic economic pressures on middle-class families, a new desire for independence (*dokuritsu*) and self-reliance (*jiritsu*) had emerged as important motives for seeking work (Tōkyō shakaikyoku 2003: 2–3).

The study also noted the impact of the women's liberation movement (Tōkyō shakaikyoku 2003: 4). What is often referred to as the "first wave"[1] of organized feminism had begun with the launch of the feminist literary journal *Seitō* (Bluestocking) in 1911 (see Bardsley 2007 for an anthology of the journal's articles). Although intended to display the literary talents of women, its contributors, including founder Hiratsuka Raichō, were dubbed "new women" (*atarashii onna*) by the media. They attracted sensationalist coverage in newspapers for their flouting of conventional views of marriage, but also provoked serious discussion of women's issues in mainstream journals, such as *Chūō kōron* (Central Review) and *Taiyō* (The Sun).

Public attention and debate were further stimulated by a shift in *Seitō*'s content under its second editor, Itō Nōe, away from mainly literary pieces toward controversial topics such as abortion, sexuality, women's work, and political rights. Although Itō closed the journal in 1916, exhausted by personal and financial pressures, she and other Seitō Society members continued to participate in public debates over women's issues, such as state support for mothers or what was called the "motherhood protection debate" (*bosei hogo ronsō*). They also led feminist organizations, such as the New Women's Association (Shin fujin kyōkai) and the left-wing Red Wave Society (Sekirankai). The New Women's Association worked for women's economic and political rights, which were lacking according to the Meiji Civil Code. It partially succeeded in gaining women's right to attend political meetings and join political organizations in 1922. A bill in favor of women's suffrage passed the lower house of the Diet in 1931, but was blocked in the more conservative House of Peers. The Red Wave Society mainly organized May Day demonstrations, linking Japanese socialists to international movements (Mackie 2003: 58–63, 79).

Two other reform movements supported young middle-class women who sought employment outside the home before marriage. Leaders in women's education and intellectuals promoting modernization, supported by government agencies, participated in the Daily Life Reform Movement (Seikatsu kaizen undō) and a boom in "self-cultivation" (shūyō) publications during the late 1910s and early 1920s. Although ultimately conservative in supporting the gendered separation of spheres, they elevated the importance of the role of the housewife as efficient manager of her household and gave her primary responsibility for educating her children and creating a happy and healthy family life. In order to fulfill this modernized role as "good wives and wise mothers" in what they called "the new era," the reformers urged young educated women to go out into society and become knowledgeable about contemporary affairs (Tipton 2009; Sand 2003; Koyama 1994).

Consequently, such movements encouraged many professional working women responding to Tokyo City surveys to see temporary work as "preparation for marriage" (katei seikatsu no junbi), providing them with opportunities for "self-cultivation" (shūyō) and "self-improvement" (jiko kansei) (Tōkyō shakaikyoku 2003: 127). Self-cultivation had many meanings at this time (see Wang 2004). To intellectuals, it suggested spiritual and cultural development in a rather abstract philosophical and moral sense. To professional working women, it could mean conventional feminine accomplishments and etiquette, but it could also mean reading, building personal character, and learning about society outside the home through work. Such knowledge and experience would prepare them to be modern housewives.

Attractions of the Department Store

Given these motivations and expectations, young middle-class women of marriageable age often saw department stores as offering more desirable experiences and attractive work environments than other types of white-collar work. Women in Tokyo City government surveys mentioned opportunities for "self-cultivation" most often as a motivation for work as a sales clerk than for other types of work. For example, in a 1922 survey, 7.1 percent of the women answered that self-improvement was the main motivation for wanting to be a sales clerk, compared to 3.8 percent for being a typist and 5.8 percent for becoming an office worker. In a 1931 survey the differences were less pronounced, but self-improvement remained a more frequently mentioned motive for becoming a sales clerk (8.1 percent) than for a typist (7.5 percent) or an office worker (7.3 percent). In addition, becoming a sales clerk was mentioned more frequently as preparation for marriage (6.3 percent) than becoming a typist (4.7 percent) or office worker (5.4 percent) (Sato 2003: Table 1, 132). These responses may also be related to the fact that many department store workers came from small retail family backgrounds (Tōkyō shakaikyoku 2003: 24).

The view of department store work as preparation for marriage also provided a noneconomic justification for middle-class women to work. It helped to overcome the stigma attached to working outside the home for this class of women. In the early twentieth century, Home Ministry official Tago Kazutani, for example, expressed the common view that middle-class women should work only if their lives or marriages were in difficulty. While observing that during the "Great War" women in Western countries had demonstrated capability in performing jobs previously thought to be men's jobs, he rejected arguments circulating in Japan in favor of expanding women's employment in order to achieve women's independence and freedom. Tago maintained that men and women had different roles to play in society; women's special responsibility and vocation (tenshoku) was to give birth and raise children. Taking up employment would undermine the division of labor and take women away from their fundamental reason for existence. In his view, if women had to work, then they should only take up jobs, such as social work, midwifery, or primary school teaching, that suited their essential mission (Tago 1919: 13–22). Although working in a department store did not fit these categories, it was considered respectable work for members of the middle classes and represented a step up for those of the lower middle class. Department store work was viewed similarly in the United Kingdom (Lancaster 1995: 141).

The vast majority of female department store workers were thus young and unmarried, expecting to become housewives in a few years' time. The 1925 Tokyo City study reported that out of 168 department store workers surveyed in 1922, 155 (92.2 percent) were single, an even higher percentage than for all 900 women surveyed (which was 83.6 percent) (Tōkyō shakaikyoku 2003: 41–42). More than two-thirds (68.5 percent) worked for three years or less (Tōkyō shakaikyoku 2003: 55). The study correlated the fact that women between the ages of seventeen and eighteen and twenty-three and twenty-four were most numerous among the 900 surveyed, with the usual age of marriage for women being between twenty and twenty-two or twenty-three (Tōkyō shakaikyoku 2003: 41).

The modern image of department stores helps to explain the particular desirability of this kind of work. Since their transformation from dry goods stores into department stores during the first decade of the twentieth century, they symbolized what was most fashionable and up-to-date, offering visions of a modern lifestyle in the commodities and entertainment that they provided (Tipton 2012; Young 1999; Tamari 2006). In the late 1920s and 1930s the buildings themselves were massive architectural wonders celebrating the latest art deco designs and décor and providing spaces for cultural exhibitions, lectures, musical and theatrical performances, gardens, zoos, and children's playgrounds, as well as elegant lounges and restaurants. Exhibitions, such as Mitsukoshi's 1927 exhibition of social customs throughout the world (*sekai fūzoku tenrankai*), offered views of exotic people and societies, while fashion shows and displays of sporting goods, Western-style furniture, kitchens, and electrical appliances showed how to live a "modern life," including goods that defined it for purchase (Mitsukoshi hyakkaten 1927: 10; *Dai Mitsukoshi rekishi shashinchō* 1932: passim). These facilities, displays, and events transformed shopping from a mundane purchase of goods into a new social experience for education, leisure, and entertainment. Working in such an environment, surrounded by beautiful fashions, housewares, and lifestyle goods, therefore presented an alluring modern image. Moreover, women's magazines played a large role in attracting young women from the countryside and from small and medium-sized towns to the city by painting a rosy picture of urban living and work that would prepare them for marriage as well as financially support their families (Sato 2003: 140).

Adding to the drawing power of department stores, the stores themselves, as in Western countries, recruited women in great numbers during the 1920s. Men had previously dominated retail sales during the Tokugawa and early Meiji periods, but, along with an expanded range of goods and revolutionary retailing methods accompanying their emergence at the beginning of the twentieth century, department stores had begun to employ women. Conscription had created a gap in workers as men left to fulfill their military service obligations, which disrupted the traditional live-in apprentice system. Then, during the economic expansion of World War I, department store managers, like factory managers (see Faison 2007), recruited more women. More opportunities for white-collar work had opened up for men, creating a labor shortage. Besides, women could be paid much less.

たしまりなに事るむしせ用着を服務事たし定一に[

り よ 日 五 十 月 九 年 十 正 大

Figure 3 Mitsukoshi shop girls in uniform, 1921. From *Dai Mitsukoshi rekishi shashinchō kankōkai* (1932, A Photographic History of the Great Mitsukoshi). Courtesy of Mitsukoshi Isetan Holdings.

Department store statistics reveal the huge influx of women workers. In 1921 female employees made up 17.5 percent of all employees in Mitsukoshi's main store in Nihonbashi, but in 1930 they comprised 42.5 percent of all employees in its new Ginza store (Matsuda 2005: 198–199). They worked not only as sales clerks, but also as switchboard operators and accounts clerks, and less-educated women worked as waitresses, escalator girls, and elevator girls. The Ginza figures are particularly high, suggesting that the employment of women contributed to the classy image that Ginza department stores, and Ginza more generally, pro-jected during the post-earthquake years, which were often called the "Ginza era" (Andō 1983: 131–134; Tipton 2007). But the trend was not limited to Ginza. In 1930 women also made up at least 40 percent of employees in four of the six big-gest department stores in Osaka (Matsuda 2005: 198–199), and over 60 percent of employees in Takashimaya's stores in Nihonbashi (Tokyo), Osaka, and Kyoto (Takashimaya hyakugojū nenshi henshū iinkai 1982: 424). In 1934 at least 622 out of 1,086 employees were women in Isetan's Shinjuku store (Hisayama 1961: 119).

The department store Isetan had relocated from Kanda to Shinjuku after the 1923 earthquake, recognizing the commercial potential of a neighborhood that was becoming a key transit point between the growing suburbs and the center of the city. Shinjuku especially grew after the Yamanote railway loop line was completed in 1925. The district boomed in the late 1920s and early 1930s because the earthquake had forced the population of Tokyo out of the central districts and accelerated suburbanization towards the west and south. Many of the new commuting suburbanites were members of the new middle classes, attracted to the modern housing developments, several of which were built by private railway companies that also owned department stores. Shinjuku Station, constructed in 1926, became the most-used train terminal in all of Asia (see Freedman 2010: 137–151). Department stores as well as other businesses in services and entertainment in Shinjuku catered to these middle-class commuters who aspired to a modern lifestyle, and employed the female members of their families.

A 1925 article by Kitazawa Shūichi in the journal *Kaizō* suggests that there were other important reasons for department stores to employ young women besides a male labor shortage and the fact that they could pay women lower wages. Kitazawa wrote that employment of attractive female workers added to the appeal and popularity of department stores. Kitazawa begins by pointing out that, among the young women going out of the home into society to work, it was the "shop girl" who has most caught people's eye. Kitazawa explicitly chose a foreign-derived term, "*shoppu gāru*," to convey the modern air that these women possess. According to Kitazawa, they attracted attention not only because of their growing numbers but also because hiring policies deliberately designed to create a "sensation" sought beautiful women (Kitazawa 1925: 172–173). Okinawa's Yamagataya department store, for example, recruited twenty "*depāto*" girls for the first time in its new Naha branch, requiring that they be "good looking and clear-headed" (Ito 2008: 251). However, it is not only the beauty of the shop girl that attracted Kitazawa, for, as he points out, there are beautiful young women who work in cafés and restaurants. To him the shop girl has many more modern qualities than waitresses. Moreover, he argues that, while the geisha was the "flower of social intercourse in olden times," the charm and beauty of the shop girl surpasses that of the geisha, and she has become the "flower of great Western cities" today (Kitazawa 1925: 174).

It is significant to note why Kitazawa regarded department store work as superior to that of café waitressing, another new and popular urban occupation. He explains that being a shop girl was "modern work" (*kindaiteki kinmu*) because it had fixed daytime working hours. Cafés, contrary to our present-day conceptions, were nighttime drinking establishments where the waitresses in the late 1920s and 1930s increasingly provided "erotic" services (Tipton 2002). Although some department stores were open in the evening, they remained primarily daytime stores. Theoretically, therefore, women had the freedom to pursue some kind of study after they left the store. And in fact, the Tokyo City government study of 1925 found that sales clerks spent their leisure time reading and playing the koto or biwa, as well as doing household chores like sewing and doing laundry (Tōkyō shakaikyoku 2003: 101). Here was reinforcement of the idea of department store work as self-cultivation. As will be evident from the later discussion, this was an overly sanguine understanding of their working conditions, but Kitazawa's association of the shop girl with the urban conditions of the "civilized countries" (*bunmei koku*) of the West indicates that her emergence was seen as a sign of national social advancement.

Certainly, in their appearance, department store shop girls conveyed a sense of modernity. Photographs of department store shop girls in the early 1920s show them in kimono uniforms, but later photographs of sales clerks, restaurant waitresses, and elevator girls show them wearing Western uniforms and hairstyles. Advertising posters also commonly depicted young female customers in the latest dresses. Yet Western dresses were still a rare sight in Tokyo. According to self-styled "modernologist" Kon Wajirō's May 1925 survey of what people were wearing, only 1 percent of women dressed in Western clothes, even in the fashionable Ginza. A later 1933 survey by Kon and his associates found this number had risen only to 19 percent (Nakayama 1987: 397–398, 413). This does not mean that kimono were unfashionable. Kimono of the 1920s and 1930s often exhibited bold colors and abstract patterns inspired by art deco and other modernist designs (see, for example, Van Assche 2005).

Nevertheless, because it was typical for only a minority of women, wearing dresses in the interwar decades represented an embrace of the modern as well as the Western, and it invited contradictory responses. On the one hand, dresses were associated with the controversial *moga*. Critics frequently linked her Western clothing, which revealed the shape of the body and legs more than a kimono, with sexual depravity. On the other hand, social modernizers advocated Western dresses for respectable modern housewives in debates over clothing reform. When considering the pros and cons of Western versus Japanese clothing for women, women's educators and Daily Life Reform advocates frequently argued that Western clothes allowed for more movement, which suited women's need to get out, be active, and socialize in the modern era (see, for example, Tsukamoto 1997: 37, 41; Saga 1924: 182–183). With other professional working women, department store shop girls thus led the way in Japanese women's slow shift to wearing Western clothing and making that shift respectable.

"The Cinderella of Occupations"

Despite Kitazawa's sense of romantic fascination with shop girls, he was not blind to their social historical significance and the problems of their daily lives. Kitazawa notes that a department store sales clerk in Tokyo made only thirty or forty yen a month, an average corroborated in the Tokyo City government surveys (Tōkyō shakaikyoku 2003: 14). This was not enough for the shop girl to live independently of her parents, although he said that there were "not a few" who had to live on their own. The 1925 Tokyo City survey recorded the wish for establishment of apartments or dormitories by several professional working women from the countryside. The difficulty of living on low salaries corresponds to a description of department store work in the United States as the "Cinderella of occupations": "at one pole, toil, tedium, and poverty; at the other, glamour, fulfillment, and financial security" (Benson 1988: 181). That comment was made by the director of the Research Bureau of Retail Training in the 1920s.

In the case of Japanese department store workers, however, the negative aspects of the work often were not offset by fulfillment and financial security. In addition to poor wages, department store work in Japan did not offer women the opportunity for long-term employment after marriage or promotion to management-level positions such as buyer or head of stock; in American department stores, in contrast, over one-third of buyers were women in 1924 (Leach 1984: 332; Benson 1988: 187–214). Nor did they become "queens of the urban proletariat," like female department store workers in late nineteenth- and early twentieth-century France, who could afford to live on their own and dress stylishly outside of work (McBride 1978: 681). In Japan the gender ideology centered on the "good wife, wise mother" ideal meant that department store managers as well as young women presumed that work would only be temporary.

Kitazawa worried about social changes that would result from young women going outside the home to work, while later commentators focused on the unglamorous reality of working in a department store. Kitazawa's concern was about the changes in ideas and attitudes, namely the spread of ideas of free love and hedonism, that he expected would come with the lifestyles of working women and commercialization of their society. Looking to social developments in London and New York, he predicted a similar trend in Japan in the development of the "modern girl" (*modan gāru*) who drinks alcohol and smokes, but he accepted this development with a kind of fatalism (Kitazawa 1925: 178).

Popular writer Ishikari Jirō was also concerned with the morals of shop girls, but rather than anticipating sexual promiscuity and materialistic consumerism, he sympathized with their working conditions in his 1932 book, *Department Stores Exposed* (*Abakareta hyakkaten*) (Ishikari 2005). Ishikari was not a scholar, and as is evident from the title, his book was intended to delve behind the ostensible glamour of department stores to expose the problems of women working in them. Ishikari was not the only writer to bring attention to health problems of female department store employees and the sexual harassment they experienced by male superiors. Social critics and reformers commonly criticized conditions that entailed long working hours (shifts of nine to ten hours), standing on hard floors, and lack of exercise or sunlight for the poor health of young female department store workers. Health problems commonly included tuberculosis, exhaustion, and headaches. Shop girls only had one day off per month, which left little time for rest, recreation, or self-cultivation. Besides leaving for marriage, these conditions might account for more than a quarter of sales clerks resigning their jobs after less than one year (Tōkyō shakaikyoku 2003: 55).

As socialist critic Yamakawa Kikue pointed out, female factory workers were protected by laws, but female department store workers and other professional working women (except teachers) were not (Yamakawa 1929: 57). As in Kitazawa's case, Ishikari and others, including feminist Ichikawa Fusae (Tōyō keizai shinpōsha 1936: 60–61), often used American practices and conditions as a benchmark for criticizing those in Japan. They pointed to American labor laws that limited working hours and required overtime payment for night work. They also recommended the American model of providing a half-hour lunch break and a fifteen-minute afternoon break when workers would be able to go outside for some exercise and sunshine.

There is sensationalism and doubtful scientific validity in some of Ishikari's critique. For example, he criticized concrete buildings because of the moist atmosphere that they supposedly created and praised American department store owners for their concern for human welfare in using natural stone (Ishikari 2005: 424). He also blamed the long hours of standing on concrete or linoleum for a "kind of special women's illness," or "*dokuji no fujinbyō*," especially, he said, since Japanese women still did not wear Western-style underpants (Japanese undergarments were wraparound garments that did not cover the crotch). In one of his so-called exposés entitled "The Tragedy of a Female Department Store Employee," he attributed the inability of a former department store worker to have a child after three years of marriage to the "*fujinbyō*" that she contracted while working in the pharmacy department of M department store for three years. Noting the importance of children for a "natural" married life, he related that this tragedy resulted in the loss of her husband's love and forced her into a less desirable position working for a café in Ginza (Ishikari 2005: 361–366).

Questionable as these explanations might be, we can nevertheless see that improvement of conditions even in modern working environments like department stores was a concern of social reformers during this period in Japanese history. Commentators also criticized the poor quality of food and dirty conditions of department store dining rooms for customers as well as workers. Reformers stressed the importance of including vitamins and calcium in diets. The attention to food quality and not just caloric sufficiency, like the emphasis on the need for exercise and sunlight, reflect the wide circulation and application of modern ideas of public health and hygiene to everyday life during the interwar decades, other modern ideas besides self-cultivation that had been promoted by the Daily Life Reform Movement (Tipton 2009; Sand 2003).

The young age, beauty, and class background of female department store workers made observers especially concerned for their moral welfare. Nevertheless, commentary on professional working women, including department store shop girls, was contradictory. On the one hand, some warned women about the sexual dangers of going out in public places and taking public transportation. Kaetsu Takako, a leader in women's education and the Daily Life Reform Movement, warned young working women not to wear flashy clothing in the streetcar that would be alluring to men: "Girls have to be aware of what they are letting themselves in for, and be strong-willed" (quoted in Sato 2003: 124).

On the other hand, other commentators assumed that working women would give in to temptation, becoming corrupted and sexually promiscuous. Yamamuro Gunpei, moral reformer and Salvation Army leader, assumed that "mixing with men, they [were] going to make mistakes when it comes to maintaining their chastity. . . . Or perhaps I should say, I think it will become a matter of course" (Sato 2003: 124). More sensationalist was a newspaper report speculating that the many young female office workers in the Marunouchi Building were "probably having sex orgies off somewhere in the corner of the office" (Sato 2003: 124).

These assumptions and Kitazawa's exclamations about the beauty of the shop girl correspond to what historian Rosalind Williams has argued regarding late nineteenth-century French department stores, that they created dreams of exotic places and luxurious consumption with their electric light and glass displays and incarnated erotic dreams in the female image (Williams 1982: 90). In the Japanese case, they were incarnated in the shop girl: perhaps a man would touch the hands of a shop girl when making a purchase; or the anonymity of the crowd would afford opportunities for close contact with the bodies of female customers. From a less suggestive perspective, such illusions are also indicative of the limited opportunities that young urban men and women had in the early twentieth century for mingling socially without parental supervision.

Yet this was the time when Western ideas of romantic love (ren'ai) and "companionate marriage" (yūai kekkon) were circulating in Japan through mass magazines, popular novels, translations of Western writings, and Hollywood movies. A translation of the book titled Companionate Marriage, by the American judge and reformer Benjamin Barr Lindsey, created a sensation when it was published in 1930 (Minami 1986: 541). Dating, known as "rendezvous" (randebū) or "abekku" (from the French word avec, "with"), was a new social practice that accompanied these modern views of love and marriage; department stores became one of the sites for dates. In fact, they featured on one of the date courses described in a "guidebook for rendezvous" (randebū no annai) (Ogawa 1988: 412–414). For fifty sen, a couple could purchase a round-trip train ticket to five department stores in Ueno, Ginza, and Nihonbashi. The guidebook gave details about items and their prices that could be purchased along the way. A department store in Shinjuku, along with cafés and nightclubs, also figured as a site for romance in modernist author Okada Saburō's "Twenty-Four Hour Love Hunter" (Rabu-hantā nijūyonji), an essay that appeared in Chūō kōron in 1931 (Okada 1931: 254–256).

Department stores thus emerged as a place where new romantic social interactions between male and female patrons were encouraged, but, as a workplace, department store managers were apprehensive about the sexual dangers presented to female employees. The modern sexual attractions of café waitresses lured young salarymen to cafés as well as department stores, but the department store was different from a café in being a workplace where men and women worked side by side. Department store managers tried to preserve traditional norms and gender roles, even though this contradicted their using young women to attract young middle-class salarymen to their stores. In one sense, traditional views of women as providers of entertainment and sexual services for men underlay the hiring of attractive young women as shop girls; at the same time the ideal of female chastity, which was institutionalized in a legal double standard regarding adultery (Fuess 2004: 77, 117; Tipton 2005), led to attempts to prevent women workers from becoming victims of sexual corruption. Store regulations did not permit male and female employees to develop romantic relationships. Takashimaya department store minimized contact by making sure that men and women did not leave the store together—women left five minutes ahead of men (Matsuda: 2005: 222). Furthermore, moral discipline inspectors monitored the behavior of shop girls, like the "floor walkers" in British department stores (Lancaster 1995: 127–131).

Nevertheless, Ishikari's exposé included reports about store executives taking employees as mistresses and about inspectors raping shop girls (Ishikari 2005: 369–371, 376–380, 387–391). It is difficult to determine how widespread such practices were. It is worth noting that Western social commentators also expressed alarm about the sexual morals of female department store workers. Many Western journalists, social critics, and novelists portrayed the department store as a dangerous space for women and assumed that female department store workers engaged in prostitution on the side (Lancaster 1995: 178–182). A prominent example was Victorian journalist W. T. Stead's 1893 study of Chicago sales girls, *If Christ Came to Chicago*, which asserted that girls' low wages and lifestyle desires pressured them to seek "the allowance of a friend . . . [but] not food but clothes, not plain clothes but finery, that is . . . the want that drives many to a life of shame" (quoted in Lancaster 1995: 179).

Japanese commentators made similar assumptions or criticisms about café waitresses and dancehall women. But they depicted shop girls as innocent victims of lecherous men. Perhaps this reflects the difference in the class background of shop girls and waitresses, the latter coming from the lower rather than the middle classes. Similarly, it may explain the difference in assumptions about shop girls in Japan and working women in Western department stores who, like Japanese café waitresses, had lower-class backgrounds (Benson 1988: 129).

Conclusion

In the 1930s, the relationship between changing women's roles and the expansion of department stores was a central topic of debate. At this time, women became department stores' primary workforce and main customers. Commentators generally supported the expansion of these large-scale stores, for they perceived them as important indicators of Japan's progressive social, as well as economic, development (see, for example, Tōyō keizai shinpōsha 1936: 56–57). In the context of such debates about women's roles and department stores, the contradictions in discourses about shop girls become even more apparent. Young middle-class women continued to be attracted to department store employment because they believed they would enjoy self-improvement through social experiences in a modern work environment, while helping their families financially. Surrounded by displays of up-to-date fashions, household goods, and exhibitions, they would learn how to be modern housewives and how to lead a "modern life." Once employed, however, the women, as well as social commentators and reformers, found the conditions far less glamorous and enriching. Long hours, strict discipline, and sexual harassment contributed to a high turnover rate among shop girls. Many were too tired after a long day to engage in any self-cultivation activities.

Consequently, while welcoming department stores as a sign of advancement, social critics deemed department stores dangerous places for the health and morality of the young female workers. Their view reflected the contradictions and conflicts in attitudes toward middle-class women working outside the home, the new urban development that characterized the interwar decades. By going out to work, professional working women were challenging the gendered separation of spheres between home and workplace. Indeed, shop girls epitomized real-life "modern girls on the go" as they moved up and out into society. Because of that, their entry into public life—mixed company with men—threatened to undermine the ideal of female chastity as well as the home-centered ideal of "good wife, wise mother." The fact that women were being drawn to and exploited in department stores, an icon of the new, modern consumer society, added all the more to the ambiguities of the discourse. Such ambiguity and anxiety were particularly acute during this period of transition to a modern, industrialized society.

Since completion of the transition after World War II, a majority, rather than a minority, of middle-class women have entered the paid workforce as the "good wife, wise mother" ideal was discredited along with the prewar imperial ideology. Nevertheless, since the gendered division of labor has remained entrenched in Japanese society, women's labor continues to be seen as temporary and supplementary, and women's mobility in public spaces outside the home continues to evoke ambivalence and controversy. As for working women themselves, like the shop girl and other professional working women of interwar Japan, they must continue to negotiate the constraints and possibilities of their labor.

Chapter Three

ELEVATOR GIRLS
MOVING IN AND
OUT OF THE BOX

Laura Miller

A short McDonald's hamburger commercial that aired in Japan in 2006 begins with a salaryman trying to get on an elevator. He pushes the elevator call button, and, although the doors tantalizingly begin to part, they close before he can board. The camera shows him making a few futile efforts to enter before switching to a shot of the inside of the elevator, where a uniformed elevator girl is cramming a hamburger into her mouth with one hand while repeatedly pushing the close button with the other hand. The words "I want to eat, now" (*Ima, tabetai*) appear on the screen. Short and funny, the scene became a YouTube hit.[1]

People loved peeking behind the scenes at the elevator girl's natural or backstage behavior. The elevator girl's job is a type of "performance" in Erving Goffman's (1959) sociological sense of the outward expression of a social role that actors consciously, and at times unconsciously, adopt. This front-stage performance is an aspect of impression management that is crafted for specific social situations.[2] Chomping on a hamburger is backstage behavior and is not something customers expect to find elevator girls doing while at their posts.

I am interested in the figure of the elevator girl (*erebētā gāru*, and its abbreviation *erega*) because it allows us to track the ways women in this occupation have been seen not only as exemplary of the female service worker, but also as a fertile example of the disparity between the crafted public image of a trained employee and her private life. As young women from diverse regional and class backgrounds move into the elevator girl slot, they are trained in codified ways of speaking and performing the role, highlighting awareness of the gap between their putatively authentic selves and new occupational expectations. Of course, all interactions involve the performance of various roles, so this polarization is not based on any real dichotomy, a point that must be emphasized. The elevator girl in her impeccable uniform, topped by a proper hat, is one of many easily identifiable occupational types that are the legacy of prewar professional working women (*shokugyō fujin*). She rides in a moving machine, and she also moves into a cultural role invested with marked class and gender associations. The *erega* has long typified a modern girl on the go.

The elevator girl's forms of mobility, therefore, are both physical and cultural. I argue that it is the predictability of her gendered performance that, paradoxically, shoves her into the limelight, while her true self remains hidden from the observer. The public witnesses the repetitive, standardized work done by elevator girls in a circumscribed space, and rarely knows her as a woman in other identities and performances. It is partly the regularity and apparent constraint of her occupation, however, that makes her such an appealing object of the popular imagination. Her job provokes questions about what she is really like behind the scripted veneer and the shipshape uniform. Is she eating a hamburger when the doors close, or even perhaps engaging in some type of sexual activity that we can only guess at?

This chapter aims to recapture a piece of Japanese women's cultural history by looking at a service job that is usually considered mindless and marginal despite its importance to the construction of department store culture. Elevator girl was one of many female professions that served as a human link between technology and its users. The elevator girl was a key figure in the department store's establishing itself as a modern temple of consumption. Surveying how the 1960s in the United States have been represented in mass media, Susan Douglas notes that few forms of female culture were identified as contributing to the era:

> According to the prevailing cultural history of our times, the impact of the boys was serious, lasting, and authentic. They were the thoughtful, dedicated rebels, the counter-culture leaders, the ones who made history. The impact of girls was fleeting, superficial, trivial. (Douglas 1994: 5)

The job of elevator girl likewise has often been viewed as a superfluous and silly occupation. In contrast, the reified male office worker, or salaryman, of the 1950s to 1980s was lauded as the focal point of economic growth and cultural inspiration. He became a national icon of pride and was even credited with establishing Japan's economic success. In contrast, elevator girls and other female service workers are treated as nothing more than spatial decorations, like the female clerks described as "office flowers" in Japanese white-collar firms.

In spite of the denigrating characterizations of her work, in popular culture and media the elevator girl's image has continued to arouse great interest. Reclaiming her history helps us to understand why, in the twenty-first century when the majority of elevator girls have all but disappeared, she continues to surface in comics, novels, films, and even types of costume play. Although the elevator girl was also part of American history, she is sometimes put forward as prototypically "Japanese" to the outside world, and foreign journalists and visitors invariably comment on her. In the 1990s the character of an elevator girl was used in language textbooks to illustrate Japanese culture for the foreign student (Tsukuba Language Group 1994). In order to explore the elevator girl's gendered labor, I take an interdisciplinary approach, drawing on materials from different time periods and using a variety of texts (histories, newspaper articles, comics, television, and other sources). I also track media representations of the elevator girl that monitor the contrast between her movement between front-stage and backstage behaviors.[3]

Among the multiple depictions of the elevator girl since 1929, many contain at their core a fascination with the juxtaposition of her work and her imagined private life or presumed true self. News reports in the 1930s latched on to the suicide of an elevator girl, discussed below, as an especially notable event that highlighted the dangers inherent in the modern girl's lifestyle. In later decades the elevator girl became the topic of adored computer games, manga, films, and various spoofs. In the hit television drama series *Tokyo Elevator Girl* (*Tōkyō erebētā gāru*, Yoshida, Katō, and Kitagawa 1992, examined in more detail below), the cute and perky workers have complex sexual and romantic lives behind the scenes.

The demure elevator girl who is really an insatiable nymphomaniac is a favorite theme in adult videos. An example is *Going Up: I Am an Elevator Girl* (*Ue ni mairimasu: Watashi wa erebētā gāru*), which is about the exploits of an elevator girl, including sex in the elevator during working hours (Aikawa 1989). The cover shows famous porn actress Shōji Miyuki wearing a demure red blazer, virginal white blouse, white gloves, and white bowler hat. Flip over the video case and there are shots of her not wearing this uniform.

An episode of the popular anime series *Crayon Shin-Chan* (*Kureyon Shinchan*, Hongō 1992, discussed below) features a professional elevator girl who turns into a blubbering crybaby when she is trapped in a broken elevator. At an event meant to showcase the film *Elevator Nightmare* (*Akuma no erebētā*, Horibe 2009), comedienne Torii Miyuki posed as a deranged-looking elevator girl. As part of the promotional stunt, she watched a screening of the movie in an elevator together with three bona fide elevator girls. Torii's bug-eyed intensity, overdone makeup, and camp parody of the demure department store lift worker contrasts with the decorous elevator girls who appeared with her.

Karl Greenfeld's (1995) exposé of the underbelly of Japanese society, *Speed Tribes: Days and Nights with Japan's Next Generation*, offers portraits of young yakuza, porn stars, and computer hackers who live marginal lives outside the Japanese mainstream. One of his featured types was a twenty-one-year-old elevator girl named Keiko. After changing out of her department store uniform, Keiko goes out clubbing in a sexy outfit (perhaps her boy-catching uniform?) where she experiments with the drug ecstasy and has sex with foreign men. A decade after the book's publication, Greenfeld admitted in an interview that the vignette about Keiko was a form of literary journalism, since she was not a real person at all, but rather (quoting Greenfeld) "was, like, a composite of three chicks" (Moorghen 2004). An important point is not that Greenfeld fabricated Keiko, but that, in his desire to illustrate the disparity between young women's private and public lives, he selected the elevator girl as the epitome of the well-bred young lady in order to contrast this with the behind-the-scenes person. Similar to this literary intervention, the elevator girl is often used as the hook upon which portraits of proper young femininity are hung.

Tracing the etymology of the term "elevator girl" is difficult because there are so many possible lines of inception. As discussed in the chapter by Freedman, Miller, and Yano in this volume, scholarship on the modern working woman frequently refers to the proliferation of the English loanword "girl," such as the kiss girl (*kissu gāru*) who exchanged kisses for a modest fee, the movie theater usher cinema girl (*kinema gāru*), and the mannequin girl (*manekin gāru*) who modeled the latest fashions, often as part of a display of other merchandise. Japanese scholars became fascinated by the use of *gāru* in new job titles and what these terms illustrated about modern life (Kitazawa S. 1925).

However, I suspect that "girl" has a longer residence in Japan than previously assumed, and that some of the occupational labels with *gāru* in them have separate histories and are not simply the outcome of one era's linguistic fad. For one thing, the loanword "girl" was already circulating in Japanese culture by the later part of the Meiji period (1868–1912). One news item reported that the terms *geisha gāru* (geisha girl), *mikado, banzai,* and *kimono* were being used around the world, evidence that words with origins in Japan had made it to the global stage (*Yomiuri Shinbun* 1909).

The term *geisha girl* was said to be something foreigners used for Yoshiwara sex workers. "Girl" also appeared frequently in media after the Girl Guides (later renamed Girl Scouts), were introduced to Japan in 1919. Although officially called Nihon Joshi Hodōdan (Girl Guides of Japan), newspapers of the time often referred to them as *gāru gaido.* In 1925, the Osaka branch of the Daimaru department store began using high-school-aged Girl Guides as saleswomen (*Yomiuri Shinbun* 1925). These surfacings of the term *gāru* indicate that it was already in play years before Kitazawa's much-cited 1924 essay.

Although twenty-first-century American travelers to Tokyo gush over their first sightings of her, the female elevator operator who was called an elevator girl appeared in the United States nearly three decades before her debut in Japan. According to an article in the *New York Times* (1902), a woman was placed in the job formerly held by a male worker who suddenly quit: "A young and pretty girl was found and she is now running the elevator in a neat white cap and apron. . . . The idea 'caught on' and girls got employment in elevators in other establishments. The elevator girl is fast becoming popular." This example is one reason we might use caution in thinking about the English loanword "girl," and when and how it entered the Japanese lexicon.

Initially the elevator girl held a critical job in operating the elevator, getting customers on and off safely, working the controls for the gears, and opening and closing the doors and metal gating. As the elevators became increasingly mechanized, department stores extended the role of operators to include greeting customers and announcing merchandise and sales on each floor. But the elevator girl is not a uniform without a biography, and her tale reveals many fascinating contradictions and insights. Somehow, we already knew that she is not always as dutiful as a spaniel and that occasionally her hair is a mess. Understanding her takes us back to the earliest incarnations of the job and to the media's uses of her persona, so I begin by looking at the history of this occupation and also at the story of one unfortunate 1930s elevator girl.

We also need to acknowledge the performative nature of the elevator girl's actions, so I follow the section on history with a short sketch of traits that contribute to the construction of her routine. My narrative then shifts to a few selected popular culture texts from the 1990s and 2000s. In each case the elevator girl is emblematic of the tension between her embodied occupational role and her agency as a person. She highlights the contrast between the outside public layer and the woman beneath.

The Box Maiden

When the Ueno branch of the Matsuzakaya department store reopened in 1929, six years after the Great Kantō Earthquake, it had many new features: heating and air conditioning, a hair salon, its own post office, and eight elevators operated by women. According to news reports, these young female employees were referred to with various titles, including *"shōkōki gāru"* (up-down controller girl), *"hakojō"* (box girl), and *"erebētā no onna untenshu"* (woman elevator driver). The name that eventually took root, however, was *"erebētā gāru"* (*Yomiuri Shinbun* 1929a, 1929b).

Japan's first electric elevator system was installed in 1890 in the twelve-story Ryōunkaku building in Asakusa. There were two cars that went from the first to the eighth floor, but within months of being installed they were shut down because of safety concerns (Nihon erebētā kyōkai 2007). The Japan Elevator Association has designated November 10, the day the elevators in the Ryōunkaku building first ran, as Elevator Day, during which they promote elevator and escalator safety nationwide.

The first elevator operators were men, and it was not until 1929 that women were recruited for the job. In an article announcing it as a "new women's occupation," the newspaper commented that the first elevator girls thought that the hardest part of their job was when the elevator stops (*Yomiuri Shinbun* 1929a). The elevator girl had to manipulate a motor controller via a projecting handle in order to stop the car. (It was not until the 1950s that fully automatic elevators not requiring an operator came into general use and replaced the manual control systems. Yet even after elevators became fully automated, most stores continued to employ elevator girls.)

A year after the *erega*'s debut, the comic artist Ogawa Takeshi (1930) took up the theme of the elevator girl in a drawing he created for the weekly publication *Comic Times* (*Jiji manga*), a series published between 1921 and 1931 that satirized current affairs and trends. In his drawing, Ogawa makes fun of the elevator girl's language and fashion consciousness, particularly her choice of footwear. In the text accompanying the image of an elevator girl extending a dainty foot, Ogawa puns on the sound *"shū"* and the putative verbal ending *"su."*

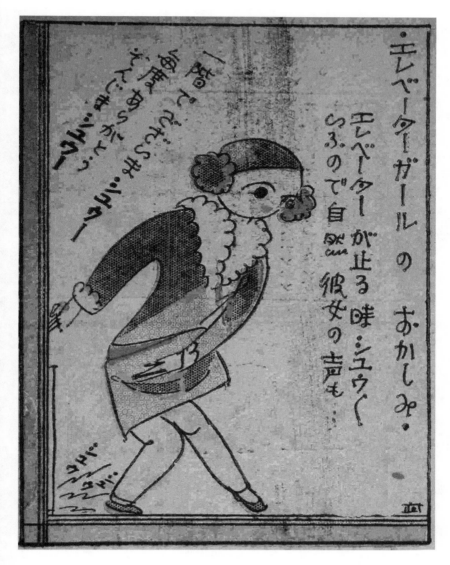

Figure 4 "Elevator Girl Humor" (_Erebētā gāru no okashimi_), illustration by Ogawa Takeshi in _Jiji manga_ (Comic Times) no. 468, October 5, 1930, page 5. Courtesy of Laura Miller, photo taken at the Billy Ireland Cartoon Library and Museum, Ohio State University.

The elevator operator was originally a male occupation, so why did the job become so completely feminized? As in the case of the department store clerk (see chapter by Tipton in this volume), managers and owners understood that having young attractive female employees do service jobs added an elegant cachet to the retail business. News reports announcing the new elevator girls were quick to note that women in American department stores also held this occupation. American department stores were often emulated, and male executives from Takashimaya, Matsuzakaya, and other stores visited the United States to learn about the latest retail trends.

The idea of getting into a small box and being quickly whisked upwards hundreds of feet must have aroused some anxiety about this mode of transport. As late as 2009, the Ministry of Land, Infrastructure, Transport, and Tourism (Kokudo kōtsū daijin) ordered that all elevators be equipped with an auxiliary brake after a fatal accident in 2006 that killed a teenage boy (*Japan Times* 2009).[4] As other chapters in this volume note, female bodies and images are attached to new technologies of warfare and transportation in order to diffuse their dangers. By having young women controlling this new vertical transport, those who wanted people to ride in large moving containers were offering a type of assurance about their safety.

Reclaiming the elevator girl's cultural history must also include a closer look at the story of an individual worker who illustrates both the allure and the dangers of this new profession. I am interested in the following short biography because it illustrates how middle-class status was undergoing a transformation from an older model to a newer one (Sato 2003: 128). As women from relatively uneducated backgrounds moved into jobs that were *scripted* as middle-class femininity performances, the disparity between class as an economic status and class as cultural attainment (or even mimicking of it through memorized elevator girl language and comportment!) was put in high relief. In addition, this story is one of many texts of the era that show a fascination with the seemingly double life that women in these new occupations were suspected of living.

The Tragic Elevator Girl

Tsuchido Shizue, described as an elevator girl in news reports, killed herself on August 14, 1934, by jumping from a seventh-floor ladder at her workplace at the Nihonbashi Shirokiya department store (*Yomiuri Shinbun* 1934). In a farewell note to her father, Tsuchido expressed dismay that she was about to be fired because of a rumor about a love affair she was reportedly having with a famous customer. In the last letter she wrote to her father she said, "The world has become hateful so I am leaving it before you." Tsuchido began working at Shirokiya in 1932 as a cafeteria worker, or "*shokudō gāru*." Two years later she started doing one-hour shifts as an elevator girl. This particular suicide captured the public imagination, and newspapers were eager to print a series of stories about the incident.

Why would the death of a lowly department store cafeteria worker who sometimes ran the elevator be considered newsworthy? Suicides of other young people during this period were not unusual, and they too were covered in the news. An increase in suicides of young people during Japan's interwar years is sometimes blamed on the eroding effects of non-Japanese ideas about romance and marriage that were promoted in popular media and films of the era. Japanese government concern with the problem was even noted in foreign news reporting (*Canberra Times* 1930). It is estimated that perhaps one-third of these suicides were same-sex female couples, so the strain on women wishing to escape a patriarchal system is particularly notable (Robertson 1999). Perhaps interest in Tsuchido relates to her having been on the scene at Shirokiya in 1932 when a famously huge fire killed fourteen female customers and workers. Although one of her feet was slightly singed, she survived the disaster because she had been working in the cafeteria, which was on the periphery of the blaze.

Fires were common enough in prewar Tokyo, but this one was said to be the impetus for a major change in Japanese clothing customs. Before the 1950s, the only undergarment normally worn beneath a kimono was a sheer slip (*hadajuban*), since a kimono does not easily accommodate the wearing of Western-style panties. According to many histories, the decline in the wearing of kimono may very well stem from the Shirokiya incident. When the fire was reported in news and historical accounts, such as Shirokiya's own corporate history (Shirokiya 1957), it was noted that female victims perished even though firemen were on hand to save them. According to Liza Dalby's (1983: 318) account of the Shirokiya incident, "several scores of women customers died in the flames despite the fact that firemen arrived in plenty of time with safety nets. The women apparently were afraid of exposing themselves by jumping and landing in ungraceful postures." It might be noted, however, that some writers have viewed this as an urban legend, and that many of the women dropped to their deaths onto the streetcar tracks below the store because the escape ropes they had hastily fashioned out of Shirokiya cloth broke or they lost their grip on them (Nakagawa and Rosovsky 1963; Inoue 2002). Inoue Shōichi (2002) adds that in other fires in multilevel buildings during the same period, many men wrote about seeing, from below, kimono-clad women descending ladders and ropes without hesitation in order to escape the burning buildings. The true cause of the Shirokiya deaths, therefore, may have had more to do with insufficient disaster equipment provided by the store rather than female anxiety about exposing their nether regions.

For unclear reasons, after the conflagration, Tsuchido was subjected to nasty gossip and ostracism among her coworkers. Two years after the fire they broadcast a rumor that she was in a relationship with Yokō Dekao, a handsome man who was part of the Warai no Ōkoku (Kingdom of Laughter) comedy theater group in Asakusa. Some newspapers implied that Tsuchido's death was related to the problem of women assuming modern occupations, which allowed them to meet attractive men and to get entangled in inappropriate relationships. In their view, Tsuchido must have lived a double life as a seemingly chaste department store worker and unstable actor's girlfriend. Media efforts to explain why Tsuchido would leap to her death never considered that the ill-fated elevator girl/cafeteria worker may have been suffering from an ugly combination of post-traumatic stress syndrome and workplace bullying.

Tsuchido caught the attention of the news media because her sad story demonstrated the dangers associated with this modern profession. The 1920s gave birth to many new female identities, all of them an implied rejection of the elite discourse of women's primary assignment to domestic space. Similar to a paradox found in other modern professions (see chapters by Freedman and Tipton in this volume), the elevator girl provided a mixed message about proper female roles. Her job was a respectable form of employment in a beautiful setting that served to buttress middle-class norms of femininity and deference. At the same time, attired in her new Western wardrobe, the elevator girl was placed in proximity to many strangers and had new opportunities to meet and perhaps socialize with people without family supervision. She is thus one of the prewar modern girl morality tales that arose from anxiety about movement of women into public domains.

Elevator girls were at times the topic of news articles in which they were cast as victims of male stalking behavior by foreign (Filipino) men, who found their kind smiles and cheerful attitudes enticing (*Yomiuri Shinbun* 1941). She also demonstrated what could happen when women from lower classes attempted to move up. The term "professional working women" was ambiguous because it was created to distinguish working women in urban jobs from female day laborers and factory workers; yet it included non–middle-class café waitresses and domestic workers (Silverberg 2007: 68; Sato 2003: 133). The category embraced relatively uneducated women such as Tsuchido, who graduated from higher elementary school (six years of elementary school plus two or three more years, unlike middle-class women who might receive a few more years of high-school-level education).

These urban women considered elevator girl work desirable because it taught them how to perform middle-class femininity. It is the scripted nature of the job that allows such boundary crossings, and even a well-bred miss who moved to Tokyo was resocialized into another type of urbanized class status. Fast forwarding from the 1930s to contemporary times, we find that although some aspects of the job have changed, the predictable bits of language and the expected gestures and movements have continued to characterize the elevator girl's performance.

Enacting the Elevator Girl

A contemporary Japanese woman who works as an interpreter considers elevator girls to be no better than unbaked automatons: "Those girls are trained to be robots. With the elevator girls, you don't see a person but a doll" (quoted in Kristof 1995). Elevator girls are given extensive training in how to comport themselves, how to stand straight, bow crisply, and speak appropriately. The department store wants to install a specific elevator girl persona through compulsory fastidiousness and training in methodical movements. But rather than seeing these as behaviors scripted for profit, some observers, both Japanese and foreign, deflect disdain onto the elevator girl herself, casting her as an empty purse. Foreigners in particular interpret the *erega* as a sign of oppressed Japanese womanhood, and her bowing is misread as subservience.

Various body movements and linguistic features constitute an elevator girl's performance. Her training is significant, as she must memorize specific gestures, bowing routines, and formulaic expressions. Elevator girls perform a type of service industry "*kata*"—standardized postures and movements normally associated with traditional arts. Yet, as Christine Yano (2003: 26) illustrated in her use of the term, *kata* training works "to fuse the individual to the form so that the individual becomes the form and the form becomes the individual." This idea captures the way that the elevator girl's presentation of self distances her from the private spaces where her movements and speech are not so highly regimented. Within studies of the sociology of work, there has long been recognition of how the ideology of "scientific management"(Taylorization), originally advocated as a strategy to improve factory production, has come to dominate management philosophy in a spectrum of occupations. In Japan, compulsory standardization of the worker's bodily comportment is especially evident in the training of service industry employees, as illustrated by Raz's (1999) study of Tokyo Disneyland.

The manager of the Odakyū department store in Tokyo told a journalist from the *New York Times* that "these girls are the first employees our customers see. We take training them very seriously" (Tabuchi 2009).[5] Elevator girls are the public face of their stores and employers, so the job is invested with intensive scrutiny and self-regulation.

Because the ambiguous space of the elevator allows strange men to enter and stand close to her, the store's training asserts a forced gentility onto their bodies and the words they use in these settings. Unlike the store clerks who work on the shop floor and are subjected to more forms of surveillance, the elevator girl is working in such a small, often hidden space that she herself is responsible for creating an imaginary barrier between herself and her passengers. One way she accomplishes this is through use of an artificial form of language, as discussed below. At the same time, a woman's possible insecurity about dealing with the public, coupled with wanting to earn a salary in a clean and attractive setting, made the training and unvarying performance not only acceptable but comforting.

Employees find security in the elevator girl script that is assigned, which requires little modification. The predictability that is ordinarily a pejorative and is denigrated as doll-like or robot-like becomes instead a suit of armor. The elevator girl's uniform functions as a "spatial curtain" in the same manner that women in Islam claim for the hijab or other forms of veiling. In an edited volume on Islamic veiling, some contributors discuss the veil's liberating function of diffusing unwanted male attention while also conferring a degree of security and privacy while in public spaces (Gabriel and Hannan 2011). The veil and the department store uniform both work to symbolically mark off an unapproachable private bubble while in public space.

In the autobiography of an elevator girl named Shinmura Miki (2009), titled *Department Store Girl* (*Hyakkaten gāru*), published as part of the Media Factory series about female service workers discussed in the chapter by Freedman, Miller, and Yano we learn about the training and work provided at Takashimaya. Much of the work that elevator girls do for the store is unseen by the public.

Figure 5 Takashimaya Elevator Girl Shinmura Miki. From *Hyakkaten gāru* (Department Store Girl) by Shinmura Miki, page 12, 2009, Media Factory. Courtesy of Katō Arata, Katō Nana of Takashimaya, Imano of Century and Company, and Kure Rena and Ambai Akiko of Media Factory.

Shinmura notes that elevator girls are hired as white-collar employees of the department store's parent firm and spend part of their working hours behind the scenes doing clerical tasks. Elevator girls work one-hour shifts with twenty- to thirty-minute breaks between them, and therefore ride in the elevator no more than three hours total a day. Shinmura's narrative reveals some interesting details about the job. For example, one of the small but critical jobs the elevator girls are given is to clean and organize the baby strollers available for customers' use.

In her study of how service workers funnel their feelings into grooves that comply with the interests of their employers, Arlie Hochschild (1983) coined the useful notion of "emotional labor." At Takashimaya, the rules and guidelines for the production of emotional labor are codified in training sessions and written materials organized around three English loanwords starting with S: sincerity (shinseritei), speed (supiido), and smile (sumairu) (Shinmura 2009: 55). These prescriptions are expected to be conveyed through a combination of language and body movement, particularly approved forms of standing and bowing. The Taylorization of department store work is described in great detail by Shinmura, who appears to welcome management's detailed attention to workers' bodily discipline. One tourist guide claims, "Japan is probably the only country in the world where department store elevator operators have been trained by the company robot to bow at just the right angle (we suspect the robot also teaches them to speak in that uniformly falsetto voice)" (Barakan and Greer 1996: 102). In another version, elevator girls supposedly must be trained with "special hinged gauges to teach them the exact angle of a bow" (Lowry 2006: 117).[6]

Whether or not these are urban myths, at least at Takashimaya human instructors teach elevator girls correct honorific speech, bowing, and stylized arm movements. They also teach them the history of the department store industry in Japan and elsewhere, and even show historic photographs of the staff at early American department stores such as Marshall Field's. Shinmura writes often of her role as not just a service worker, but as a curator of the store's history. Through such training, Takashimaya encourages elevator girls to take pride in their work and to see their job, and their emotional labor, as integral to the creation of the department store as an attractive, welcoming space for consumers.

The elevator girl is a perfect example of a specific form of feminized labor that includes a crucial visual component, the uniform. Over time her uniform became a fetish item for the public as well as the department store companies, who invested heavily in designing and promoting them. The department stores use costume as a way to make their low-paying service jobs more attractive to prospective employees as well as to create a certain elegant ambience for their customers. Brian McVeigh (2000: 115) noted that even some young people like uniforms because they indicate pride in group and workplace identity.

To assist in projecting meanings of both femininity and competence, the elevator girl's uniform is the product of much thought and planning. Most of the uniforms combine elements from other service jobs, livery with corded trim and brass buttons, together with skirts and high-heeled shoes. During Sogō Department Store's decades of economic success, before its financial collapse in 2000, the company commissioned a designer to create all the uniforms worn by female clerks and elevator girls (Kurosaki sogō memoriaru 2001). The fashion designer Shimura Masahisa created new elevator girl outfits for each of the four seasons, and all the uniforms were changed approximately every two years. One of his designs, the winter uniform for 1992, was the model for the costumes worn by Miyazawa Rie and the other actresses in *Tokyo Elevator Girl* (Yoshida, Katō, and Kitagawa 1992). When the television drama series aired, Miyazawa's sparkly champagne-colored miniskirt, paired with an eggshell white jacket, black stockings, white pumps, black bowler, and white gloves, was considered daringly glamorous.

The change in uniforms worn by female department store workers is often included in corporate histories. Elevator girls at Takashimaya did not start to wear the jaunty hats that later became one of its trademarks until 1944 (Takashimaya hyakugojū nenshi henshū iinkai 1982: 441). In 2001, Takashimaya in Nihonbashi held a one-day fashion show of its past elevator girl uniform designs, and outfits worn between 1972 and 1999 were modeled by working employees (*Asahi Shinbun* 2001). Takashimaya changed designs every three to five years and kept old uniforms in the store's archive, where they were brought out of storage for the show. Customers were heard saying things such as "How nostalgic" and "They really changed a lot, didn't they." The oldest uniform on display dated to 1972 and was worn by an elevator girl named Yajima Hiromi, aged twenty-two, who noted that it was older than she was.

The elevator girl fashion show indicates that customers as well as those working for the department stores are keenly aware of the connection between the uniform and the job. Although elevator girls are becoming scarce, their uniforms live on in perfect reproductions for sale online to fans, sex workers, and costume players. A store in Osaka specializes in selling women's lingerie, uniforms, and used sailor suit schoolgirl uniforms and underwear. Their website includes an "elevator girl corner" with a selection of uniforms from all the large department stores for prices ranging from $200 to $400 (Love and Lady 2010).

In a well-known and condescending article, Nicholas Kristof (1995) immortalizes the elevator girl's voice thus: "The Voice is as fawning as her demeanor, as sweet as syrup, and as high as a dog whistle. Any higher, and it would shatter the crystal on the seventh floor." Of course, the chirpy voices of female service workers are intentionally forged, and while somewhat higher than the speaker's normal speaking voice, they are not always in the highest decibel range. Vocal pitch is the result of both unconscious and conscious cultural training. The voices of female service workers such as television commercial narrators, station announcers, public service announcers, and elevator girls reflect a culturally expected "service voice."

These voices are not as uniformly high-pitched as observers later recall, and they vary depending on a number of factors. For example, Yumiko Ohara (2004) tracked the variation in pitch found in the service voice that changes depending on the participants in the interaction. According to Shinmura (2009), as part of their training, elevator girls practice speaking in a somewhat higher-pitched yet clearly enunciated voice in order to make their speech easier to understand. The higher pitch also discourages passengers from engaging in conversation by alerting them that the attendant is only available for speech related to her role as a formal spokesperson for the store.

In the Osaka Hanshin department store in Umeda, the elevator girls do ten minutes of vocal exercises in the morning and practice a nasal intonation, valued in the Kansai area as an indicator of refinement, in order to sound upscale (*Yomiuri Shinbun* 2008). The service voice of the elevator girl is often confused with the falsetto voice of the "fake child" or *burikko* (Miller 2004). A high-pitched, wheedling voice is often correlated with the "*burikko*," a derogatory label used to describe women who exhibit feigned naïveté. In both cases, women "doing" a *burikko* performance or "doing" an elevator girl role are drawing from a common gendered system of linguistic femininity. In the case of the *burikko*, however, there are additional features that mark her speech, such as use of a baby-talk register and novel morphemes from youth culture.

The elevator girl, however, uses predetermined announcements that are based on the refined speech of middle-class speakers of the standard (Tokyo-based) dialect. They are explicitly taught to use honorific speech, which even middle-class women often need to learn as adults (Miller 1989).[7] Shinmura (2009: 59–63) describes diligently studying honorific forms and being tested on their use. This training in a register of the standard dialect symbolically places elevator girls in a modern, urban space and marks their role as an official, codified one.

The nature of the elevator girls' work, which includes memorized greetings and announcements, easily allows for regional and class mobility. The brief, scripted encounters with customers demand performance but not lengthy attention. Dialects are submerged in the memorized formulaic routines spoken in the standard dialect. They are delivered shorn of as much of the underlying non-Tokyo accent as possible. Indeed, Shinmura (2009: 31) recalls having to do a microphone test as part of her training.

The expectation on the customer's side that an elevator girl will perform a certain way is apparent on those occasions when she does not do so. One example of this is found in a magazine article on peculiar women in the workplace, titled "The really weird Office Ladies in my company" (CanCam 1996). One of the obnoxious types is labeled the returnee woman (kikoku onna), and readers share stories about the type of coworker who uses her new cultural capital in arrogant or off-putting ways, such as speaking in English after returning from a stint overseas. Notwithstanding the supposed cachet accorded to foreign travel or living experience, returnees from abroad are reproached for speaking English in the wrong contexts. A four-frame comic accompanying the article featured a returnee woman elevator girl who uses English.

In frame one, a man enters the elevator and she greets him with "Hi." In the second frame he requests the second level basement floor, and she says "Okay." In the third frame she turns to punch in the floor while saying "B Two." In the final frame he thinks to himself, "Oh, right, the second level basement floor is B-2," while she turns, presents a saucy hip thrust, and winks while saying "good" (gū). The requirement that the elevator girl stay with her scripted speech, which has almost become a reified object itself set apart from the person who utters it, is most apparent when she fails to adhere to it.

Because the young, attractive elevator girl is always precisely put together in her hat, gloves, scarf, and perfectly coordinated blazer and heels, her overdone feminine beauty has become a figure ripe for feminist parody. It is not surprising that some observers see her as a bit too standardized. Her mannequin-like façade is viewed as repressive by photographer Yanagi Miwa (2007) in the Elevator Girl series, in which she has the models pose with expressionless faces as if they are devoid of agency. In an interview that took place in her Kyoto studio, Yanagi talked about her motivation behind the elevator girls project (Geijutsu Shinbunsha 2001). She saw the stiff, constrained images of the elevator girls as symbolic of the suppression and standardization of women in various occupations in Japan. She deliberately made the models she used for the project behave like dolls. At the beginning, the project took the form of museum performance art events, but eventually Yanagi switched to photography because of a desire to put the models entirely under her control and make them as much like mannequins as possible. Yanagi takes the public face of the elevator girl as her starting point, but her critique stops there and never imagines what might be behind the *erega*'s script. Many other popular culture texts, however, like to contrast the formal persona with the private, hidden person behind it.

Moving from Front Stage to Back Stage

One interesting treatment of the elevator girl allows the viewer to spend time with the women behind the uniform. This is the television drama series *Tokyo Elevator Girl*, which starred the frisky but scandal-ridden Miyazawa Rie (Yoshida, Katō, and Kitagawa, 1992). The narrative was also published as a paperback novel with the same title by the television series scriptwriter Komatsu Eriko (1992). The story is one of many of the era that relate to the theme of "*jibun sagashi*" (finding oneself). In this genre young people make self-discovery their primary goal in life rather than pleasing their parents.

Marvin Sterling (2010: 192–198) writes about the varieties of texts that feature *jibun sagashi* in their titles or as a major theme, noting that more than fifty books were published from the early 1990s onward. The target audience was primarily young people and those undergoing life-course transitions. To some degree this media niche stems from the collapse of the bubble economy, especially between 1990 and 1991, even though the metaphor of looking for the true self was present in some 1980s popular song lyrics and elsewhere and can even be dated back to the vogue for personal fiction (*shishōsetsu*) that arose in the early twentieth century and continues to be a popular genre in Japan.

The main character played by Miyazawa is a recent high-school graduate named Sawaki Tsukasa. Tsukasa (I use her first name because that is how she is most often addressed and referred to in the series) pursues her dream of leaving her hometown on Shōdoshima in Shikoku for life on her own in Tokyo. Only nineteen years old when the story begins, Tsukasa matures during the course of her first year in Tokyo working as an elevator girl. Her two friends at the department store have convoluted adult lives behind their perky smiles. One is another elevator girl named Naoko, a spunky type who unabashedly pursues sexual liaisons with men. Naoko falls for one handsome character and continuously pesters him to go out with her. Naoko comes from a solid working-class family from a blue-collar neighborhood, where she lives with her widowed father, who runs a Chinese-style restaurant. Many of the comic scenes in the series are of Naoko and her exasperated father arguing about her late hours and wild ways. Tsukasa's other pal is Miyuki, a dreamy information desk receptionist who, in contrast to Naoko, is delicate, reticent, and soft-spoken. Yet even this paragon of femininity has an affair with the department store section head and ends up getting pregnant and having an abortion.

At the beginning of the drama Tsukasa somewhat priggishly observes the love affairs and behind-the-scenes tricks of her female coworkers. She befriends a married man from Osaka named Yoshimoto who lives in her apartment building. Their first encounter takes place at a laundromat, and a few days later Yoshimoto visits Tsukasa's department store on business and sees her in the back office area when she is not in her elevator girl uniform.

Yoshimoto: Miss, why are *you* here?

Tsukasa: I work here.

Yoshimoto: Oh . . . what do you do?

Tsukasa: *erega.*

Yoshimoto: Huh?

Tsukasa: Elevator girl.

Yoshimoto: Oh, you can catch a rich husband that way.

Tsukasa: Well, that was in the old days, maybe there are still cases where they marry some company president, but I haven't heard anything like that.

Yoshimoto: Yeah, that's true, this is the era of the stewardess.

The dialogue suggests that husband-catching was one motive for working as an elevator girl and as a stewardess (see chapter by Yano in this volume). By the end of the series, Tsukasa is taking off from work for play days with Yoshimoto and arranges an overnight trip with him. The drama underscores the life of the elevator girl as full of its own ups and downs, framing her as a young woman somewhat detached from the expectations of propriety constraining the good girl from the good family. Open to play and performance outside the decorum imposed by her uniform at work, she is on the lookout for doors opening to all kinds of fleeting adventure.

The drama also provides an inside look into the elevator girl's workday and her treatment by male colleagues and female coworkers. At the formal, obligatory morning gatherings (*chōrei*), elevator girls are given pep talks or admonished by smarmy and badgering male supervisors. At training sessions, senior elevator girls drill the new hires in proper greeting routines and posture, and inspect their appearance. The series also dramatizes how elevator girls must clean the baby strollers at the end of the day, a task typical of the job. In one memorable episode, an elevator girl mops up a stroller where a child has had a toilet accident, then uses the same cloth to wipe off the suit of the universally despised male supervisor. Like the scene of the hamburger-chomping elevator girl in the McDonald's commercial, this one, too, trains attention on the elevator girl's potential for covert resistance.

One other interesting character in *Tokyo Elevator Girl* is the elevator girl adulator, a creepy male nerd (*otaku*) who has learned the lift worker's script by heart and likes to board the elevator with her and perform "her" routine. Such mimicry points up the elevator girl's distinctive speech as an integral part of her uniform. Rather than accepting this speech as merely a warped form of femininity, we should consider the elevator girl's manner of talking to be a register, a form of speech used in specific situations and having distinct grammatical, lexical, and phonological traits.

When speakers shift from one language, dialect, or register to another, it is called "code switching" by sociolinguists. There are numerous interactional functions that can be served through code switching, such as showing co-membership in a group and marking a change in social situations. In many scenes Tsukasa switches to her *erega* register whenever she wants to end or avoid a conversation with one of her coworkers. The code switching signals that she is "doing" her elevator girl role so is not willing to perform other identities such as coworker, potential girlfriend, or pal. The adulator likely envies the complex stance, both assertive and elegant, that this speech role confers on the *erega*. As a man, he may only imitate, but never genuinely perform this role.

In the novel version of *Tokyo Elevator Girl*, we learn that Tsukasa thinks elevator work was pleasant and prefers it to the clerical tasks she does in the back office when not working a shift on her car. At one point she is "grounded" for her involvement with Yoshimoto, which had become a topic of workplace gossip. She asks herself what it means to be an elevator girl who does not ride an elevator and realized that not being able to ride the elevator would make her consider quitting her job. One downside of elevator work, however, that Tsukasa worries about is that the long hours of standing will make her legs become too large and muscular (Komatsu 1992: 10).

At the end of the series, Tsukasa's sister writes to her to ask: "What did you find in Tokyo? Friends? Lovers? You own lifestyle?" As a typical text in the *jibun sagashi* genre, it is not surprising that in the final episode Tsukasa philosophically accepts that her unfulfilled romance with Yoshimoto was just one episode in an unfolding quest for her own path and that she is not eager to accept an offer of marriage from an attractive salaryman, either. The year 1992, when *Tokyo Elevator Girl* was aired, is notable because another elevator girl also appeared in a highly popular television program, *Crayon Shin-chan*. Here, the elevator girl's role as feminine protector of her passengers lends itself to comedy.

Crayon Shin-chan is a manga and anime series (Usui 1992) about a precocious five-year-old named Nohara Shinnosuke, who often mortifies his family with his eccentric speech and behavior. In the 1992 elevator girl anime episode that aired on TV Asahi (Hongō 1992), Shin-chan and his parents are on a shopping spree at a department store. They enter an elevator where a pretty, long-haired elevator girl, her eyes kept demurely downcast, announces each floor. Customers call out their intended stops, and when Shin-chan asks for the 137th floor, she tells him there are only seven floors in the building. This exchange leads Shin-chan to imagine there is more of a connection between them, and when his parents exit the elevator he stays behind to flirt with her. Completely smitten, Shin-chan asks if he can ride with her in the elevator for a while and begins making inappropriate suggestions. A female customer and her young son get on the elevator, and then it suddenly malfunctions, coming to a stop between floors. The elevator girl tries the telephone, but that too is broken. Meanwhile, Shin-chan's mother is sobbing and demanding that the store supervisor rescue her son, claiming that her little boy must be petrified. The supervisor says, "Please don't be worried. The elevator girl is with him; she's part of a very experienced staff. I'm sure she is taking good care of your son."

The next scene shows the inside of the elevator, where Shin-chan is perfectly calm but the elevator girl is kneeling on the floor crying uncontrollably, lamenting her fate and even her decision to become an elevator girl. In order to raise their sagging spirits, Shin-chan decides to teach the others a provocative and silly dance and song about "little buttocks" that one should wiggle and slap. When the elevator is repaired, the worried parents and staff gather in front of the elevator doors to greet those trapped inside. The doors open and the onlookers are confronted with the swaying backsides of all four of the occupants, who are also slapping their own bottoms and singing the "little buttocks" song. In this episode, the well-trained elevator girl is exposed behaving in unanticipated and unprofessional ways, while the little boy remains unflustered.

Elevator girls who are usually more professional than the one found in the *Crayon Shin-chan* episode may nevertheless reveal their private sides in other novel situations. Again, the assumed femininity and docility of the elevator girl lead to fantasies of a true self that is radically different and even malevolent. Mizutani Fūka's (2009) manga entitled *Melancholy of the Wolf* (*Ōkami no yūutsu*), which appeared in *Tsubomi*, a quarterly anthology that features female-female romance stories, is about a predatory elevator girl. This genre of manga, called "girls' love" (*gāruzu rabu*) by publishers, was originally produced by male artists and intended for a mostly male audience. More recently, however, the genre has diversified, and *Melancholy of the Wolf* is targeted to a mixed audience of male and female readers. In this story the tall, elegant Sakurai recalls that from her days in kindergarten she has loved only women, and they in turn find her irresistible and cool. At her job in a small department store she considers her workplace to be prime hunting territory. Sakurai muses that "Everyone, everyone is my prey."

One day Sakurai is at her post in the elevator when a young woman wearing a frilly beribboned dress, lacy bonnet, and laced-up boots boards the elevator car. She is one of the subculture types known as Gothic Lolita. This style features clothing based on designs from the Victorian era combined with a gothic sensibility. The ensemble often includes bouffant skirts, pinafores, and ruffled blouses, much of it edged with lace and ribbon. An embellished bonnet or other headgear such as the one worn by Sakurai's Lolita is de rigueur.

Miss Lolita turns her back on Sakurai once she boards the elevator and stares intently at an advertisement for teddy bears on the wall. Noting this, Sakurai asks if she's decided on a doll and directs her to the third floor. But the Lolita ignores her and gets off the elevator without responding to her. This behavior upsets Sakurai, who decides to go looking for the Lolita. Asserting to herself that "It is the start of hunting time!" and "There's no girl who has not fallen for me!" Sakurai sets off in hot pursuit of the Lolita. She asks coworkers if they've seen her and is directed to the exit. Sakurai dashes outside frantically in search but finally gives up and returns to work, where she is admonished by her male supervisor. She is back on the elevator when Miss Lolita suddenly reappears, smiling fetchingly. Miss Lolita apologizes and tells Sakurai that she got tired of walking around and wonders if it is all right to ride for a bit. The final frames of the manga depict Sakurai and Miss Lolita holding hands as they ride the elevator together.

In this manga, the elevator girl Sakurai steps away from her cool façade to the extent that she is reprimanded by her boss and becomes emotionally distraught about being ignored by a potential love interest. The tableau presents two figures recognizable in their uniforms, yet pushes the reader not to take the uniform at face value in the case of either individual.

Nostalgia for a Dying Profession

Only a few department stores still employ elevator girls, but those that do value them as a critical marketing device. Odakyū in Tokyo retains fourteen full-time elevator girls, yet to a few foreign journalists she is emblematic of wasteful extravagance. One columnist questions why a country like Japan has so many "exquisitely engineered inefficiencies," including elevator girls and other people who are "spending valuable time doing things that don't need to be done" (Gross 2009). One wonders if men were getting paid for this job if the derision would be quite as intense, or if their performance would serve as another celebratory moment of praise for Japan's consumer-pleasing service industry.

Yet this figure that provokes contempt from foreign journalists still manages to elicit attention as a prototype of decent female labor in past decades. Despite her disappearance from most urban spaces, the elevator girl's footprint remains embedded in mass consciousness. Shinmura (2009: 30) lovingly describes Takashimaya's retro-style elevator doors of gold brass and glass and writes about the store's slogan, "Never changing so always new" (*kawaranai noni, atarashii*). Nostalgia and pride in the elevator girl is a recent phenomenon. It is interesting that in 2010 Matsuzakaya features the innovative hiring of elevator girls in 1929 on its official website.[8] The company history of 1982, however, does not list elevator girls in its timeline of notable store events for the year 1929 (Matsuzakaya Nanajū Nenshi Henshū Iinkai 1981: 336).

Some younger women find the figure of the elevator girl an appealing icon to emulate at a safe distance. The elevator girl is a popular dress-up figure in costume play, such as the parody 2009 cover of *Special Best Vol. 1* (*Suppesharu besuto* vol. 1) by the popular girl group Berryz Kōbō, in which all seven members are attired in magenta elevator girl uniforms and pink and black bowlers (Berryz Kōbō 2009c; see the chapter by Freedman in this volume for more on Berryz Kōbō). Elsewhere others pretend to be elevator girls, as in a photo of a young woman who is standing in her apartment doorway with her arm extended up, palm facing inward, in a stereotypical elevator girl pose. On the photo she has written "going up" (*ue e mairimasu*). Dressing up as an elevator girl is also found on "print club" (*purikura*) self-photography sticker art. Some arcades with print club booths provide costumes for girls who want to dress up before taking their photos. In addition to Elevator Girl, other popular outfits include Stewardess, Mini-Skirted Policewoman, Nurse, Santa, and Bride (Miller 2005).

Miyazawa Rie revisited her role as an elevator girl in a series of Glico chocolate commercials aired in 2009. Miyazawa, thirty-six years old, plays the role of Wakame-chan, a character in the Sazae-san anime. In the commercials, Wakame-chan has landed a job in an old department store as an elevator girl, and having Miyazawa play this part is a type of nostalgic parody of her former hit role. The elevator girl serves as an allegory about the impact of modernization, making many feel as if they are being pushed to assume new behaviors that feel layered on to a self that, underneath, is more authentic. As a visible example of the literal changes in dress, mobility, and technology, she becomes a focus of modern tensions.

The *erega* work and the uniform mask the hidden self, thus allowing the observer to imagine or install their own fantasies of the woman under it. As noted above, however, while the idea of the two sides to an elevator girl (her uniformed self and her un-done self) is present in popular culture, I do not believe that there is a "true" elevator girl self that exists when she is not at her post. As sociologists and anthropologists are quick to note, all human actions are culturally constructed and performative, even the seemingly behind-the-scenes actions performed in privacy. But perhaps because our view of the elevator girl is from an outsider's perspective, we are missing something. Could it be that the apparent homogeny is deceivingly liberating? Rather than simply camouflaging the individuality beneath, the predictable scriptedness of the role offers an avenue for women to participate in public jobs without having to reveal individual aspects of their personalities or identities. This trained façade also allows advancement for working-class women and for women from small towns who want to move into the ranks of the seemingly well-bred. Since all public roles entail a degree of performativity, this is not to say that there is a "true" versus "fake" display involved here. Rather, the elevator girl slot does not rely on extensive orality or exquisite cultural capital, so serves as a useful avenue for women who want to move into an urban lifestyle. There might be a liberating metamorphosis involved as well, as her vulnerability in the public gaze is masked or protected by the uniform and scripted speech.

Beyond an expectation that service workers are performing an occupational role that is partly artificial, the elevator girl's persona is so noticeably scripted and managed that she easily becomes the object of multiple fantasies and eroticized attributions. Tsuchido at Shirokiya in the 1930s, and the fictional elevator girls found in popular culture texts (Tsukasa in *Tokyo Elevator Girls*, the long-haired *erega* in *Crayon Shin-chan*, and Sakurai in *Melancholy of the Wolf*) all illustrate both the attractions and the dangers of the job. In these cases there is fascination with the disparity in their professional behavior and what they do when not enacting the script.

At the same time, the availability of the elevator-*kata* or script enables young women, especially those who have no possibility of landing a high-status job or marriage, the opportunity to participate in the middle-class imaginary. Department store customers experience their own aspirational dreams through consumption of its luxurious displays. These ideals about class mobility and attainment that the store promotes have already been adopted by the elevator girl through her training and costuming. Doing her job, while attired in a beautifully tailored *erega* uniform and speaking the formal Japanese phrases she has been trained to use, places her at the center of the dream that the store aims to sell. Class, regional differences, and even youthful insecurity melt away in the freedom offered by the elevator girl's performance.

Chapter Four

SWEAT, PERFUME, AND TOBACCO

The Ambivalent Labor of the Dancehall Girl

Vera Mackie

In his 1931 novella *Dancers and Drawers* (*Dansā to zurōsu*), Tada Michio describes an enchanting figure, a dancehall girl on the streets of Tokyo: "With a cheeky bob and slim legs. With stockings of a color that matches her skin so well she looks like she's not wearing any. Her shoes are patent leather with high heels. Her gaudy salmon pink dress flutters in the wind as she steps along the pavement" (Tada 1931: 1).

Kawanishi Hide's (1894–1965) woodblock print of a dancehall from 1930 presents another intoxicating scene. The print is composed of fields of a few strong colors: red, yellow, green, black, and white. The figures of women in vivid dresses overflow the edges of the rectangular print, giving a sense of abundance and excess. The black jackets and trousers of the men highlight the bright colors of the women's dresses, while these shapes and colors are reflected in the glossy dance floor below. In the background is a stage where musicians play trombones and trumpets, and the gaudy colors and strong lines of the picture somehow suggest the swing of the music. Dancehall girls are seated around the edges of the dance floor, waiting for the next patron to purchase a ticket to dance.[1]

Such scenes from popular culture reflect a fascination with dancehall girls in 1920s and 1930s Japan. These women appear regularly in the visual culture, literary works, and popular sociology of the time, and dancehalls also provide a backdrop for satirical cartoons depicting the foibles of the "modern girl." While the dancehall girl is regularly represented in the writings and art works

Figure 6 "Dance Hall" (*Dansu hōru*), print by Kawanishi Hide, 1930. From the collection of the University of Sydney Gallery. Reproduced with the permission of Kawanishi Yūzaburō.

of others, her own voice and her own experiences are somewhat more elusive. In order to get a sense of the working lives of such women, it is necessary to read between the lines of a range of sources: fiction, popular culture, popular sociology, visual culture, and ephemera.

The dancehall is a contradictory site for the enactment of practices of labor and leisure. For the male patrons, the dancehall is a site of commodified leisure, where they can purchase the company of a female dancing companion for a short time. For the dancehall girls, however, the dancehall is a site of labor. Their company is a commodity to be purchased. Dancing is hard work, and the dancehall is a workplace structured by power relationships shaped by gender, class, ethnicity, and racialized positioning. These dimensions of power determine which men can purchase the company of which women, so that the binary gender relations of male purchaser and female provider of services are mediated by class and ethnicity.

The dancehall is also symptomatic of Japan's place in the world. The practices of the dancehall were transmitted from the United States in the 1920s to the rest of the world. Dancehalls and taxi dancing were adopted in the urban centers of Japan, as well as in other major East Asian cities such as Shanghai.

The history of the dancehall thus takes us from the major cities of the United States to Europe and East Asia, reflecting the movements of people, products, practices, and ideas under conditions of colonial modernity (on colonial modernity, see Barlow 2004: 7 and 1997: 1–20). The appearance of the dancehall girl in these sites reflects the gendered and ethnicized power relations of each place.

The Dancehall

The taxi-dance hall was invented in the United States during the Prohibition Era and provided a space where men could socialize with women without alcohol. The first taxi-dance halls were in port cities on the West Coast but soon spread to Chicago, New York, and other major cities. Men would buy tickets to dance with the women, who came to be known as "taxi dancers." Like taxi drivers, they provided services for a limited amount of time, in turn, to whoever could pay the charge.

The dancehalls revealed some of the gendered, classed, and ethnicized dynamics of the major U.S. cities and provided the site for one of the classic sociological investigations of the Chicago School: Paul G. Cressey's *The Taxi-Dance Hall* (1969 [1932]). The clients of these dancehalls were often men who were marginalized in society and could not otherwise hope to interact with women in a casual way. For example, immigrant men from the Philippines, at that time a U.S. colony, frequented the dancehalls as one of the few places where they could socialize with white women (Parreñas 1998: 115–134). Right from the start, the dancehalls were a site where the dynamics of imperialism and colonialism were revealed.

As the dancehall was introduced to Japan in the 1920s, special-purpose buildings were constructed, although some dances were also held in hotel ballrooms.[2] Several books appeared on the architecture of dancehalls, which had to be suited to the purposes of social dancing, while complying with regulations designed to discourage unseemly mixing between men and women off the dance floor (Nagai 2004: 659–679).[3] The dancehalls provided an opportunity to experiment with new architectural styles and interior decoration. They were located in major cities like Tokyo and Osaka, former treaty ports like Yokohama and Kobe, and other major entertainment centers. The Takarazuka Hall (Takarazuka Kaikan) in Western Japan, for example, was in the latest art deco style. The dancehalls were places where the newest international fashion and accessories could be seen, worn by young men and women often referred to as "modern boys" and "modern girls." The dancehalls flourished from just after the Great Kantō Earthquake of 1923 until they were suppressed with increasingly moralistic regulations in the 1930s.

Kon Wajirō and his colleagues in "Modernology," who conducted ethnographies of the places and practices of daily life, described the various dancehalls in Tokyo in their 1929 *New Guide to Greater Tokyo* (*Shinpan dai-Tōkyō annai*), reporting that the halls generally charged an entrance fee of around fifty *sen*, although the entrance fee might be commuted if dance tickets were purchased. Dance tickets cost ten *sen* in the daytime, when music was provided by phonograph records, and twenty *sen* at night, when there was a jazz band. The dancers pocketed around 40 percent of the fee. The Tokyo Dance Research Institute (Tokyō Buyō Kenkyūjo) in the Kyōbashi neighborhood was one of the older dancehalls, rather formal, and with a Filipino jazz band. The Union Dancehall in Ningyō-chō had a "hedonistic" and "cheerful" atmosphere but charged an entry fee of one yen, as well as a fee for dancing tickets. The Kiraku-kan in Shibuya had only twenty or so dancers who seemed like beginners, and neither the dancers nor the patrons were very skillful. The Kokka in Shinjuku had an air of decadence, while the Iidabashi Dancehall (Iidabashi Buyōjo) had a more serious (*majime*) atmosphere. The Ikeuchi Dancehall (Ikeuchi Buyōjo) in Sugamo Shinden boasted of being the oldest dancehall in Tokyo and had rather a warm, "domestic" (*kateiteki*) feel (Kon 2001 [1929]: 287–291).

The Florida Dancehall in Akasaka, described as being as large as the Moulin de la Galette in Paris,[4] had a Hawai'ian band (Kon 2001 [1929]: 287–291). Florida is perhaps the best known of the Tokyo dancehalls and has been immortalized in the photojournalism of Hamaya Hiroshi (1915–1999) and the paintings of Enomoto Chikatoshi (1898–1972) (Brown 2012: 258–263). One of Hamaya's well-known photographs provides a behind-the-scenes glimpse of a dancehall: a barely clad woman is seen from behind as she gazes at her reflection in a mirror, resting her elbows on a ledge in front of the mirror. She is perhaps checking her makeup before her appearance on the dance floor, or perhaps taking a moment to rest between dances. Enomoto's series of large fan-shaped paintings prepared for the Gajō-en wedding hall in Meguro in Tokyo (Brown 2012) depict the women of the Florida Dancehall. One woman sings into a microphone, while a pair of dancers in revealing dresses clutch small purses where they keep their dance tickets. All of the women in Enomoto's paintings have bobbed and permed hair, wear rouge and lipstick, and have fine plucked and penciled eyebrows in the style of the modern girl (for more on this style, see Mackie 2010b: 996–1011; Mackie 2012: 53–57).

The *New Guide to Greater Tokyo* provided a taxonomy of the dancehalls and other entertainment venues in the metropolis, while other writers and artists provided a taxonomy of the different kinds of people found there. The Modernologists' casual references to Filipino and Hawai'ian dance bands suggest wide-ranging circuits of mobility for the jazz musicians. Jazz bands played on the ocean liners that plied the Pacific and East Asia, and some of these bands played in Osaka or Yokohama dancehalls while docked in these port cities (Atkins 2001: 60).[5] Dancehall girls, too, moved between these sites, as we shall see below.

The Modern Girl and the Dancehall Girl

The dancehall girl may be seen as one manifestation of the figure known as the "modern girl." The rise of the modern girl roughly coincides with the rise of the art deco and modernist styles in the period of reconstruction after the Great Kantō Earthquake of 1923 (Mackie 2010b: 906–1011; Mackie 2012: 53–57). She is associated with the spaces of the café, the cinema, the theater, the department store, the ocean liner, and the dancehall. In visual culture we see her driving, shopping, swimming, playing sports, smoking, drinking, and dancing.[6] Advertisements often present the modern girl as both a consumer of modern products and a spectacle to be consumed (Mackie 2010a: 91–116).

The modern girl has a distinctive style: Western dress with short skirt, a cloche hat, shoes and stockings, pearls, beads, rings and earrings, lipstick, rouge, and beauty spots. The modern girl herself can be seen as an icon of modernity, and the shape of her bobbed hair also came to function as a metonym. The figure of the modern girl decorates the sheet music of the 1920s and the matchboxes used to advertise cafés, cabarets, and dancehalls (Mackie 2012: 53–57). The dancing legs of the modern girl in her short skirt also function as an icon in this context (Silverberg 2007: 53).

Dancehall girls were also, of course, working women. Most visual and literary representations, however, focus on their attractiveness to the male client and consumer, rather than on the conditions of their labor. The *New Guide to Greater Tokyo* describes the attraction of the dancehall for the male patrons:

> On looking at the swirling pleasure in the white-hot mass of men and women in the dancehall, there is no doubt that anyone who could dance would want to join in, to keep dancing to the sound of that cheerful jazz music with a young woman in your embrace. . . . To get close to a waitress (*jokyū*) in a café, in one of the high class cafés in Ginza, for example, takes quite some time, and even then

the rules forbid even holding her hand. In the dancehall, however, just for the price of a bottle of beer, one can openly hold hands with a woman and dance madly with her for a few minutes without anyone trying to stop you. . . . There is no other entertainment so modern (*kindaiteki*), so cheaply available, and such good exercise (Kon 2001 [1929]: 287).

These reflections suggest that, in the popular mind, the dancehall girl was connected with other modern women's occupations, such as actress, artist's model, café waitress, and cabaret dancer. What these occupations share is some form of commodification of women's bodies and sexuality. There are also, however, hierarchical differences: the company of the dancehall girl is apparently cheaper than that of the café waitress.

The names of many of these occupations were formed through neologisms employing the suffix "*gāru*" (from the English "girl"), such as "*sutekki gāru*" ("stick girl," a woman who could be hired for a short time to accompany a man on a walk) (*Examiner* 1929: 18). "*Gāru*" was used for women in service jobs (see chapters by Tipton and Miller in this volume). Other terms used the suffix "*jō*" (literally "daughter" but also translatable as "girl"). The term "*dansu-jō*" (dancer, taxi-dancer) is thus a hybrid term, formed from the Japanese transliteration of the English word "dance" (*dansu*) and the Sino-Japanese "*jō*."[7]

The café waitress, by contrast, was linguistically domesticated, with the use of the Sino-Japanese term *jokyū* (waitress, literally "woman who serves"). The labor market for these service industries was paralleled by other labor markets.[8] Other women worked in factories or as domestic servants, while more elite women with a higher school education might work as teachers, shop assistants, or telephone operators (Tsurumi 1990; Hunter 1995).

While the Japanese media debated the morality of the modern girl in all of her manifestations (see the chapters by Freedman, Miller, and Yano and by Tipton in this volume), international correspondents in the Anglophone media reported on the spectacle of the bobbed-haired, short-skirted women in the dancehalls of the major cities of Japan (Point True 1928: 19; *Cairns Post* 1928: 11; *Morning Bulletin* 1929: 8; Uenoda 1930: 13–21; *Queenslander* 1933: 35; *Brisbane Courier* 1933: 7). Most of these journalists saw the dancehalls as exotic spaces and the dancehall girls as exotic figures. While the practices of taxi dancing and the figures of taxi dancers were familiar from other major international cities, the dancehall became an exotic site when relocated to Japan, and the dancehall girl became an exotic spectacle in the eyes of the Anglophone viewer. The dancehall girl was simultaneously a figure of modernity for the Japanese metropolitan male, and a figure of exoticism for the Anglophone male. For the Japanese male, the dancehall girl was "other" in terms of her gender and class. For the Anglophone male, there was in addition an ethnicized otherness. All of these male viewers, however, could reaffirm their masculinity through the power to purchase the services of the dancehall girl for a short time.

Although the dancehalls seemed glamorous to many of the male patrons, mainstream society often looked on the dancehalls with a judgmental gaze. In October 1925, artist Kitazawa Rakuten (1876–1955) depicted a modern girl on the cover of the satirical magazine *Jiji manga* (Comic Times) [see Figure 7].

Figure 7 Cover illustration by Kitazawa Rakuten, *Jiji manga* (Comic Times) no. 234, October 12, 1925. Image courtesy of the Billy Ireland Cartoon Library and Museum, Ohio State University.

Rakuten was commenting on a seventeen-year-old woman, Fukaya Aiko, who had shot her lover "Ricci" with a gun. The cartoon reveals the cultural associations of the dancehalls in 1920s Japan: a space where both sexes mix, young people wear Western dress, and cross-cultural encounters take place. The insouciant modern girl in cloche hat, bobbed hair, and form-fitting dress dominates the foreground of the frame. She plays with her scarf with one hand while her other hand rests on her hip. A man and woman are seen in one corner of the cartoon, obviously judging the deviant modern girl and demonstrating the respectable standards she is being measured against. The respectable woman wears a kimono, and her husband wears a Western-style suit. Their faces are creased with concern at the antics of the modern girl, the focus of their concern shown in a balloon above their heads. The balloon shows a couple dancing in a dancehall, their posture echoed by another whimsical couple, a champagne bottle dancing with a champagne glass.

Moral reformers coalesced with the Home Ministry, calling for the reform of cafés, cabarets, bars, and dancehalls. Because dancehalls were controlled by municipal governments, these campaigns took place at different times in different cities. The crackdowns in Osaka in 1927 led to a boom in dancehalls in post-earthquake Tokyo, until the Tokyo metropolitan government, in turn, exercised its own controls (Atkins 2001: 58).

Social critic Tosaka Jun (1900–1945) noted the contradictory attitudes of the Home Ministry. While it suppressed cafés and dancehalls—which were associated with non-Japanese culture—licensed prostitution districts were allowed to continue as before (Tosaka 1983 [1936]: 44–47, cited in Silverberg 2007: 76). The Home Ministry and Tokyo Metropolitan Police exercised increasing control in campaigns between 1928 and 1930, and again in 1934 and 1938, closing down dancehalls by 1940 as part of the mobilization of the populace for total war (Garon 1997: 107–108; Atkins 2001: 63–64; Silverberg 2007: 76).

Gender and Class on the Dance Floor

The dancehall is an ambiguous and ambivalent space: a place of leisure and entertainment for the male clients, but a workplace for the female dancers. A 1924 print by Nomura Toshihiko (1904–1987) depicts a different view of the dancehall from most other contemporary representations, for it does not actually show anyone dancing. Two women sit on chairs, no other men or women in sight. They wear the short skirts and bobbed hair of the modern girl. They slump in their chairs, their heads cast down. It seems they are resting between dances.⁹ Their posture highlights the fact that they are working women, and that dancing is, in fact, hard work for them. The print is in somber tones of dark red and green, in contrast to the vibrant colors of Kawanishi's dancehall. The name of the dancehall on the window behind them is "Break Away" (in English), perhaps ironic in its associations. Does it mean that the dancehall is a place where men can "break away" from their everyday lives, or does it suggest that the women would like to escape from their ambivalent situation?

The *New Guide to Greater Tokyo* documented the working conditions, economic conditions, and profound ambivalence of the dancehall:

> The young dancers, around the age of twenty, have to dance from two o-clock in the afternoon until eleven o-clock at night embraced by men in a whirlwind of sweat, perfume, and tobacco. Supposing that they dance continuously from afternoon to evening, around sixty dances, they could pocket four out of every ten *sen*, which would give them two yen and forty *sen*; and if they danced another hundred times up to eleven o'clock, then they would keep eight *sen* from each twenty *sen*, meaning they could take away eight yen for the night. So, they could make a maximum of ten yen per day. However, a dancer would have to be very popular to dance that much, and even so, there are few women who would have the stamina to keep dancing like that, so they would likely have to refuse half of those dances, and might come away with around five yen for the day. While the men dance cheerfully, happy with this pleasure in tangible form, the women dance in their dance partners' arms with a rather pained cheerfulness, their eyes burning brightly, but with a cold, ashen taste in their mouths. (Kon 2001 [1929]: 290–291)[10]

The power dynamics of the dance floor are revealed in several scenes of author Tanizaki Jun'ichirō's 1925 novel *Chijin no Ai* ("A Fool's Love," translated in 1986 under the title *Naomi*, the name of the main female character, Tanizaki 1925, Tanizaki 1986). The novel focuses on the relationship between a white-collar salaried worker, Jōji, and a woman known as Naomi. Jōji comes to know Naomi in her work as a waitress in a café, and he eventually marries her in the expectation that he can train her to be his ideal companion: schooled in English, singing, and social dancing. Naomi has been described as the archetypal "modern girl," and several scenes in the novel are played out on the dance floor. (For further discussion of the dancehall scenes in this novel, see Mackie 2009: 3–9; Gralla 2010: 88–106.)

These scenes reveal a shifting hierarchy shaped by class, gender, and racialized positioning. There is a taxonomy of different types of women in the novel. The most refined of middle-class Japanese women are not encountered on the dance floor. The Russian countess and dance teacher, Madame Shlemskaya, suggests the complex history that brought Russian refugees to Japan via Shanghai (Sawada 2001: 31–46). The actress Kirako seems a charismatic and refined figure in the world of the dancehall but, as an actress, she would be beyond the pale from the point of view of respectable middle-class families (Tanizaki 1986: 92).[11] Jōji's partner Naomi is a long way from the refined middle-class ladies and the "white countess" Madame Shlemskaya, but may be placed in a hierarchical relationship with the other women encountered in the dancehalls. Naomi can look down on another woman, Mā-chan, who presents a carnivalesque image of mismatched colors, much more vulgar than Naomi (Tanizaki 1986: 83–84). Even lower in the hierarchy would be the women who dance for a fee. Naomi is not a dancehall girl, but she does have a background as a café waitress and comes from a family associated with the "water trades" (mizushōbai).

Dancing provides Jōji with an opportunity to observe various women at close hand—not only to look but also to experience this proximity with all of his senses. Madame Shlemskaya is associated with the whiteness of fabrics such as georgette and precious stones such as diamonds (Tanizaki 1986: 60–61), but Jōji also has a more earthy response to the experience of dancing with her. In his comments on Madame Shlemskaya's body odor, Jōji articulates commonly held views of racialization at this time. Non-Japanese bodies were thought to have a distinctive smell, due to the consumption of animal products, such as milk, butter, and meat. Indeed, one epithet used to describe Europeans and Americans was batā-kusai "smelling of butter." This passage also, however, expresses the closely linked attitudes of anxiety and fascination, fear and desire (Hamilton 1990: 14–35), which are revealed in Jōji's encounters with white women on the dance floor.

> What's more, [the countess's] body had a certain sweet fragrance. . . . I'm told that Westerners do have strong body odor, but to me, the faint, sweet-sour combination of perfume and perspiration was not at all displeasing—to the contrary, I found it deeply alluring. It made me think of lands across the sea I'd never seen, of exquisite, exotic flower gardens. 'This is the fragrance exuded by the countess's white body (shiroi karada)!' I told myself, enraptured, as I inhaled the aroma greedily. (Tanizaki 1986: 69)

In the dancehall, Jōji casts his taxonomic eye over a series of women, placing them in a strict hierarchy according to racialized standards of beauty. The dancehalls of Tokyo, then, provided a site where men and women of different classes and nationalities could mingle, but these encounters often served to highlight hierarchical differences rather than overcoming them.

Men and women in the Tokyo metropolis could also imagine visiting dancehalls in other exotic places, as depicted in Toyoharu's painting of a dancehall in Marseilles from 1923 (reproduced in Brown 2012: 259), or Tani Jōji's (real name Hasegawa Kaitarō, 1900–1935) fictional depiction of the entertainment world of Manhattan (Tani 1927; cited in Omori 2003: 239–245). While the dancehalls and ballrooms of the United States and Europe were distant dreams, the dancehalls of Shanghai were somewhat closer to the metropolis of Tokyo. Artists and novelists from Japan depicted scenes of dancing with Japanese, Chinese, and Russian women in places like Shanghai's New Carlton Hotel.

Colonial Modernity and the Dancehall

In 1924, artist Yamamura Kōka (1885–1942) produced a color woodcut depicting the dancehall of the New Carlton Hotel in Shanghai.[12] In this scene, two women are seated at a round table. One has bobbed hair; the other wears a red hat. Both wear Western dress, but the embroidered jacket draped on one of the chairs suggests the fashion for Chinoiserie. Several couples dance in the background of the picture, the women all with similar bobbed hair. The male dancing partners are barely visible, and the women are seen from behind, giving them a sense of anonymity. The lack of individual features of the women dancing in the background also suggests a degree of interchangeability between the taxi dancers. The ethnicity or racialized positioning of the dancing women is unclear, but at least one of the seated women appears to be "European," possibly Russian. With their bobbed hair and Western dress, the women clearly reference the style of the modern girl.

Several scenes in Yokomitsu Riichi's (1898–1947) novel *Shanghai* also take place in dancehalls.[13] Several of the dancehall girls in the novel are Japanese, and they dance with patrons from all over the world, including the Japanese businessmen who are the main protagonists. Yokomitsu's novel suggests, then, the regional mobility of both men and women from Japan at this time, but does not go into detail on the routes and circumstances that would have brought such women to Shanghai (on regional mobilities, see Driscoll 2010; Itō 2006; Matsuda 2006).

Tada Michio (1931: 14), in *Dancers and Drawers*, relates stories of women who went from dancehalls in the Tokyo metropolis to Shanghai, having been advanced the cost of their travel and their clothing. Yokomitsu's dancehall portrays a confusion of different nationalities:

> An American was holding a German. A Spaniard was holding a Russian. Portuguese bumped into people of mixed blood. A Norwegian kicked at the legs of a chair. Englishmen caused an uproar with a shower of kisses. Inebriated people from Siam, France, Italy, Bulgaria. Sanki alone, his elbows resting on the back of a chair, was staring like a frog at the voluptuousness of people of all nationalities entwined in the strands of tape. (Yokomitsu 2001: 80; for a similar description of the various nationalities encountered in a Shanghai dancehall, see Tada 1931: 14.)

Historian Frederic Wakeman notes that Shanghai became "a city of tawdry, sordid dancehalls" (Wakeman 1996: 108). He described the changing fortunes and changing composition of the dancers and patrons of the notorious Carlton Hotel in Shanghai, not so different from Yokomitsu's fictional depiction of a Shanghai dancehall:

> "The old Carlton closed. It opened again at once as a dancehall with Russian hostesses, a risqué floorshow, and became a cabaret of sailors." Public dancing during the 1920s had been more or less monopolized by White Russian women, but around 1930 dance halls on the Western model began to open up in Shanghai and other Chinese port cities with Chinese *wunü* (dance-hall girls). . . . Eventually, toward the end of the 1930s, Shanghai would have 2,500 to 5,000 taxi dancers. (Wakeman 1996: 108)

Historian and literary scholar Leo Ou-fan Lee describes Shanghai in the 1930s as "the cosmopolitan city par excellence . . . the center of a network of cities linked together by ship routes for the purposes of marketing, transportation and tourism . . . an international cultural space in which not only Britain and France but also Japan played a significant role" (Lee 1999: 409).

Under the terms of the unequal treaties with the Euro-American powers in the nineteenth century, certain ports in Japan and China were designated as "treaty ports," where international traders could gain access to port facilities, ships could take on fuel and water, and their nationals were exempt from prosecution by the local legal system under the principle of extraterritoriality. By the turn of the century, Japan had successfully renegotiated its treaties with the

United States and the European powers and had in turn forced a similar treaty on Korea, before finally annexing Korea in 1910. Such cities as Shanghai, Yokohama, Nagasaki, Hakodate, and Kobe were linked with international trading routes. The routes that linked these cities referenced the overlapping circuits of European, U.S., and Japanese colonialism and imperialism in the East Asian region. Ocean liners plied these routes, transporting tourists and traders, jazz bands and dancehall girls between the treaty ports. Yamamura Kōka's print of the New Carlton Hotel in Shanghai provided viewers in Japan with the image of an exotic site, a projection of the dreams of the men of the metropolis.

Dancehalls were subjected to increased control not only in mainland Japan but also in Manchukuo from 1938, and closed down by 1940, as the government cracked down on activities that were not seen to contribute to the war effort (*Courier Mail* 1938: 14; *Townsville Daily Bulletin* 1938: 11; *West Australian* 1938: 15; Russo 1938a: 18; Russo 1938b: 6).[14]

Postscript: The Return of the Dancehall Girl

After Japan's defeat in 1945, military forces from the United States, United Kingdom, and other Allied countries occupied the nation until 1952, under the Supreme Commander of the Allied Powers (SCAP), General Douglas MacArthur. Once Allied troops landed on Japanese soil, dancehalls sprang up again after their wartime suppression. The dancehall proprietors revived the practices that had been outlawed just a few years before, this time with the occupying soldiers as their clients.

In January 1946, the *Nagasaki Shinbun* reported on the opening of the Roseland Dancehall to cater to Allied troops stationed at Sasebo (*Nagasaki Shinbun* 1946, cited in Kovner 2009: 794). The international Anglophone media also reported on the entertainments available to the Allied soldiers (*Argus* 1946: 3), usually from the point of view of the soldiers and often referencing knowledge about the entertainment districts of Japan's major cities before the outbreak of war: "Meanwhile, if you are a non-Axis white, and provided you have American dollars or American dollar backing, you can have almost as swell a time as old Japan hands had before the war" (*Courier-Mail* 1946: 2).

At times the tone was highly moralistic. A "Special Correspondent" for *The West Australian* reported on the "taxi dance racket" as early as December 1945, describing dancehalls apparently run by the Recreation and Amusement Association (RAA, *Tokushu ian shisetsu kyōkai*) (Special Correspondent 1945: 11; see also Percival 1945: 9).[15] While most entertainment establishments were placed off limits to troops, the "Special Correspondent" reported that soldiers were allowed to enter the "Oasis of Ginza" because alcohol was not served there (in the Australian vernacular, the Oasis was "dry"):

> Troops descend to the hot cigarette-smoke-filled basement, 50ft below street level, and choose their partners from 500 simpering Japanese girls in gaily coloured kimono. They purchase strips of two-yen tickets, each of which entitles them to a three-minute dance to a slick Japanese orchestra playing latest American dance hits. Obedient to their training, the taxi-dancers make themselves bright and agreeable partners and collect their tickets at the end of each three-minute dance. . . . It should not be imagined that all [the price of the tickets] goes to the taxi dancer, or that taxi-dancing is a lucrative pastime for the tiny doll-like dancers. On the contrary. They are bound to their service by an original debt for their clothing, which includes a beautiful kimono that may cost 1,000 yen, and by the fact that outside exists unemployment and hunger. The dancers live dormitory style in sections of unbombed city buildings, and are provided with their frugal rice meal by their employers. And for this food and shelter they pay from the 150 yen a month . . . allowed them from their earnings. (Special Correspondent 1945: 11)

The description of the ticketing system suggests that the practices of the 1920s and 1930s were revived in the Occupation period, and that the house still collected most of the proceeds from the dance tickets. While the dancehalls of the 1920s and 1930s had been associated with modernity and Western dress, the Occupation-era dancehalls catered to Allied expectations of exoticism. The Special Correspondent writing for the *West Australian* described the women as "simpering" and "doll-like." The dancehall girls variously wore kimono, Chinese-style dress, or Western dress. A "Member of the Occupation Force," reporting on dancehalls for *The Mercury*, described the scene: "Paper streamers, festoons, and garlands of all colors in profusion give an air of gaiety. The soft lighting, diffused by multi-colored "Chinese" lanterns and glass shades, lends an exotic aspect to the scene" (Member of the Occupation Force 1946: 3).

Sumi Seo Mishima, in her memoir of postwar Japan, reports on women in dancehalls wearing "sarong style evening gowns" (1953: 155) and recounts the sad stories of the dancehall girls:

> [M]any of these dancers for hire were war-widows, who had been burnt out or repatriated from the Continent. Each had a sad story to tell of how she had been

stranded on this growing crust of postwar Tokyo—a series of tragic, wasteful quarrels with her parents-in-law, accounts of hellish repatriation journeys from a far outpost of the collapsed Japanese Empire, recollections of nights spent penniless, foodless and shivering in the street with her little children, and so on. (Mishima 1953: 155–156)

Reports on the dancehalls in occupied Japan also reveal tensions between the different armies involved in the Occupation:

In the larger cities, such as Osaka, there are cabarets that really are large dancehalls, having a few extra attractions such as drinks, waiters, and stage shows. These places are even more expensive than the dancehalls, especially if the visitor avails himself of the facilities for drinking. . . . The Americans patronize these cabarets in large numbers, but the British troops, with their smaller incomes, could not patronize them to this extent even if available in their area. (Member of the Occupation Force 1946: 3)

The suggestion that the dancers were indentured to the dancehalls in order to repay debts highlights the extreme poverty of Japan in the immediate postwar period. Accounts from the 1920s and 1930s do not often describe such indenture in the dancehalls, although this had been common in brothels and in factories. The involvement of the Japanese government in setting up the RAA dancehalls contrasts with the repressive moralism and nationalism of the wartime regime that had closed down the dancehalls in the late 1930s. There are, however, continuities in the wartime provision of military brothels for soldiers of the Japanese army and the postwar provision of various forms of "entertainment" for the occupying soldiers under the auspices of the short-lived RAA.

The shifting history of the dancehalls in 1920s, 1930s, and 1940s Japan reflects the shifting gendered, classed, and racialized dimensions of Japan's place in international circuits of power. In the 1920s, the dancehall showed Japan's place in the international transmission of cultural forms and practices, with Tokyo taking its place alongside other major global cities. The dancehalls of post-earthquake Japan were places where the latest international fashions could be seen, while the buildings themselves were sites for experimentation in the latest modernist, art deco, and art nouveau styles.

In the 1930s, the dancehalls were sites for cross-cultural encounters. Patrons in Tokyo, Yokohama, and Osaka danced to the music of Hawai'ian and Filipino jazz bands, possibly learning to dance from "White Russian" immigrants. Dancehalls in Shanghai reflected the intersecting circuits of European,

U.S., and Japanese colonialism and imperialism. For readers and viewers in the Tokyo metropolis in the 1930s, the dancehalls of Shanghai seemed accessible because of Japanese economic and colonial power.

In Occupied Japan, the floor of the dancehall was one of the places where new forms of Euro-American hegemony were enacted, in practices that drew on early twentieth-century forms of commodification, reimagined through new forms of Orientalism. The figure of the dancehall girl moved through all of these spaces, subtly reimagined in each new decade, gazed on by a series of dancing partners and represented by artists, photographers, novelists, and sociologists, but rarely invited to speak for herself.

PART II

Models and Modes of Transportation

Chapter Five

"FLYING GEISHA"

Japanese Stewardesses with Pan American World Airways

Christine R. Yano

The cover of the May 1, 1967, issue of *Life* magazine (Asia edition) and an accompanying feature story proclaimed, "Newest Stewardess Fad: A Japanese in Every Jet." Both the cover and the story included photos of an array of Japanese stewardesses from eleven international carriers.[1] Standing dead center and smiling broadly was Abe Hiromi, a Japanese stewardess wearing the Tunisian blue uniform of the American corporation, Pan American World Airways. Abe's placement in the photos was no accident. At the time, Pan Am was the undisputed leader, trendsetter, and symbol of prestige in global aviation. It is understandable that of all the airlines represented by the women, it would be Pan Am, by way of Abe, that grabbed the center-stage position.

However, there is more to the story than this. In an interview with me, Abe recalls her own personal media savvy: understanding the spotlight, she took it upon herself to maneuver into the center position in any group shot. She did this to capture the stage, not so much for herself as for the airline that she represented and proclaimed as number one. Thus, Pan Am's spotlight in this and other representations came about as a combination of both corporate strategy and personal initiative on the part of its employees.

Both the corporation and the individual worker were constantly engaged in Pan Am's public relations, sharing a belief in the worthiness of the endeavor. In this, Abe was exemplary. The spotlight of the *Life* magazine article shone multiply—on Japan, on Japanese women, and inevitably on Pan American World Airways. In effect, Abe (and other Japanese stewardesses for Pan Am) inhabited that triple spotlight, and in the process created subject positions for themselves. Abe and others flew as paragons of the airline—what Najeeb Halaby, Pan Am's president from 1969 to 1972, dubbed "flying geisha." Halaby's expression "flying geisha" drew little from actual knowledge of geisha but instead relied greatly on widespread Western stereotypes of Japanese women as subservient handmaidens to men's desires. This was Halaby's fantasy: the ultimate in gendered service mixed with racialized exotica. Halaby's fantasy did not include technical knowledge, emergency training, or CPR procedures that were critical components of the job. It did not include maneuvering into positions of the camera's frame to beat out personal or corporate competitors.

Indeed, the actual Japanese women in Pan Am's Tunisian blue uniform were far from exotic handmaidens. Halaby's fantasy did include the public relations moment that each stewardess inevitably lived on the global stage that was Pan Am. *Life* magazine may have trumpeted "a Japanese in every jet," but Abe's actions demonstrate ways in which Japanese women and jets fueled a dialogic interaction between gender, mobility, and modernity in postwar Japan.

This chapter critically traces Abe and other Japanese Pan Am stewardesses' positioning at the forefront of an era. I ask, what did it mean to suggest not only the presence of "a Japanese in every jet," but that the jet-borne Japanese of international note should be a woman? What made gender, mobility, and modernity a particularly potent combination? I take the Japanese international stewardess as a case study of globalism during the Jet Age, a period of incipient cosmopolitanism for Japan and much of the industrial world. Through personal interviews with Japanese former Pan Am stewardesses and an investigation of archival materials (including a book of memoirs written by members of the Pan Am Alumni Association), I analyze these Japanese women's experiences flying for Pan Am as a strategic mix of the traditional and the modern, the old and the new—that is, the very modern international stewardess job, relying on women's performance of old-fashioned femininity, particularly racialized within the Japanese context.

The Three Strands of the Story:
Gender, Mobility, and Modernity

The three strands I tie together here deserve brief separate mention. Gender is critical to the discussion and analysis in multiple ways. These include the stereotypical assumptions made about women as servers ("flying geisha"), the exoticization of the Japanese woman, and the gendering of Japan as woman.

Corporatist gendered assumptions imbued women with certain access to the world outside of Japan, working as exemplars of "tradition" within a service profession that boasted of its newness.

Furthermore, the story of Japan's international stewardesses must be contextualized within the politicized frame of the 1960s and 1970s, in much of the industrial world globally. This was a period of highly public activism, from student uprisings in Japan and elsewhere, to racially based protest movements and rising feminism in Euro-America. The women's liberation movement was taking hold, especially in the United States, emphasizing equal pay for equal work, and disavowing beauty contests as demeaning to women's worthiness on criteria other than appearance (see Bardsley in this volume). At the same time, this liberation included the sexual freedom afforded by greater access to and ease of birth control ("the pill" and intrauterine devices). Women's liberation activists often denounced sexualized female images, including that of the stewardess.

That image erupted riotously in the mid-1960s and 1970s with the publication of *Coffee, Tea, or Me: The Uninhibited Memoirs of Two Airline Stewardesses*, a fictionalized account purportedly by two flight attendants, Trudy Baker and Rachel Jones, but actually ghost written by Donald Bain (Baker and Jones 1967).[2] Although Pan American World Airways itself purposely kept some distance from such a freewheeling sexualized image of the profession, the scent of the "Coffee, Tea, or Me" image and slogan pervaded the industry and the times. The image fit the times so well: attractive women finding libidinal pleasures outside the home in a fast-paced life that took them seemingly everywhere. Japanese women—including those who flew—presented contradictions and contrasts. As seen by Euro-Americans, they were exotic women from afar, trained—or even more pointedly, assimilated—by an American corporation. They represented nostalgized figures of dutiful women who knew how to serve, especially in contrast to Western "liberated" women who only knew how to serve themselves. And yet they, too, were traveling women in a profession considered at the forefront of the age. This story takes these gendered dimensions as a starting point and ground upon which to inscribe the women's stories.

Mobility is another important strand, particularly as a key symbol of an era. As geographer Tim Cresswell (2006: 1–2) points out, mobility itself bundles its own contradictions—linked to concepts of progress, freedom, opportunity, and modernity, alongside concepts of deviance, resistance, and shiftlessness. Indeed, both the celebratory and critical aspects of mobility inform this research. The twinned aspects help us understand ways in which the Japanese international stewardess could simultaneously be interpreted in Japan as a glamorous icon of the time, as well as a suspect "bad girl" for leaving Japan.

Mobility during this postwar era was enabled through government rule. On April 1, 1964, the Japanese government officially lifted international travel restrictions imposed since the days of the Allied Occupation. The lifting of the ban allowed Japanese to more fully participate in the Jet Age, an era linked to social changes wrought by movement itself. These changes included the upward mobility of individuals and groups of people, as well as an expansion of Japanese citizenry's sense of the postwar world, enhanced by rising incomes and enabled by foreign travel. The numbers of Japanese traveling abroad rose rapidly from 128,000 in 1964, to 500,000 in 1969, to over four million by 1979 (Carlisle 1996:12). A critical year within this rise was 1971, when for the first time, the number of outbound Japanese travelers exceeded the number of inbound foreign travelers to Japan (Carlisle 1996:12). Although initially the majority of Japanese travelers were businessmen, with the rise of packaged tours and middle-class disposable income, growing segments of the general populace in Japan began to consider international travel within their purview.[3]

Enhanced mobility thus created the "contact zone"—in Mary Louise Pratt's words, "social spaces where cultures meet, clash, and grapple with each other, often in contexts of highly asymmetrical relations of power"—that became the Japanese international stewardess's workplace and playground (1991: 33). That contact zone included the physical spaces of airline training facilities, airplane cabins, airports, and hotels in foreign ports of call, as well as the discursive spaces of advertisements, media, and literature. In these various contact zones, Japanese international stewardesses navigated the demands placed upon them as part of their newfound mobility.

And finally, the strand of modernity emphasizes the place of science and technology in contributing to a public sense of newness and excitement of the era. Advertisements and public relations campaigns highlighted the speed, quiet, and safety of jets. Technological and industrial achievements, such as the first commercial transatlantic flight in a jet, made headlines. In this atmosphere, men occupied the forefront, as scientists, engineers, industrialists, and pilots became heroes. Stewardesses became the glamorous "trophy-wife" accouterments to a life spent within the high-speed jet stream. These were women on the go, undoubtedly, but their participation rested in a gendered set of expectations of the modern life. High speeds shrank the globe in a time-space compression (Harvey 1990: 240),[4] enhancing the possibilities for international communication and cooperation.

In a Cold War era of ideological warfare, the U.S. government saw international travel as critical in fostering "education for overseasmanship" that "would not entail the learning of new information so much as the cultivation of new feelings" of empathy for other peoples (Klein 2003: 21). Overseas travel, then, carried the hopes of such affective learning (a "sentimental education," as Christina Klein puts it) to meet both humanistic and political goals (Klein 2003:23). These goals placed Asia in the midst of Cold War concerns. Modernity encompassed jets that made overseas travel possible, but it also included the growth of a middle class and the creation of economy fares by Pan Am that made that travel affordable.

Modernity also references a particular historical figure in Japan, the "modern girl" (*modan gāru*, shortened to *moga*) from the 1920s and 1930s. The *moga* of the 1920s and 1930s was based in media images of women who did new things in new places. In very public urban spaces, they lounged in cafes, strolled Ginza's newest shops, and took on an air of Western cosmopolitanism, much like their flapper counterparts. In short, they moved through urban spaces flaunting new consumer-based agency.

I borrow the term "modern girl" as a heuristic device, linking the Jazz Age of the 1920s and 1930s to the Jet Age of the 1960s and 1970s in Japan. During both of these eras, women became the spectacle of a particular kind of modernity built through the possibilisms of mobility and consumption. In this regard, the characterization of interwar years "modern girl" by the cross-disciplinary, cross-areal Modern Girl Around the World Research Group (quoted in the chapter by Freedman, Miller, and Yano) is worth repeating: she projects "an up-to-date and youthful femininity, provocative and unseemly in its intimacy with foreign aesthetic and commodity influences" (2008a: 9). These elements of modernity, youth, femininity, foreign contact, and consumption link flappers and international stewardesses within a useful analytical frame.

The Jet Age of the 1960s and 1970s created a particular position for the Japanese woman, not as a passenger so much as a server. What became known as the "cocktail generation"—that is, middle- to upper-middle-class whites whose stereotypical lifestyle included nightly, after-work infusions of alcohol and occasional forays into fantasy escapism in tiki-lounge culture—of the 1950s and 1960s framed Asia alongside the Pacific and other far-off destinations as a broadly characterized jet-set fantasy of exotic drinks and equally ex-

Figure 8 First group of Japanese flight attendants to be trained in Pan Am's International Training College, Miami (*1966*). Photo courtesy of Jane Euler, President of World Wings International, Inc.

otic women (Adinolfi 2008: 52). Among these, the Japanese woman—based on Euro-American interpretations of the geisha—became the ultimate symbol of gendered service.[5]

Hiring Japanese Women as "Flying Geisha"

Pan Am's hiring of women of Japanese ancestry was not altogether new.[6] This practice began in 1955, when Pan Am undertook to hire Japanese American women for Japanese language service, in order to compete with Japan Air Lines, which began flying internationally in 1954 (Yano 2011). But the negotiations of language and race were always problematic: many Japanese Americans could not speak Japanese fluently or were not adept at the special speech of honorifics (*keigo*) expected within native Japanese service culture.

When the U.S. immigration laws on employment changed in 1966 to allow hiring foreign nationals, Pan Am jumped at the chance to hire Japanese women. Whereas Pan Am previously had to check Japanese American hires for their ability to speak Japanese, when hiring Japanese nationals the company had to test for their English language competency. Hiring for English language ability meant that Pan Am was necessarily tapping into an upper-middle-class stratum of elite women (as I will explain later). The first Japanese women hired by Pan Am in 1966—a group of seven—became media sensations, their photos in newspapers throughout Japan.

The sensation of Japanese Pan Am stewardesses—in other words, what made them newsworthy in Japan—lay in the global recognition their hiring brought. In effect, the hiring of Japanese women by Pan Am and other international airlines was yet another national achievement for Japan on a global stage, taking place within the context of the nation's dramatic entry into postwar modernity through its "economic miracle." It meant that Japanese women could occupy the same rung of glamour—albeit within a service industry—that other, primarily white, women could, circling the globe with the best of them on an airline that claimed the number one spot.

Japan's pride in these women lay in the indisputable reputation of Pan Am at the time as the leading airline of the world. The 1964 Tokyo Olympics had brought a similar national pride in global representation, as Japan proved itself worthy of hosting and participating in the leading international sports event in the world. Just as Japan could bask in the glory of the Olympics, now could it point to its international stewardesses with Pan Am as proof that the nation could hold its own against others. Japanese international stewardesses thus signaled a particular kind of global achievement.

The *Life* magazine article of 1967 provided a litany of qualities that purportedly made Japanese women well suited to the job:

> While the Japanese airlines have always been aware of the attributes of Japanese women, the foreign carriers only lately have discovered their unique talents. "It is her air of serenity and gift of grace that makes the Japanese stewardess such a sought-after member of the airlines' crew," says one Lufthansa official. An Air India representative adds admiringly: "Their ability to stand up to strain better than others is a major asset. . . . A Japanese woman knows how to serve and desires to serve," says Ursula Tautz, Lufthansa's chief of stewardesses (*Life* 1967: 42–43).

Indeed, the *Life* magazine article reinscribes Halaby's "flying geisha" ideal: working efficiently and unobtrusively to serve others while imparting nothing less than an "air of serenity" and "gift of grace."[7] The "flying geisha" ideal situated Japanese women as exemplars of what some of her Euro-American counterparts had left behind—a feminine position rooted in patriarchal hierarchy. In short, taking the submissive, gendered role of a server became a source of praise for Japanese stewardesses. Within the context of global travel, *Life* magazine's coinage of the "Japanese in every jet" phenomenon suggested that amidst the dizzying ultra-modernity of the Jet Age, Japanese women could provide a nostalgized presence of good, old-fashioned, racialized servitude.

Granted, stewardesses in general acted as a reassuringly "domestic presence" aboard the latest in technology, as historian Kathleen Barry explains the job: "A stewardess's foremost duty was to mobilize her nurturing instincts and domestic skills to serve passengers . . . [as] guests in their own homes" (2007: 12). Barry's description takes into account attitudes toward air travel that have hovered around the practice since its beginnings—a combination of fear and excitement that was allayed by the calming presence of the stewardess.[8] The airplane cabin, then, became a living room in the air, and the stewardess, its hostess. If the airplane cabin was a space domesticated in part by the stewardess, then the Japanese woman among them held a particular position as one well accustomed to such domestic duties. Unlike her Euro-American "swinging" sisters, the reputation that Japanese women held was one of modesty and domesticity. This was particularly important as passenger lists grew to include more women and children.

The airplane cabin thus held the gendered and racialized tensions of the era, at least as presented in the media. On the one hand were "coffee-tea-or-me" Euro-American stewardesses purportedly living the swinging lifestyle of the jetsetter. On the other hand were "air-of-serenity-gift-of-grace" Japanese stewardesses who remembered their household and hostessing duties. The Japanese woman, then, performed as the cabin domestic, serving others rather than using the job as a self-serving platform. These media constructions, built on Euro-American stereotypes of the period, reinforced the contradictions of the cabin.

For Japanese passengers and stewardesses alike, however, the Pan Am cabin could never quite serve as their own living room. With World War II in the not-so-distant past, with the Allied Occupation (1945–1952) an even more recent memory, this living room was a complex, borrowed space. Flying Pan Am certainly represented prestige for Japanese, but it was the giddy prestige of poached privilege that only reinforced their place within it. Seated next to white passengers in first class, Japanese travelers could share the wine and caviar equally.[9] Yet they retained the lingering assumptions of race and nation that pervaded the cabin. Even on an international carrier such as Pan Am that prided itself on its broad cultural knowledge, Japanese often felt themselves to be poachers in the cabin space that belonged more fully to white Americans and Europeans.

Having Japanese stewardesses on board may have brokered the gap between Japanese passengers and that borrowed space, but stewardesses, too, faced their own sense of poaching. With Halaby's "flying geisha" as a backdrop, all stewardesses performed traditional roles of service and hospitality. As Arlie Hochschild puts it, those roles were constituted in emotion management, and sold as product: "The emotional style of offering the service is part of the service itself" (1983: 5). For Japanese stewardesses, however, this ideal carried a racialized note, especially on an American carrier. The emotional style of their workplace performance reflected gendered assumptions of servitude profiled within foreign stereotypes of Japanese women. In short, performing the "flying geisha" role before an audience of foreigners naturalized Japanese women's place on board Pan Am's jets.

The women's opportunities to travel internationally with Pan Am surpassed those of Japanese men, but came with demands that they perform in roles that emphasized racial and national distinctions. Wearing Pan Am's uniform represented women's membership in a sorority of airborne professionals and provided them with firsthand experiences in practices and stereotypes that set them apart. The issues of race, culture, and gender intersect with social class and nation as well.

Flying during the 1960s was expensive, especially in comparison with the lower fares that came with deregulation from 1978 through the 2000s. With the exception of those on group tours, passengers flying internationally were typically upper or upper middle class, whose expectations of service matched their own status position. The fact that class relations paralleled hierarchical relations between Japan and the United States only amplified the racial and national differences in status between the Japanese stewardess and her American employer (as well as other stewardesses and passengers, who were primarily Euro-American). Furthermore, more men than women traveled, often for business; therefore expectations of service followed intertwined gender, nation, and class lines. The demands placed on Japanese stewardesses thus came not only from the company and its training but from the structural position of passengers based in gender, class, race, and nation. In short, the Japanese stewardess flying for Pan Am entered a position that was overdetermined even before she stepped aboard the plane.

Mobility Embedded as Class-Based Practices and Dreams

It is important to delineate more clearly what the Japanese Pan Am stewardess's position was, especially as a factor in shaping corporate and personal subjectivities. In other words, the women who flew for Pan Am themselves came from particular class positions. Their English language facility was one class indicator. But so, too, was the scope of their dreams.

Coming from elite families meant holding elite dreams as part of their milieu and times. As Appadurai argues, "Fantasy is . . . a social practice: it enters in a host of ways, into the fabrication of social lives for many people" (1996: 198). These dreams were part of the social lives of these women. In speaking of their Pan Am aspirations, they use tropes such as "freedom," of wanting to go "beyond Japan" in order to know and experience what was on "the other side of the horizon." These tropes sound out postwar fantasies whose archaeology includes wartime suffering, Allied Occupation, miraculous reconstruction, and mid-1960s emergence as a global citizen capable of staging an Olympics and building high-speed trains. Would-be stewardesses' fantasies of freedom and going beyond national borders paralleled Japan's. Furthermore, the women's dreams of mobility paralleled global fantasies of international travel fostered by the Jet Age itself. Inasmuch as these fantasies of global travel were Japan's and the industrial world's, they held resonance as part of the elite women's practices.

In fact, many of these women lived amidst an embedded expectation of cosmopolitanism: the women's dreams were part of a family heritage. Akemi (who worked for Pan Am from 1968 to 1986),[10] for example, describes her background: she had a geologist father who traveled worldwide and lived in Singapore while she, her mother, and her siblings lived in Tokyo; her aunt attended university in Los Angeles and married a non-Japanese there. Within this context, Akemi's dream of becoming an international stewardess was a matter of course.

Sumie (with Pan Am 1967–1972) likewise recounts a family background of international expectations:

> In my lifetime I always knew that I would be coming to America because my
> grandparents had been here. So was my grandfather's younger brother, and
> my grandmother's younger brother was also in England. In my family people

have gone in a hundred years before to America, to England, to Germany for various study and work. So when my mother's father returned to Japan, he raised my mother saying that she would come to America someday. And when my grandfather passed away and that dream didn't come true, she still came [to America] even though she was a mother of three and was forty-three years old. So I was left in Japan with my grandmother and two brothers, knowing that I was going to make it there [overseas] one day!

Sumie's family's reaction to her Pan Am employment: "They were excited, very. They backed me up 100 percent."

Not all families welcomed their daughter's dream of becoming a stewardess. However, the objections that some families raised were not to the travel; they disapproved of the class implications of the job. Satō Kumiko from the first group of stewardesses in 1966 recalls:

> I told my family that I wanted to become a flight attendant, and they strongly opposed this. I was not expecting such a reaction from them. Their reason was, "It is manual labor. Serving meals and drinks for a living is out of the question!" I had never experienced such rejection by my family before, so I was in a state of deep shock. But at the same time I felt a strong sense of rebellion. I had no one on my side, so I had no chance of winning this. After much deliberation, I decided to seek advice from my uncle on my mother's side, and thus I began my lonely battle with my family. Thanks to my uncle's help, my persistence was rewarded with my family agreeing to let me fly for one year. This is how I joined Pan Am as a member of the first group of Japanese stewardesses in 1966. (Satō 2004: 102)

This kind of objection followed the stewardess profession from its inception. The service nature of the position was by definition déclassé, no matter how seemingly glamorous. Even while sharing some of the white-gloved practices of elite culture, the undeniable fact was that the stewardess was there as a service provider, not a partaker. The structural hierarchy offended some upper-middle-class parents, especially those to whom position mattered. Their daughter could visit some of the same places, stay at the same hotels, and do many of the same things that jetsetters in far-flung places around the world did, but it was a service job that got her there.

Flying for Pan Am meant opting out of a safer, more predictable life close to home. The women who chose to become stewardesses were elite daughters whose families had invested in their education and who might have worked as teachers or nurses, if temporarily. However their main future trajectory and primary social responsibility was to marry and to do so within the bounds of shared class privilege. Working for Pan Am did not fit this scenario. It meant not only traveling the globe in the name of work, but also relocating to Honolulu, which was the Japanese-language base for Pan Am operations. Taking the job meant placing oneself temporarily out of circulation as a potential marriage choice in Japan at the exact moment when elite women ideally might be making those choices or being chosen—that is, after formal post–high school education. Instead, Pan Am represented foreign employment that would take them away from Japan. Most stewardesses followed the ideal scenario presented by both the women and their parents, which was to work for a few years, then quit and get married.[11] However for several women I met, the stewardess lifestyle became habit-forming. They married late or, in a few cases, not at all. Inadvertently, they had become career women.

The prestige of working for Pan Am was matched by the elevated pay scale. Quite simply, Pan Am paid far better than other airlines in Japan and provided women the opportunity to earn even more than many Japanese men of equal education. One boon to their salary was that the women were paid in dollars. As Saeko (with Pan Am 1971–1981) points out, when she was hired, "The yen was 360 to the dollar. So my first salary, including per diem and all that, was close to a thousand dollars a month. But when I calculated it in Japanese yen, it was a lot of money! About 360,000 yen. And my classmate, his starting job was about one-fifth of that!" Employment with Pan Am thus offered American-based prestige combined with American-level pay. Here was mobility on a social and economic level that performed on a global stage.

Some of the women's narratives also reveal the individuated practices and aspirations that led to Pan Am employment. Hiroko (with Pan Am 1966–1986) from Kitakyushu describes herself as a "vagabond with wanderlust," fascinated with foreign cultures since childhood. During the war, after she and her brother found a small downed plane in a ditch, they would sit in it and dream of flying to far-off places. She recounts: "I daydreamed all the time whenever I saw planes taking off. I was intent upon traveling the world. I always dreamed what would it be like on the other side of the horizon." While at the prestigious Dōshisha University in the 1960s majoring in English literature, she experienced the "Hawai'i fever" that engulfed Japan at the time, fueled by films such as Elvis Presley's *Blue Hawaii* (released in Japan in 1962), popular Japanese actor Kayama Yuzo's *Hawaii no Waka Daisho* [Hawai'i's Young Guy] (1963), and older songs such as "Akogare no Hawaii Koro" [Dreams of Hawai'i] (1948).

Hiroko, like many others of her generation, learned ukulele and avidly played Hawai'ian songs such as "Blue Hawaii" and "Aloha 'Oe." She says, "Everyone's dream was to go to Hawai'i!" Mobility for Hiroko meant an expansive global stage that would allow her to meet a wide range of people and fulfill her dreams fostered through books, movies, and songs.

Another former Japanese stewardess who began with Pan Am in 1966, Noriko, credits "curiosity" with drawing her to Pan Am. She says, "I was always interested in anything going on outside of Japan. My curiosity level was far beyond average." Because of her desire to see things "outside of Japan," she rejected considering any job with a domestic airline. She explains, "I always wanted more freedom than [what] the Japanese carriers [would allow me]." Likewise, another Japanese stewardess explains, "I wanted to travel to foreign countries right away, so I decided to join Pan Am which had the most flights overseas at the time" (Suzuki 2004: 110).

Dreaming Big: Corporate Loyalty and Cosmopolitanism

For these women, Pan Am represented the freedom of mobility gained through American-led cosmopolitanism. Sumie says, "I looked at Pan Am as very luxurious. Everything about Pan Am was bigger, fancier, more history." That "bigger, fancier" assessment refers to the global prestige of Pan Am in parallel with that of the United States at the time. "More history" refers to the fact that Pan Am represented the developments of the twentieth-century more prominently than any other airline through its path-breaking technological innovations, ties to the U.S. government during World War II, and international humanitarian missions in Berlin, Vietnam, and elsewhere. The big dreams that Pan Am enabled drew on the airline's own ambitions as personalized in the women's narratives.

One woman who flew in the 1970s reminisces: "I believe Pan Am was loved all over the world, because it was symbolic of the United States!" (Arima 2004: 17). As Saeko points out, "You have to remember, the 1960s, 1970s, America was up there. Rock and roll, Elvis, [and everything]." The women speak of Pan Am and the United States in glowing terms, interchangeably and uncritically. Neither one mentions the turbulence of the Vietnam War, violent student unrest, and other noteworthy conflicts of the period that made the image of the United States far more complex than simply being "loved all over the world."

This kind of uncritical attitude was characteristic of the women I interviewed and similar to the words I read in a book of memoirs compiled by the Pan American Alumni Association of Tokyo in 2004. They were very much a self-selected group—ever the diehard fans of the airline that employed them in their formative, young-adult years and placed them at the forefront of the Jet Age. Some of their loyalty and enthusiasm reflects the time in their lives that they were employed by Pan Am—a liminal period, post-education, pre-marriage, pre-children, relatively free of responsibilities except to themselves. Pan Am provided them with the heady experiences of international travel at exactly the moment when they may have best appreciated it. It is not that the women thought the airline (or the United States) was without problems. Some of them became involved in union activism; all of them had to explain to themselves and others how the airline fell from such heights to sell its Pacific routes to United Airlines in 1986, and eventually shuttered its operations amid bankruptcy in 1991. Yet the women's loyalty to the company is critical to this story of gender, mobility, and modernity.

I understand their loyalty as a function of many aspects common to former Pan Am employees I have met at company reunions, parties, meetings, and interviews. They wax nostalgic over the prestige of the company, the many perquisites of the job, and the interpersonal relationships their employment made possible. Wherever they went, Pan Am was a brand name that garnered respect and often praise. They proudly basked in the spotlight of their company.

Pan Am employees generally felt that they were a privileged bunch—privileged to be one of the select few, to be working alongside other select individuals, to be rubbing elbows with elite customers, and to be working for a company that treated them well. This was prestige tied to an age in which commercial aviation was at the forefront of public attention globally. International travel was supposed to transform the world, and Pan Am's place within it ensured its employees' place in an epoch-making endeavor.

Within this halo of remembering, stewardesses waxed nostalgic. At least while age and marital restrictions were in place until the end of the 1960s, stewardesses were a young group. Even when those restrictions were lifted, Japanese societal pressures on women to marry and to relinquish their jobs upon marriage were particularly strong for middle- and upper-middle class women, from which stewardesses were drawn. Thus they worked for Pan Am at a period in their lives when they likely held relatively few other responsibilities. Filling that liminal period with the heady experiences of round-the-world travel had a tremendous, lasting impact on the women.

Pan Am was the only exclusively international carrier, at least among American companies, meaning the flights were typically long. If the industry allotted jobs by number of flight hours (i.e., flying a certain number of hours per month), then working long-haul trips meant fewer trips overall. Long-haul trips typically held higher prestige in the industry, and were staffed by personnel with greater seniority, from pilots to cabin crew. In short, the hierarchy of air travel, with domestic, short-hop travel at the bottom and foreign, long-distance travel at the top, placed all of Pan Am's routes at the top. Pan Am's employees inhabited that upper echelon along with the airline and its routes.

And among them, stewardesses held a critical place as the face of the airline. They interacted with the public most directly in the most media-centric of positions. Besides serving as hostesses in the air, stewardesses acted on behalf of the public relations wing of the company, appearing in uniform at public relations events and photo shoots. Japanese stewardesses were among these. The uniform was critical to the performance, acting as a walking signboard for the company. Wearing the uniform, smiling the "Pan Am smile,"[12] the stewardesses became living logos. Being placed in the position of representing the company lent itself to being a loyal, corporate person, taking the company's needs as one's own and seeking the spotlight to promote the company. This was the case with Abe Hiromi, immortalized on the *Life* magazine cover. She found and claimed the "sweet spot" of the photo for Pan Am, dead center.

The Japanese stewardesses shared many experiences generating corporate loyalty with other Pan Am employees. However, I argue that Japanese culture imposed elements tied to gender, mobility, and modernity that amplified and refracted that sense of privilege and the aura surrounding Pan Am. Given Japan's wartime history and its spectacular emergence into the global limelight in the mid-1960s, the women who flew for Pan Am felt themselves swept to the forefront of this emergence. They appeared there—selected, trained, groomed, and uniformed—specifically as Japanese women, gaining a foothold in history.

Furthermore, these Japanese women were truly leaving home—that is, Japan—at a time when the practice was not common. The process of leaving home/Japan became critical in defining who they were and what they would become. As Doreen Massey points out, "Many women have had to *leave* home precisely in order to forge their own version of their identities" (1994: 11; italics in original). I contend that for Japanese stewardesses, the impact of leaving and thereby forging their own identities carries particular weight, given the history of the opening up of the era to globalism in Japan.

If Pan Am held prestige in the Japanese public's eye in the 1960s, then being hired by the company was not only a personal achievement for Japanese women but also a national achievement. The Japanese stewardesses became celebrities in their hometowns, national media, and corporate newsletters. Part of their celebrity within Japan rested in situating these women at the global forefront of technology and society—flying jets, meeting world leaders (even as servers), traveling to glamorous places, and doing glamorous things (getting haircuts at Vidal Sassoon's salon in London, attending the opera in Paris, and eating orange crepes at the Raffles Hotel in Singapore). What made these activities even more of an achievement was the place of Japan in relation to the elite of the world. What Japanese stewardesses achieved represented a tremendous national leap. Theirs was mobility of a different, but no less significant, sort. In fact, it was a leap into modernity—or at least into the practices of one of the very modern industrial countries, the United States. Furthermore, this was a leap directly into an American corporation as one of its employees.

Through Pan Am employment, Japanese stewardesses gained a foothold in modernity and mobility from the inside, as a representative of an American corporation, and even at times of the United States itself. One woman recalls:

> The day of the moon landing (July 21, 1969, Japan time) after I finished my breakfast in the hotel, the Pan Am branch office called me on an urgent matter. I headed to Sogō Department store . . . to the top floor where Nihon Terebi (Japan TV) studio was located. They wanted me along with others to be part of the television program to watch the news from the moon. The Pan Am crew appeared in uniform on the program. I thought I was really lucky to be there to witness the astronauts on this historical moment. . . . I was just a college student a few months prior. And now, living in America, visiting places all over the world, which is a dream come true. And in addition to this, that I got to watch the moon landing, live, while in my Pan Am uniform, simply made me cry with joy!" (Kawauchi 2004: 74)

As Pan Am stewardesses, women such as this became the mediated presence of Japanese achievement in a form of globally recognized assimilation, wearing the uniform of a prestigious American company, taking on a profession at the forefront of mobility, and occupying a position in close proximity to the highest achievements in America's modern technology. This was a spot reserved for women. Flying for Pan Am meant gaining global citizenship as a member of one of the leading American corporations of the day. The fact that Japanese women gained this citizenship more readily than Japanese men speaks to the gendered, racialized aspects of the period. Being present to publicly view the moon landing was the Japanese stewardesses' accomplishment of citizenship. The headiness of this experience was more than enough to garner corporate loyalty and became the basis for future nostalgia.

Lusting After and Beyond Donna Reed

Besides gender, mobility, and modernity, Japanese stewardesses' corporate loyalty should also be framed within "*akogare*" (longing, yearning, desire) for the West, and more specifically for America (dubbed *Amerika*). As anthropologist Sawa Kurotani points out, "*Amerika* is not just a Japanized pronunciation of the English word. It is a complex historical formation of the cultural and political other, a mirror against which Japan came to imagine its own totality as a modern nation-state" (Kurotani 2005: 167). In many ways, the *akogare* for the West may be considered an attitude derived from reverse Orientalism, or here, Occidentalism, defined by James Carrier as "stylized images of the West" (1995: 1). The complex formation of the West as political "other" in relation to Japan includes a modern history of centrifugal and centripetal forces, ambivalent desirings that yearn for and reject the United States as a model.

During the postwar era, mass media productions from the United States became a source of Japanese dreams. Saeko recalls: "I remember watching *Donna Reed Show*.[13] She shows up doing a vacuum cleaner, with a skirt like this [demonstrates a full skirt], and wearing high heel shoes, and impeccable hair, and I thought, my god, is that what they do? I was curious! . . . It's definitely *akogare* [longing], but I didn't want to be Donna Reed. I wanted to see her and see if they really do that." Saeko, like others, viewed Donna Reed voyeuristically, as an aspiration of modern living, American-style. Training and flying with Pan Am meant edging that much closer to the model—learning how to set the Donna Reed table, to clean as she did, to style one's hair and wear a shirtwaist dress, and to walk indoors with high-heeled shoes (against Japanese rules about the purity of indoor spaces). Pan Am brought these women within spitting distance of what was perceived as the American-dream lifestyle.

Pan Am training school in Miami also brought them face to face with women they perceived as looking, speaking, and acting a lot like Donna Reed or her European counterparts—in Pan Am uniform. Saeko, for example, recalls being stunned: "All the instructors were very pretty, slender, tall. It's the typical Pan Am image, and I go—omigod!" As Anne Cheng notes, "The mastery and assumption of female beauty by a nonwhite woman must also announce her remoteness from the norm of beauty, which is white female beauty" (2001: 55). Thus Saeko was both stunned to be faced with the images of white women she had previously seen on the television or movie screen, or in person, as well as fully cognizant of her racialized inability to meet the standards set by the images.

Saeko continues, "Pan Am training school was just totally a finishing school for me to go into this—this America." Her characterization of Pan Am as a finishing school is a sentiment echoed by several former stewardesses, both Japanese and non-Japanese. In some ways that characterization outlined the particular niche from which airlines often drew for flight attendants: middle- and upper-middle-class women who could be groomed to mingle with elites, without necessarily coming from the highest social echelons (i.e., the upper class) themselves. For these women, Pan Am could serve as the cosmopolitan finishing school they had not yet attended. Indeed, Pan Am taught Western-style makeup, hair grooming, dress, and conversation; it taught women how to set a Western table, serve hors d'oeuvres (caviar, cheeses), pour wine, and offer after-dinner drinks. The Pan Am cabin presented itself as the epitome of Western refinement professionalized to the point of routine practice, thousands of feet in the air. The effect was dizzying.

In fact, the Pan Am finishing school taught them practices that went well beyond the knowledge and experience of most Americans. Although the Japanese women arrived in Miami thinking they might be learning the ways of *Amerika*, their training was aimed at serving a global elite, not the average American. Knowing about chilled salad forks, caviar, and aperitifs responded to the expectations of those in global positions of power, including world leaders, movie stars, and heads of international corporations. Even Donna Reed might have been in awe.

Men—including passengers and pilots—were a major part of this global encounter. Some women got an intimate look at elite lifestyles through off-the-job practices, including dating and subsequently marrying white men. Unquestionably, flying for Pan Am placed Japanese women on a global stage of desirability. In taking the position of stewardess, these women accepted the sexualized and often racialized terms of their employment. Many of them "married up"—in anthropological terms, they practiced hypergamy—including at least one who married a (white) Pan Am executive. Others married laterally in terms of socioeconomic position, but by marrying a white American, their marriage might also have been seen as hypergamous—racially, nationally, and culturally.

All the women I interviewed who stayed in the United States married white Americans or Europeans. Those I met in Japan married Japanese men—typically business executives (and one Buddhist priest)—and often quit their jobs upon marriage, as was common practice. I asked Sumiko if her family objected to her marriage to a white man:

> No, no, no. In fact my father . . . would say that being short was a handicap. . . . So for me to have children who would be taller, would be to marry outside of your race. That's what he said. So . . . to make our race better, he said, we have to mix. . . . I didn't say anything, but I heard him and I kept it in me. So when it came time to tell him that I was marrying my husband, a white person, 6′6″, I knew he wouldn't object to it.

For Sumiko's father, Pan Am could be seen as a source of eugenics, improving his family's racial stock by interbreeding. (This view contrasts with the more typical attitude in Japan that Japan's strength lies in its racial purity.)

The practice of Japanese international stewardesses forming liaisons with white men gained notoriety in a book published in Japanese by Takahashi Fumiko, a former Pan Am stewardess with a degree from Columbia University

Figure 9 Japanese flight attendant Takahashi Fumiko posing in the cockpit. Photo courtesy of Takahashi Fumiko.

and a white American husband. Entitled *How to Date a Foreign Man* (*Gaikokujin dansei to tsukiaihō*, 1989), her book draws on her experiences traveling globally as a Pan Am stewardess to provide tips about attracting men (usually elite white men) in twenty-five different countries (see Kelsky 2001: 162–167).

Japanese stewardesses, such as Takahashi and others, may have initially been lusting after the lifestyle of Donna Reed (or after her husband), but clearly they surpassed their model. Instead of staying at home and cooking dinner for their husbands, they learned how to cook omelets in a cramped first-class kitchen while flying between Karachi and Beirut. Instead of vacuuming the wall-to-wall carpet of their two-story home, they flew on the inaugural flights of new aircraft and walked on the red carpet laid out for them and other V.I.P.s upon landing. While Donna Reed served macaroni and cheese, they served cuisine from Maxim's of Paris. They may have even married men who looked something like Donna Reed's television-handsome, doctor-husband, Dr. Alex Stone; but their husbands were likely far more worldly and well-traveled than the doctor-husband on-screen. In short, whereas Donna Reed was home-bound, these Japanese stewardesses claimed the world as their home. They understood mobility as part of their lifestyle, whether at work or play—inhabiting a new, modern category of glamour found in work-as-play.

Mobility as the Hallmark of Postwar Japan's New "Modern Girl"

What, then, can we say about these postwar "modern girls"? Gender—as tenuous public accomplishment—defined the critical spotlight of the national imaginary. That spotlight rested in the public gaze upon them, celebrities symbolic of an era of rapid change. In fact, it is the rapidity of the change that ties them to the ambivalences surrounding postwar Japan, particularly in gendered terms. Pan Am's Japanese stewardesses represented very public women, highly visible aboard international carriers, themselves icons of the Jet Age. In part, it is "modern girl" international stewardesses situated within the visual economies of postwar Japan that helped define the era (see Modern Girl Around the World Research Group 2008a: 12).

They also represented working women with jobs outside the home, often in glamorized service positions. Pan Am's Japanese stewardesses represented foreign prestige in Japan through an American corporation, even as they performed the Japanese woman. In the late historian Miriam Silverberg's words, they inhabited an important liminal category of "Japanese-but-Western"

(Silverberg 1991b: 249). Growing up and looking Japanese, trained in Western ways, they were Pan Am's marketing dream.

Finally, Pan Am's Japanese stewardesses represented women on the move—into and out of Japan—physically traveling the world and relocating to the United States, some staying there, socially inscribing a position of global visibility. The jet cabin and foreign ports of call became theatrical spaces at the forefront of postwar mobility and modernity. In simple terms, mobility thrust these "modern girls" into the limelight as complex sites of prestige and transgression. As the modern girl-on-the-go, she performed the exotic, new-but-old-fashioned, Asian woman aboard the most advanced fleet in the air. That she did so amidst rising feminist critique and union activism among flight attendants in the United States clearly etches the politically charged, retro-poignancy of her performance. She worked just this side of change: avoiding taking a critical stance herself, she lived a lifestyle that might be considered both a sign of postwar Japan's achievement and a challenge to its norms.

These women engaged in processes of what Bruce Robbins calls "emergent cosmopolitanism"—that is, "(re)attachment, multiple attachment or attachment at a distance" (1998: 3). This version of cosmopolitanism both performed and enabled their move "to the far side of the horizon" as a function of modern women on the go in a world swirling with contradictions. Indeed, during the Jet Age, to be modern was to be on the go—that is, to be mobile as a central defining feature of one's life.

In Japan, a country that had only recently allowed its general citizenry to travel internationally, the practices of mobility tended to be caught in structures of male privilege. This is exactly where the international stewardess job filled the gap. Flying for Pan Am gave Japanese women the means to be mobile and modern in ways not offered to men. The fact that the position may have been conceived within stereotypes of old-fashioned femininity and then racialized as the particular purview of Japanese women may have been less important to the women who took advantage of their Pan Am moment. What did matter to these modern girls is that they found the means to go, round the world and zigzagging the globe many times over, representing simultaneously Japan, America, and Pan Am.

Riding the coattails of American corporate prestige and power, they labored under critical negotiations of gender, mobility, and modernity tied to race and nation in overdetermined ways. However, like Abe maneuvering into position in the *Life* magazine photo shoot, these "emergent cosmopolitans" inhabited and eventually understood the limelight of the Jet Age. Striding through the airports of the world's capitals, Pan Am's Japanese stewardesses worked the stage to the emergence of their own pursuits.

Chapter Six

BUS GUIDES TOUR NATIONAL LANDSCAPES, POP CULTURE, AND YOUTH FANTASIES

Alisa Freedman

In Japan, it is taken for granted that every tour or charter bus is staffed with a uniformed female worker who assists the male driver, explains sites en route, leads walking tours from designated stops, and entertains passengers. Often referred to by the Japanese-English title "bus guide" (*basu gaido*), the job derived from the more arduous occupation of bus conductor—known by the diminutive "bus girl" (*basu gāru*)—begun in 1919 and ended by the early 1970s when the use of "one-man buses" (*wanman basu*), staffed only with drivers, became the norm.[1]

The jobs of bus girl and bus guide influenced each other in practice and intersected in literature, film, and popular culture. While bus girls were integral to the daily commute, bus guides are encountered in moments that mark escape from ordinary routines. Bus guides implicitly give "permission" to passengers to move out of their roles as workers, students, parents, and the like and to become leisurely explorers. The guide turns the depersonalized touristic experience into a more interactive and comfortable event. Most tour bus passengers in Japan are domestic residents, not foreign tourists, and class trips consisting of bus tours are an essential part of the secondary-school curriculum. Bus guides thus feature in memories of Japanese life in ways different from other working women. Guides not only show Japanese national history, they shape it.

The job of bus guide was seen as fashionable from the late 1920s until the escalation of the war in the mid-1930s, when buses were considered an expensive mode of transport and Western uniforms glamorized difficult service

Figure 10 Participants in the first Hato Bus Contest, March 1951. Photo courtesy of Yamada Ayumi and Katō Nanako of Hato Bus.

labor. The job was most desirable between the 1950s and early 1970s, when bus girls reached their greatest numbers and taking vacations, especially honeymoons and family trips to places associated with Japan's cultural history or current progress, became a middle-class luxury. As vehicles associated with travel represented Japan's advance in the Jet Age, the women who worked on them symbolized national development and pride, as Christine Yano discusses in her chapter on stewardesses.

In fictional accounts and most likely in reality, bus guides were usually hardworking women younger than twenty-five (the age viewed as the cutoff for marriage) who had been raised in the countryside and had left home seeking employment in the city, where they usually lived alone. Bus guides appeared as model workers in narratives advancing the idea that hard work will always be rewarded, a notion that propelled postwar Japanese society. In the front of the bus or circulating with the passengers while walking up and down the aisle for the duration of the ride, bus guides are the focus of passengers' vision, even more so than the scenery outside, and this sense of seeing has turned these women into objects of fantasy. Similar to the more prestigious flight attendants and ubiquitous bus conductors, bus guides have been conceptualized as both ideal employees and erotic icons, thus exposing contradictions inherent in women's roles in the workforce.

I survey an array of sources—films targeting women, toys marketed to men, songs sung in the first person, and memorabilia—to present a composite portrait of bus guides, disclose disparities between their images and lived realities, and demonstrate how the job has had an impact on views of Japanese women. First, I explain how the job of bus guide is predicated upon notions of modernity, gender, mobility, and proper social interactions during pivotal moments in the growth of twentieth-century Tokyo. Second, I reveal how images of bus guides from the past influence culture today, often as idealized visions of youth. I argue that bus guides form a lens through which to view the relationship between service employment, women's physical and social movements, and notions of home. They comment on different values associated with the Tokyo metropole and the rest of the nation. I examine texts synchronically to understand how the circulation of images exposes patterns and contradictions inherent in gender roles and diachronically to observe how images come to represent the times in which they are produced. I present more than a catalogue of facts and fictions about working women. Instead, I show what popular culture teaches about society, politics, and economics.

Tour Buses and Tokyo Modernity

To better understand the integral role bus guides play in society and culture, it is important to know the history of Japanese tour buses and reasons why women were hired to work on them. Larger than commuter vehicles, with more windows and seats higher off the ground, tour buses are designed to provide passengers with new ways of seeing and thinking about landscapes. They encourage the people on board to reflect on how places construct their personal and national identities. Tour buses promote feelings of superiority by lifting passengers above the street level and drawing attention to their privileged gaze.

Tokyo Motorbus (Tokyo Shigai Jidōsha, renamed Tokyo Noriai Jidōsha in 1922), the company that regularized the city's commuter bus service and introduced the job of bus girl, offered Japan's first tour buses (first called *yūran senmon noriai jidōsha*, *yūran basu*, and *tenbyō kōkyū jidōsha*) on December 15, 1925. The Tokyo Electric Bureau (Tokyo Denki Kyoku), operator of the city streetcars, had become the first municipal bus company in 1924, and the Tokyo Motorbus's powder-blue buses began to suffer in the competition. Like trains, the Tokyo bus network comprised government and private lines. Since the start of Japanese mass transportation, routes and tickets have been color-coded, making them recognizable and alluring and distinguishing classes of passengers. Tokyo Motorbus chose to paint their tour buses, slightly larger versions of their affectionately named "Blue Buses" (*aoi basu*), reddish brown. Because the color was too similar to that of vehicles for the Imperial family, they were repainted yellow. "Yellow bus" became the nickname for tour buses in prewar Tokyo. Some had light-blue stripes on top to make them more visible from the windows of tall department stores and office buildings, and perhaps to remind customers of the company's commuter buses. In 1927, glass panels were installed in the ceilings. Today buses have cataloguing numbers on top.

Beginning on June 17, 1926, Tokyo Motorbus offered half-day tours on set routes to avoid the hassle of collecting fares at each destination. During the 1930s, additional bus companies sold an increasing variety of tours, including a night ride in 1937 that ended after a few months because of the war and resumed in 1951. Tickets for all were expensive. For example, in 1932, a full-day Tokyo Motorbus city tour cost around three yen and thirty *sen* for adults (with a discount of one yen for children), equivalent to around 15,000 yen today (Hato Basu 1984: 5). At the time, train fare from Tokyo to Osaka was six yen and six *sen* (Hato Basu 1984: 15 and 283). Perhaps the idea for Tokyo tours came from Europe, where bus companies offered tours to survey damage and recovery in London and Paris after World War I (Hashizume 2006: 65). Airplane tours, lasting ten minutes and costing an exorbitant five yen, were offered from November 1929 in Tokyo, Osaka, and Fukuoka (Kōdansha 1998: 34).

Advertisements for the first bus tours promoted a look at Tokyo reconstruction after the 1923 Great Kantō Earthquake and at the vestiges of old Edo, the city that became Tokyo, all expertly explained by a guide, who was a major selling point of the tour. Originally, bus guides were male graduates of top universities, who earned high salaries. After female bus guides were first used on tour buses in Beppu, a hot-springs town on the southernmost island of Kyushu, in 1927, only women were hired for the position. A main reason was that they could be paid much less than men, and, like bus conductors, they were believed to be kinder to passengers (Masaki 1992: 20–21). That year, Tokyo Motorbus replaced its male guides with women chosen from the ranks of Blue Bus conductors. Qualifications for being a female guide, especially from around 1932, included having a residence in Tokyo and having finished high-school (Hato Basu 1984: 21). Then, as now, applicants took an examination, which includes written and oral components.

The first Beppu guide was Murakami Ayame (1910–2009), a graduate of an elite girls' high school who worked on the Kameoi line for six years, helping develop and popularize the use of scripted narration to skillfully explain the significance of sites in a rhythm and cadence that harmonized with the movement of the bus. She also sang folk songs associated with the places the bus passed. Murakami's speech became a model for bus guides nationwide and was made into a record played on the radio in 1933 (*Nishi Nippon Shinbun* 2009). Radio broadcasts of female bus guide narrations about famous places (*yūran basu no meisho annai*) were a staple of 1930s programming. Tour narrations not only entertained and educated passengers but also increased their emotional ties to the Japanese landscape.

Some aspects of the job in the 1930s still apply today. Like other female service workers described in this volume, from the start, bus guides wore uniforms. A selling point of the job, the uniform made these workers instantly recognizable, showed they were trained professionals doing serious labor, and promoted buses as stylish transport. In the late 1920s, when Western clothing was still rare, Tokyo Motorbus guides wore beige dresses, different from Blue Bus and city bus conductors, who dressed in navy blue with white and scarlet collars, respectively. Increasingly, guides and drivers wore white gloves, still a metonym for high-class service in Japan. According to anthropologist Emiko Ohnuki-Tierney, gloves also protected workers from directly handling money and tickets that might be full of germs, or "people dirt" (*hitogomi*) (Ohnuki-Tierney 1984: 31). A guide's gesture of directing passengers' attention to scenery by genteelly using the palm of her right or left hand, rather than pointing her index finger, became a visual sign of the job and an indication of good manners.[2] (See, for example, the bus guide from 1960 on the left side of the book cover.) To be more conspicuous, guides carry flags, which specify the name of the bus company (or in the case of charter buses, the name of the group that hired the tour), when they lead passengers, who customarily wear tags with similar designations, on walking tours. While the bus traverses duller stretches of road, they distract passengers with jokes, quizzes, and anecdotes, and on longer trips they lead them in games or karaoke to pass the time.

Guides were responsible for many of the same duties as conductors, with the notable exception of collecting fares. Both sets of women helped passengers on and off, announced stops, cleaned buses, and maintained a comfortable atmosphere, all responsibilities that continued into the postwar period. They had to be polite to difficult passengers, including those who refused to pay the fare or were inebriated, and those who ogled and tried to touch them. They had to work well with the driver. An important part of the job was telling the driver when it was safe to start and stop the bus. A term associated with bus girls and guides is "*orai*," from the English "all right" (a word in the Japanese vocabulary since the nineteenth century but rarely used), the call that all was clear for the bus to proceed.[3] Like conductors, guides typically stood on moving buses, but after the revised Japanese Road and Transportation Law (Dōro Kōtsu Hō) went into effect on June 1, 2008, they have been required to sit, seatbelts fastened. This has changed the nature of the job and the guide's visually dominant position on the bus and, accordingly, the passengers' relationship with both the guides and the passing scenery.

Postwar Hato Bus Guides and National Pride

The Tokyo metropolitan police banned tour buses in September 1940 because of gasoline rationing and war damage, but city government encouraged their resumption in the years following the war and during the Allied Occupation. During the war, women continued working as bus conductors and even served as drivers. Japan's premier tour company, Tokyo's Hato Bus, was founded with government assistance as the New Japan Tourism Company (Shin-Nihon Kankō Kabushiki Kaisha) on August 14, 1948, and began offering half-day tours of Tokyo at 250 yen per ticket on March 19 the following year, with a staff of five female guides, who wore beige like their predecessors employed by Tokyo Motorbus (Nakano 2010: 42).[4]

The motto "Speed, Peace, and Safety" (*supēdo to heiwa, soshite anzen ni*) was written on the side of the buses, which held thirty-five passengers and were yellow, as they are today (Tokita 2008). The company was officially named after its logo, the "*hato*" or dove, in 1963. The word "*hato*," also translated as pigeon (a bird that is the same shape), was used in names for other luxury vehicles at the time, including the long-distance, super-express Hato train from 1950 and the later *shinkansen* (bullet train) route that replaced it. The term "Hato Girl" (*Hato gāru*), used for Hato Bus guides, also signified Hato train pursers, who were modeled after Pan Am stewardesses. The image of the dove was not new in Japan; the Hato Sabure cookie had been around since the end of the Meiji period. Other tour and community buses, such as those in Osaka and Saitama, are called Hato Buses, but they are unrelated to the Tokyo company.

The first guided Hato Bus tours sought a panoramic look at Tokyo neighborhoods in order to show the city was both rising and beginning to prosper after the destruction of war and to commemorate places that had been lost. The company started offering a range of historical tours designed to inspire nostalgia for the past and to explain the modern features of different eras. Hato Bus experimented with innovative ways to see Tokyo and to make the best use of its guides in explaining the cultural meanings of the sites. Offerings included the 1964 Olympics tour, the 1983 Tokyo Disneyland tour, and tours that featured golf and kabuki. Some of the most popular tours since the 1960s have been the geisha tours, such as the Hanamachi Geisha Tour and the Oiran Show, which includes dinner in a traditional Japanese restaurant and dance performances.[5] The "open-roof bus" (*ōpen basu*) used from 1965 was seen as a novel idea at the time (Hato Basu 1984: 119 and Tanaka 2011: 87). When business hit an all-time low in 1989, Hato Bus refigured its tours and began using new buses with seats raised five centimeters. This was in response to customers' comments that the tours make them feel more special when they are towering over traffic (*Trends in Japan* 2003). Hato Bus recorded around 650,000 passengers a year in 2009 and employed 1,008 people as of June 2011 (Hato Basu 2011). To celebrate their sixtieth anniversary in 2009, Hato Buses retraced their first tour at the original price of 250 yen; all seats were reserved for retired bus guides, mostly older than age sixty.[6] The company held fashion shows of uniforms from throughout the decades. Fashion shows also featured uniforms of other professions, such as elevator girl (discussed by Laura Miller in this volume).

Scenes of Japanese residents enjoying bus tours became a way of conspicuously displaying Tokyo's development in 1950s literature and film. One of the most famous depictions is in Nobel laureate Kawabata Yasunari's *Being a Woman* (*Onna de aru koto*), a middlebrow novel serialized in the *Asahi* newspaper in 1956 and 1957. The characters gaze at a changing Tokyo from the bus window, as the guide explains, "This city of Tokyo not only puts on a different face for each of the four seasons, it is in constant flux, even over the course of a single day" (*Asahi News* 2008).

In his 1953 poignant family melodrama *Tokyo Story* (*Tokyo monogatari*), director Ozu Yasujirō includes an approximately two-minute bus tour that allows audiences to pause and consider an awe-inspiring busy city that is prospering at the expense of tearing families apart and changing values of youth. In a scene that functions almost like a mini-film and a break in the narrative, elderly parents from the countryside have come to see their children, who relocated to Tokyo and have become too busy or unwilling to make time to see them. The parents take a bus tour with their daughter-in-law, the wife of their son who died in the war and the only member of the younger generation who treats them with respect. The father, who sits across the aisle from his wife, is the only passenger wearing a hat, further distinguishing him from the crowd. Side and ceiling bus windows frame the passengers and show Tokyo's tall buildings rising around them. The focus on buildings serves as a transition to the next sequence, in which the three characters climb an office high-rise to get a different view of the city. They look out at the various directions in which their children have moved, showing how scattered they now are. Modernity is also linked to the verticality of the high buses and skyscrapers, not just to horizontal space.

Ozu's sequence is strikingly similar in urban images, music, and guide narration to the mid-1960s documentary *Tokyo Sightseeing* (*Tokyo kenbutsu*), with the English subtitle *Mammoth Tokyo*, which was featured on the website for the sixtieth anniversary of Hato Bus. The film captures the tour from the perspective of a fashionable young Tokyo couple as they listen attentively to the bus guide, an attractive woman who appears to be in her early twenties, and gaze out the window. The man smokes cigarettes on the bus, and the camera periodically focuses on the Mitsubishi logo on the inside of the bonnet bus (the round-top diesel buses first manufactured in 1948 that are a fixture in photographs from the 1950s). The tour showcases other new forms of transportation, including morning rush-hour trains packed with salarymen leaving Tokyo Station, the *shinkansen*, airplanes at Haneda Airport, and the monorail.

There seem to be conventions for filming bus tours. In both films, only the voice of the bus guide is heard. She controls how the city is seen. Her voice serves as a narrative link between the moving landscape and the subjectivity of the passengers who observe it.

Bus Guides as Tourist Attractions

Bus guides have been as big an attraction as the sites they explain. In other words, their bodies are considered as important as their voices. To cultivate the image of guides as pretty, talented, and knowledgeable, Hato Bus held annual beauty and talent contests for more than ten years beginning in March 1951. The winners, who were also judged on their tour narrations, were photographed for newspapers and became teachers for newly hired guides (Hato Basu 1984: 75–77).

Over the decades, guides have undergone intensive training that entails learning polite greetings, voice intonations, personal grooming, bus safety, bus company facts, geography, history, folk songs, and quizzes and games to play with passengers. In 1969, Hato Bus offered a bridal tour (*buraidaru kōsu*), during which guides modeled kimono and taught etiquette for women who were soon to be married (Tanaka 2011: 75). Laura Miller notes that one Tokyo tourism company offered beauty tours for men, in which they received haircuts, facials, and manicures, among other beauty treatments, and had formal portraits taken by a professional photographer (Miller 2006).

Several newspaper articles and websites profiling the work ethic and pride of Hato Bus guides from the 1950s were published as part of the company's sixtieth anniversary celebration.[7] These articles, the corporate bias of which should be acknowledged, provide insight into the job and how it has been idealized, and reflect the company's stereotyping of women. Like airline stewardesses globally, bus guides do not accept tips. Instead, these women are described as receiving personal satisfaction through serving others and the cultivation of their physical appearance. Sumida Mieko, for example, became a tour guide in 1959 after preparing for her future career as a member of her high-school broadcasting club. Her favorite memories are helping passengers to recall loved ones they lost during the war and bringing them to tears with songs as the bus traversed patriotic sites, including Yasukuni Shrine (*Asahi News* 2008).

Similar values, along with details of bus guide training, are depicted in a 2008 illustrated book profiling popular Nara area bus guide Kijima Arisa (born 1983), published by Media Factory as part of a series on female service workers who wear uniforms, including *shinkansen* pursers and elevator girls (see the chapter by Freedman, Miller, and Yano). Kijima, a talented tennis player who enjoys singing, became a bus guide on the advice of her high-school guidance counselor. She entered the Nara Kotsu Bus company right after graduation from a high school in Fukuoka in March 2001 and began work after three years of training. Kijima chose to work for Nara Kotsu Bus because she enjoyed a bus tour of Nara as a child and liked the company's checked uniforms (Kijima 2008: 19).

Historically, Japanese companies have trained their own workers, rather than sending them to schools, but this customary employment practice is changing owing to the economic climate and increasing use of short-term workers in twenty-first-century Japan. Kijima gives a detailed account of the manuals she was required to read and the manners she needed to cultivate. Like other guides, she was trained to always smile, thus shielding her passengers from the difficulties of the job. Kijima's smile won praise from her passengers and more commendations than her coworkers (see, for example Kijima 2008: 107–122).

ご指名！ No.1 Bus Attendant in a Historical City *KIJIMA ARISA*
古都のバスガイド
木島亜里沙

Figure 11 Bus Guide Kijima Arisa on the cover of her Media Factory Book. Kijima, 2008, *Goshimei! Koto no basu gaido* (*Number One! Bus Guide to the Old Capital*). Photo courtesy of Kikuchi Keiko of Media Factory.

Japanese schools and companies motivate workers by ranking them, and the women profiled in the Media Factory series have all won honors for their jobs. It is implied but not stated in the books that pride also comes from triumphing over one's peers. No male staff members appear in Kijima's book.

Articles and books about bus guides can be read as emphasizing the "*ganbaru*" ethic, the notion that diligence and perseverance will always be rewarded that has motivated individuals to try their best to succeed in the groups of family, school, and work that form the backbone of Japanese society. This ethic reflects the cultural belief that seemingly ordinary people can become heroes by improving themselves through excelling at a feat with the help of a coach and other players, who in turn learn from their examples. Discussions about the success of bus guides always include mention of their good rapport with passengers. This underscores the importance of interpersonal relations and the role of the guide as providing the human touch that personalizes the bus ride experience.

Popular culture has also recognized the narcissism that comes from being the focus of people's adoring gaze and has turned the stereotype of bus guides knowing they are being watched into a cultural joke. For example, in a 1968 television commercial cartoon narrated by comedian Norihei Miki for the Momoya Company's Nametake murasaki marinated mushrooms, a bus guide is the object of satire. As the bonnet bus winds along a steep mountain road, the bespectacled guide tells her passengers where to look, but instead of showing them the natural scenery, she presents Nametake murasaki in her right hand and a bottle of warm sake in her left. She then dances and sings a jingle at the front of the bus, as the passengers applaud. A male passenger yells out, "That's good!" She coyly accepts the praise, only to be corrected by the driver who sternly states that the compliment is meant for the Namatake murasaki. Furious, the bus guide flails her arms, trying to strike the driver. The driver, distracted, grabs at the wheel to keep the bus from swerving off a cliff. Perhaps in parody of a stock shot in films that feature buses, the final image is of the bus driving into the distance; a sign reading "The taste is *orai!*" can be seen plastered on its back (Momoya-Kawasaki City Museum 2006).[8]

Bus Guides as 1940s and 1950s Film Protagonists
In three 1940s and 1950s feature films, the job of bus guide represents the efforts of women to achieve personal pride and social mobility through their employment. First, I analyze a pair of films by director Naruse Mikio (1905–1969), praised for his empathetic portrayals of the daily lives of women from the lower

middle classes and for adapting fiction serialized in magazines for women into film: the comedy *Hideko the Bus Conductress* (*Hideko no shashō-san*, 1941), based on a novella by Ibuse Masuji, and the family drama *Lightning* (*Inazuma*, 1952), taken from a Hayashi Fumiko novel. Naruse lightened the endings of both dark stories, but his heroines are not happy at the resolutions. A rarely viewed third example is the 1958 *Tokyo Bus Girl* (*Tokyo no basu gāru*), directed by Sunohara Masahisa (1906–1997) and written by Nishijima Dai, staff members of the Nikkatsu Studio. The film comedy, which was quickly made and critically panned, is best known for the song that inspired it and is not readily available; I have only been able to obtain the script. In all three films, tour narration is a plot device and cinematographic tool. All three fictional bus guides live apart from their families and view work as a means of self-improvement. Commercial cinema offers access to public perceptions of bus guides and the desires of working women.

Hideko the Bus Conductress
The scopophilic pleasure and potential dangers of watching a tour guide, along with the envisioned glamour and real troubles of the job, are humorously shown in *Hideko the Bus Conductress*. Hideko Okoma, with a rosy complexion and sweet voice, is a nineteen-year-old conductor on a beat-up bus along a dull stretch of road between Kofu City and Fujiyoshida City in Yamanashi Prefecture, southwest of Tokyo in a scenic mountainous area of lakes near Mount Fuji. Hideko is the only reason the bus is able to attract even a few passengers. The company president uses the bus as a front for less legal ventures.

Ibuse's novella *Miss Okoma* (*Okoma-san*), serialized in the monthly magazine *Girl's Friend* (*Shōjo no tomo*) from January to June 1940, is a parable about how money can corrupt, and the title character is known only by her last name "Okoma," a homophone for a pawn in the Japanese chess game of *shogi*. She is not to be emulated; instead, she is to be pitied. Naruse gave his heroine, a better role model, the first name Hideko, after the seventeen-year-old lead actress Takamine Hideko (1924–2010), with whom he was collaborating for the first time and went on to cast in seventeen films.[9] Differences between the novella and film speak to distinctions between the media of magazines and cinema. The importance of being honest expressed in *Miss Okoma* was a topic widely discussed in *Girl's Friend*, a magazine that sought to teach its generally middle-class subscribers proper conduct while entertaining them. The film is largely a vehicle for Takamine's star power. The film is shown from the point of view of

Hideko, while the novella is told from the male bus driver Sonoda Genpachi's perspective. Both versions promote loyalty, a theme of literature and cinema produced in the early 1940s, but neither directly mentions the war.

After hearing a radio broadcast from Tokyo of bus guide narrations about famous places, Hideko asks Sonoda to approach the dishonest but wealthy company president, who represents the upper classes in the film, with the idea that she explain the places their bus passes as a means to enliven the ride and attract passengers and thereby ensure the survival of their route. Because Hideko and Sonoda are only paid for the days they work, both are forced to find second jobs—Hideko as a maid at the hardware store where she lives as a boarder and Sonoda at a greengrocery. In Ibuse's story, Sonoda also works at a *shogi* club, alluding to the author's well-known hobby and the fact that these laborers are pawns.

Hideko and Sonoda hire a Tokyo novelist, Ikawa Gonji, whom they had met when he left a notebook on the bus, to write the narration. Ibuse Masuji was perhaps parodying his own role as an author by giving his character a name similar to his own. Ikawa coaches Hideko on the proper way to read his verbose text, but Hideko finds it difficult to stay in proper timing. Ibuse quotes the long passages in Ikawa's script that detail the cultural significance of sites along the bus route. Ibuse did this either in parody, out of love for places where he used to fish, or to satisfy wartime literature censors, or all of the above; he shows that even seemingly banal places have meaning as part of the Japanese homeland. Naruse omits these passages and does not show any of the beauty of the countryside but instead focuses on the old road, which contrasts with Hideko's radiance.

The climax of the story—Hideko's narration as a guide on the bus and the accident that ensues—is depicted differently in the story and the film. In the film, the accident occurs when Hideko is practicing the script for the first time. Ikawa is the only passenger aboard. The camera shows both Hideko happily explaining the sites and pans of the countryside as seen out the side and back windows of the bus. Listening intently to Hideko, Sonoda passes people waiting for the bus without stopping. This joke is repeated twice and reveals that Sonoda cares more about Hideko than about earning money for the company.

Because Sonoda is enraptured by Hideko's narration, he almost hits a boy who suddenly runs into the street. He stops the bus short, throwing it off balance. The front and back wheels on one side catch the top of a tall stone wall at the edge of the road. Hideko bravely but rashly runs out and tries to push the bus from behind to prevent it from toppling. The wall crumbles, and the bus falls, plunging Hideko into the wheat field below. She injures her arm but is able to quickly return to work. However, the bus is out of commission. Sonoda reports the accident to the company president, who is more concerned about the state of the bus than of Hideko. What angers the president most is the possibility of not collecting insurance money, for the bus fell after it had stopped and the passengers had gotten out. He tries to bribe Hideko and Sonoda into lying to the insurance company. They refuse to commit perjury, and Ikawa comes to their rescue. He blackmails the president, who then agrees to fix the bus.

In a humorous and poignant final scene, Hideko and Sonoda hope to try out the tour for the first time in front of passengers on their bus, which has been fixed and returned to service. Hideko cannot start because a group of girls is singing. After they get off, the only passenger remaining is a blind man. Hideko is finally able to give her speech to three men dressed in hiking clothes, who listen intently and smile at her. In a crosscut scene, the viewer learns that the president has sold the bus to a rival company, which will only use it on occasion for its least desirable routes.

Hideko and Sonoda lose their jobs, but the audience is spared the sight of their disappointment and fear. Instead, they are left with a joke about tour narrations not being as exciting as the radio makes them seem. The story, which speaks about the replacability of laborers under capitalism, ends instead on a humorous note that puts audiences at ease. Like many other films about buses, the last shot is of the bus driving into the distance to strains of cheerful music, further lightening the weighty subject matter. In Ibuse's darker ending, Hideko is hospitalized after breaking her leg instead of her arm, thus curtailing her mobility. She and Sonoda face a moral dilemma: whether to lie in order to get money to pay her hospital bills or to uphold their honor. They lie. In the end, Hideko, who sports a much shorter skirt than before, and her bus are fixed in order to be "sold." When she tries her narration for passengers, they find it boring.

Visual parallels are made between Hideko and her bus. Like her bus, Hideko has a modest appearance, reflecting her honesty, innocence, and frugality. Because she cannot afford leather shoes, she wears *geta*, clogs for kimono, with her uniform, an incongruence that helps garner empathy and is shown in cinematic close-up. The incongruence is not just in wearing Japanese shoes with a Western-style outfit; it is also in symbols of tradition versus modernity and poverty versus wealth. The cover drawing for the 1959 book edition published by Kadokawa is a pair of *geta*. The bus is an important compositional device in the film; many shots of the countryside scenery are framed by its side windows. In several scenes, the camera shoots out the back window to humorously capture the dull stretch of road and the confused people along it.

Lightning

In *Lightning*, also starring Takamine, Naruse furthered the image of bus guide as an independent woman who exemplifies diligence and industriousness, neatness but not extravagance, and uses her job to achieve physical and social mobility that could change her life. The film is based on a 1946 novel by popular author Hayashi Fumiko about a mother and her four grown children—three daughters and one son who have different fathers, all of whom are absent.[10] The youngest daughter, Kiyoko, played by Takamine, has witnessed the emotional and physical pain men have caused her mother and her sisters, a fact she reiterates in the many scenes of family arguments.

Kiyoko is determined to find happiness outside of marriage. When her family pressures her to marry a man she dislikes, Kiyoko defiantly refuses, an effort that proves successful in the film but fails in the novel. The men, including Kiyoko's younger brother who has returned from fighting in the war, are slovenly, dishonest, and tempestuous. The exception is Kiyoko's father, whose sincerity is represented by the real ruby ring he gave Kiyoko's mother. Kiyoko works as a Hato Bus guide, a job that provides her with the financial means to move away from her family.

With her salary, Kiyoko rents a room in Setagaya on the second floor of a house owned by a widow with grown children. The spacious streets and green suburban neighborhood is a striking contrast to the congested downtown (*shitamachi*) where Kiyoko's mother and siblings live and work. The Tokyo areas are juxtaposed using sound and images of movement. While the Setagaya scenes are set to vibrant piano music, Kiyoko's family house is full of arguments. Shots of downtown workers in motion, walking and riding motorbikes to sell goods or preparing shops for business, are used to transition between sequences. Kiyoko's neighbors are a brother and sister around her age who support each other. The brother, a teacher, performs domestic tasks, thereby allowing his younger sister time to practice piano. He represents a new kind of man and potential love interest for Kiyoko. As a parallel, Kiyoko's mother rents a second-floor room to a young woman, who is also working as a teacher. Naruse seems to equate the professions of bus guide and teacher: both are jobs in which women can unabashedly show off their knowledge to an audience. Kiyoko remarks that she likes books and studying, and it is implied that she might have become a teacher if she had been given more education.

The film opens with a scene of Kiyoko narrating a Hato Bus tour of Tokyo's fashionable Ginza neighborhood, the streets of which are seen through the driver's windshield and the passengers' side windows. After showing scenery, the camera focuses on Kiyoko. In the middle of the film, the audience is treated to part of Kiyoko's tour of neighborhoods along the Sumida River, a striking visual contrast to modern Ginza. The bus thus becomes a way of framing districts that represent Tokyo's consumer culture and remnants of older daily life. Passengers, mostly pairs of elderly men and women, thank Kiyoko as she helps them off the bus. These couples contrast with Kiyoko's mother, whose domestic life was much less peaceful. During a climactic moment, Kiyoko accompanies her older sister Mitsuko to visit the woman who claims to have had a child with Hiroko's recently deceased husband Ryōhei and who wants part of the 55,000 yen in insurance money Hiroko has received. The sisters travel by commuter bus, and the Tokyo landscape is a backdrop in the windows behind them. Kiyoko seems more vulnerable and less authoritative as a passenger and pedestrian than as a tour guide.

Life away from her family does not bring Kiyoko the happiness she desires. Kiyoko argues most vehemently with her mother at the end of the film, criticizing her for having children with so many different men. Kiyoko seems a progressive woman but an ungrateful daughter. The neighbor's piano provides the soundtrack to this dramatic scene set in the interior of Kiyoko's Setagaya room. The flash of lightning that gives the story its title represents Kiyoko's decision not to have the kind of life her mother and sisters have. After making amends and laughing together, Kiyoko and her mother walk side-by-side through Setagaya.

The film starts with a bus tour and ends with the characters walking. They seem more comfortable enjoying daily life on Tokyo streets than in the role of guides who have risen above it. Walking also allows Naruse to position characters side-by-side. Here, as in most other scenes of *Lightning*, Takamine is dressed in the summer uniform—white blouse and navy skirt—of a Hato Bus guide.

Tokyo Bus Girl

Tokyo Bus Girl, given the English title *Girl on a Bus*, was released during the heyday of Hato Bus guides but when commuter bus companies were having trouble recruiting and retaining conductors. The film was inspired by the October 1957 popular song of the same name by the budding star Columbia Rose (Koromubia Rōzu, named for the Columbia Record Company), who played a bit part in the film.[11] This fifty-four-minute feature movie, completed on July 12, 1958, and released ten days later, is a story of mistaken identities and chance encounters, all involving a beautiful young Tokyo tour bus guide, Satō Mineko, who realizes the need for money and treasures her job, but values romantic love and the admiration of her passengers more than material things.

The most honest characters in the film, Mineko and her fiancé Tachibana Gorō, are from the countryside. Mineko came to Tokyo to find employment, while Gorō is a university student who wants to become a teacher. He works as a bus cleaner to pay for his education. The characters who most desire money include a real estate agent selling land on Uranus and a salesman selling household appliances that represent the good life; these greedy men are from Tokyo, Osaka, and the made-up country Slanvania. Throughout the film, Mineko is presented as a conscientious and competent bus guide, an occupation she likes. This is shown in scenes of her leading tours of Tokyo, including one to attentive junior high school students.

The theme song, still a staple of karaoke and a feature of nostalgia sites for bus companies, is sung from the perspective of a tour guide: "Heading from the city streets to Yamanote with young dreams and love. I am a Tokyo bus girl, dressed in a navy blue uniform" (Japanese lyrics quoted in Hato Basu 1984: 280; and Nakano 2010: 106–107, for example). The guide alludes to the fact that she represents the droves of young Japanese women who came to Tokyo to work during this time of large-scale development, seeking better lives than they had in the countryside. The lyrics lament female workers' disillusionment with urban life, as symbolized by the bus guide's difficult passengers, but praise their pride in their jobs and the uniforms that represent them. Although the bus guide tolerates drunken passengers who bully her and make her cry, she knows that she must keep a cheerful demeanor. As stated in the refrain, the guide, just like her bus, must cheerfully go on. Popular songs about workers sung in the first person provide insight into emotional experience and encourage people to see their jobs differently.

Tour Bus Guides as Toys and Idols

Toys are an additional tool for gauging public perceptions of bus guides and the emotional labor they perform. In the early twenty-first century, twentieth-century bus guides have become figures of nostalgia and fantasy. On one hand, the proliferation of bus guide dolls and costume play can be read as part of the very successful commercial trend of depictions of childhood in Tokyo during the 1950s and 1960s. Examples include the cross-media phenomena of *Always: Sunset on Third Street* (*Always: San-chōme no yūhi*, a long-selling manga by Ryōhei Saigan that was made into live-action films in 2005, 2007, and 2012) and illustrator Lily Franky's 2005 autobiographical novel *Tokyo Tower: Me, Mom, and Sometimes Dad* (*Tokyo tawā: Okan to boku to, tokidoki, oton*, adapted into television dramas in 2006 and 2007 and a movie in 2007). On the other hand, the bus guide, although slightly older, possesses many of the same associations as the "*shōjo*," or girl, an image of innocence and budding sexuality and a subject of much Japanese popular culture. As I will explain, differences between eroticism and nostalgia in the case of bus guides are created through marketing and audience.

Hello Kitty—arguably the most recognizable character in the world and the symbol of Japanese "cute" or "*kawaii*" culture—has been featured inside and outside Hato Buses since 2005.[12] "*Kawaii*" is a particular kind of cute that entails vulnerability and the need to be treasured and cared for (Windolf 2009). This is conveyed, I believe, by the fact that most *kawaii* characters look directly at you. In Japan, characters are used to represent places and ideas, thus making them easier to remember and softening their sterner associations.[13] Different versions of Hello Kitty as a Hato Bus guide were marketed in 2001, 2003, 2005, and 2007.[14] Despite her commercial ties with Hato Bus, Kitty has dressed in the uniforms of other bus companies, and her partner Dear Daniel has modeled as a driver. In a similar series, Kewpie (a doll introduced to Japan from the United States in 1913) models local customs, including different generations of Hato Bus guides—figures marketed on key chains, cell-phone straps, and other stationery goods for the sixtieth anniversary of the Hato Bus.

While Sanrio and Kewpie pitch to female consumers, the model vehicle conglomerate Tomytec markets bus guide and train pursuer action figures to men. They especially target collectors of transport memorabilia and of "beautiful girl" (*bishōjo*) figurines, two, and in this case overlapping, subgroups of "*otaku*," or avid fans who define themselves through their pursuit of hobbies (see, for example, Freedman 2009). These figures can be read as part of a consumer industry creating fantasies about women in uniform (see Sabine Frühstück's chapter in this volume). Starting in 2005, Tomytec produced several series of figurines of female conductors on local train lines (*tetsudō musume*, affectionately called "Tetsu-musu," with the English name "Young Ladies of the Railway") and commuter bus guides (*basu musume*) in boxes marked for ages fifteen and above. Tomytec began producing collections of tour bus guides in April 2008 representing companies across Japan. The dolls, six in each series, wear uniforms of different transport companies and are posed as if they are in the midst of doing their jobs.

The dolls for the Hato Bus series of June 2009, in honor of the sixtieth anniversary, wear suits from 1972, 1975, 1980, and 1991. Each figure is sold randomly for 525 yen, so that the customer does not know which girl he has purchased until opening the box. They have big eyes and small mouths characteristic of manga and anime characters and are given names, birthdays, hobbies, and body measurements all carefully catalogued on the Tomytec website and on collector cards that come with the dolls. For example, the last name of the Hato Bus guide Ueno Hiromi, who models the uniform from 1972 in the Hato Bus anniversary series, refers to the panda in the Ueno Zoo that was top news that year. Her first name seems the kind that would belong to a popular singer of the 1970s. She is strict with the new hires she trains and is faithful to her job, and, according to the card, when not in her Hato Bus uniform, she likes to wear hot pants (Tomytec 2008). Ueno's narrative alludes to the appearance of bus guides as characters in pornography. One recent example is the October 2008 photograph book by singer and actress Nakamura Chitose. This book, in which Nakamura dresses alternately in bus guide uniforms and bathing suits, was sold only in digital format with the tagline "Let's go on a bus date just the two of us. . . . Give the tour narration just for me!! ☆☆" (*Futari dake no basu dēto. . . . boku ni kankō annai onegaishimasu!!* ☆☆ [exclamation points and stars in the original title] (Nakamura 2008).[15]

Last, two songs about bus guides by groups that are part of the Hello! Project (*Harō! purojekuto*) further demonstrate how bus guides have figured into childhood fantasies of love and represent adult role models in human relationships. The Hello! Project, begun in 1997 and managed by the Up-Front Agency, is a large umbrella of all-girl bands, whose members are younger than twenty and dress alike. Singers "graduate," rather than leave the Hello! Project, and are replaced with almost exact replicas. Popular music in Japan is dominated by groups of either all-male or all-female singers and dancers. The large numbers of members (reaching around forty-eight in the case of AKB48, who were promoted on the sides of tour buses in Singapore in October 2011 but are not part of the Hello! Project) ensure an idol for every personality type and fashion taste. The two songs described below, written by Hello! Project producer Tsunku, are most likely appreciated more for their catchy rhythms and their singers' cute appearances than their lyrics, for they have not been used for programs that have to do with tour buses.

First, the September 2001 childish "Mini Moni Bus Guide" (*Mini Moni. Basu gaido*) sung by the eponymous group Mini Moni, which generally lasted from 2000 to 2004 and targeted younger fans, was one of the most commercially successful subgroups of the prime Hello! Project band Morning Musume. All members were shorter than five feet, and collectively they were known for their unusual animated music videos and live concerts. The accompanying video shows the four singers dressed in checked bus guide outfits (member Mika Todd, the driver, in a pants suit) in a bus shaped like their pink rabbit mascot.[16] In lyrics that rhyme, they sing about ordinary events in the day of a bus guide and that of an average six-year-old—they smile as they greet passengers, clean up their toys, and eat nutritious bananas—all in a bus "that is not candy" (Mini Moni 2001a). The song infantilizes bus guides but proves they are instrumental in maintaining order; thus they are as useful as they are cute.

The chart-topping twentieth single "Youth Bus Guide" (*Seishun basu gaido*) by Berryz Kōbō is a fitting way to end this tour of bus guide images and show how different ways of seeing these women—as ambassadors of the national landscape, model workers, erotic icons, youth fantasies, and figures of nostalgia—coalesce. Berryz Kōbō, or Berryz Workshop, formed in 2004, is one of the most popular, prolific, and longest-lasting Hello! Project bands. It became the first Japanese band with all members under the age of fourteen to perform sellout concerts at the Saitama Super Arena. From April 2009, "Youth Bus Guide" was the closing theme for the TV Tokyo network anime series *Inazuma Eleven* (*Inazuma erebun*) based on the 2008 soccer-themed Nintendo DS game of the same name, which does not seem to have much to do with buses. The animated theme song sequence ends with three girls sitting on a blue-colored bus, which is perched atop a soccer ball.

The song is sung from the point of view of a high-school boy who becomes infatuated with his bus guide on a class trip. He falls in love with her appearance and voice and envies the microphone she holds. (It is hard not to read the microphone as a phallus.) He is jealous of the kindness she shows to his classmates, whom he views as rivals for her love:

> But goodbye. My heart aches. I want to talk with you more. Bus guide, to us youth, you are radiant. I want to be reborn as a microphone. I want you to myself. That voice, that smile—everything. I fall for you each time our eyes meet. Let's take a picture to remember. (Berryz Kōbō 2009a)

In the music video released by Dohhh Up on May 17, 2009, the Berryz Kōbō girls cross-dress in the uniforms of high-school boys.[17] They gawk, wearing glasses and using telescopic lenses, camera, and other devices to extend their vision, at a bus guide played by Tokyo Television announcer Oe Mariko. The video is crosscut with Berryz Kōbō members dancing in what seems like space-age, micro-miniskirt versions of the 1970s Hato Bus uniform. The video starts with a bus tour narration's typical welcome and ends with the guide blowing a kiss at the passengers who long for her. Berryz Kōbō members promoted the song by dressing as guides and touring Tokyo on a red double-decker bus with their pictures emblazed on the sides. The other "A side" (instead of a B side) of the Berryz Kōbō single is "Rival," a theme referred to in "Youth Bus Guide." Berryz Kōbō have worn stylized versions of other workers' uniforms; for example, they dressed as elevator girls on the cover of their first greatest-hits album (January 2009) *Berryz Kōbō Special Best, Vol. 1* (*Berryz Kōbō suppesharu besto volume 1*).

Recordings of women's voices announce stops on commuter bus lines, providing an aural memory of the now nonexistent job of conductor. On Japanese buses, tour guides have not been replaced by recordings and headphones. If a guide were not on the bus, passengers would feel uncomfortable and sense that something is amiss. Girls can dress as Hato Bus guides and boys as drivers in KidZania Tokyo, an entertainment and educational center that replicates a town in which children can play different jobs to earn back the expensive 3,000 to 4,000 yen per child admission fee with fake Kidzos money.[18] Although aspiring singers and announcers become bus guides to train for their future careers, the job is no longer a top choice. Yet bus guides, in reality and in representation, continue to exemplify the emotional labor that female service workers perform and the associations between mobility, modernity, and gender discussed in this volume.

The bus guide domesticates public space but does so with the professionalism of the uniform. She becomes the mother, sister, daughter, and object of attraction. In many ways, the job is similar to that of elevator girl. Both workers recite scripted speeches dependent on vocal manipulations. Over time, they have been nostalgic and sexual icons. They have been made into figurines and featured in popular songs, novels, uniform fashion shows, films, parodies, and more. The difference is in the spaces that they occupy. On a moving bus, the guide acts as a mediator between people and landscape, pointing out what passengers should see. Through narrations and gestures, she gives meaning to scenes framed in bus windows and those traversed on the walking tours she leads from scheduled stops.

As demonstrated by real-life examples, such as Kishima Arisa, and by film protagonists, guides act as intermediaries in the cities in which they themselves are trying to find their place. The real tasks of and symbolic significance ascribed to bus guides provide answers to why female mobility has become associated with sexuality in the popular imagination and discourses about the city and the role of mass transportation in constructing this notion. They speak to the meanings of service in Japan and the intimate relationship between gender and the homeland.

PART III

Modern Girls Overturn Gender and Class

Chapter Seven

THE MODERN GIRL
AS MILITARIST

Female Soldiers In and Beyond
Japan's Self-Defense Forces

Sabine Frühstück

In her seminal essay "The Modern Girl as Militant," Miriam Silverberg (1991b) described the modern girl as a glittering, decadent, middle-class consumer who, through her clothing, smoking, and drinking, flouted tradition in the urban playgrounds of the late 1920s. Silverberg found the identity of the modern girl to be based on her embracing of this cosmopolitan look. As a marker of capitalist modernity, the modern girl was a consumer culture icon, suffusing once-banal objects with an intense aura and occupying new social thought through the positions she took in advertisements. What she expressed, Silverberg wrote, was sometimes historically repressed or could be appropriated for differing ideological ends.

In a concluding commentary on a 2008 book by the Modern Girl Around the World Research Group, Silverberg (2008: 354–355) addressed anew the question of who these women were and modified her original response in light of the findings of scholars around the globe. Her answer was that the Japanese modern girl had been multivalent. On the one hand, she was a phantasm projected onto the social landscape by male critics who were made increasingly anxious by the sociocultural changes taking place all around them. On the other hand, she was also a living and breathing being who wanted to engage in the cultural and social revolution. The labor and mobility of working women in the 1920s and 1930s also helped define Japanese interwar modernity. Hence, in Silverberg's modified understanding of the modern girl, there are those whose commitment to change was limited to a change of clothing, those who were activists, and those whose everyday actions challenged the sociopolitical order (Silverberg 2008: 356–357).

Like the modern girls of the early twentieth century that Silverberg described, female service members of the Self-Defense Forces (Jieitai, SDF) embody some of the most pertinent sociopolitical issues of current-day Japan regarding gender, labor, and mobility. I am not suggesting that modern girls simply exchanged their flapper dresses for military uniforms. Rather, the reason that I believe it is fruitful to adapt the early twentieth-century modern girl icon to the current-day context of female service members is this: many female service members made the decision to take their lives into their own hands in an attempt to liberate themselves from the gender and class restrictions of the predominantly rural communities from which they came. In doing so, they shunned some of the most persistent social conventions of contemporary Japan and overcame their families' pronounced objections to their professional choice to join, at least temporarily, the SDF.[1]

Becoming a service member means being mobile and willing to move to bases anywhere in Japan every two or three years. This geographic mobility is often accompanied by class mobility: some women see the SDF as their only shot at moving up socially. Once in the SDF, they find themselves in a military establishment that heavily invests in the gender management of its public image in ways that reflect its ambiguous constitutional status. (Article 9 of the Japanese Constitution prohibits Japan from going to war and from having a standing army altogether.) Female service members pursue their careers in a media and popular culture environment that mirrors, even exacerbates, the hostile attitudes they encounter within the military itself.

I begin this chapter by describing the ways female service members narrate their experiences in and around the military. I then address the question of how the military employs female figures in its visual self-presentations, including recruitment and materials for public relations purposes directed beyond the recruiting pool. In the final section, I examine a number of representations of female service members that circulate in popular media beyond the formal control of the public relations apparatus of the SDF.

Rather than solidifying any neat separation of "living, breathing" service members from their representations, I propose that it is analytically more useful to view the three spheres as being engaged in the co-production of these modern girls as militarists. As we shall see, their agency is always already compromised, and the authenticity of their selves remains in play and am-

Figure 12 A female service member on a disaster relief mission in Northeastern Japan after the March 11, 2011 earthquake and tsunami. She is depicted with a child she assists in front of a makeshift bath provided by the SDF. (*TakarajimaBessatsu 1780-gō: Jieitai vs. Higashi Nihon daishinsai*, special issue, no. 1780, The Self-Defense Forces versus the Great East Japan Earthquake, 2011, pp. 8–9)

biguous.[2] Their militarism is distinctly molded by the legal framework that guides the SDF and the collective experience and vision of the missions in which they engage.

Most important for the purposes of this chapter, their ambiguous existence leaves them—like the early twentieth-century modern girls—with a pronounced understanding of themselves as women (and as service members). Elsewhere I have argued that their military experience molds them into anthropologist Hugh Gusterson's (1999) "feminist militarists," for whom the experience of exclusionary practices raises their consciousness and makes them determined to struggle against discrimination and for a more complete incorporation into the military (see Frühstück 2007b: 86–114). Here I explore how female service members, the public relations apparatus of the SDF, and the popular media manipulate the gap between the military's promise of a meritocracy and its practice as (also) being governed by gender. I suggest that the gradual and limited integration of female service members is permeated by a rhetoric about the SDF's greater *modernity* than other institutions in Japan, which are cast as lagging behind modern trends.

At the same time, many female service members pursue and experience their careers as the result of their social and professional *mobility*. In other words, laboring for a very specific arm of the state, female service members have been *on the go* in a number of ways: they have been pursuing upward social mobility and economic independence by virtue of their choice of profession and workplace; they have been challenging the gendered order of mainstream society that marks the military male and masculine; and they have been at the forefront of modern womanhood by pursuing careers.

As in most military establishments in the postindustrial world, the integration of women into the SDF has been a strictly regulated process, unilaterally driven by the needs of the military rather than by attempts to create equal career opportunities for women (Enloe 2000; Laura L. Miller 1998). In Japan, the first women who became eligible to enlist in the new national military after World War II were nurses. They were admitted to clerical positions in the Ground Self-Defense Force (Rokujō Jieitai) in 1967 and in both the Maritime Self-Defense Force (Kaijō Jieitai) and the Air Self-Defense Force (Kūjō Jieitai) in 1974. A first breakthrough beyond the nursing profession was prompted in 1974 by the recruitment shortage of men. Subsequently, in 1978 women were granted access to training as medical doctors and dentists.

In addition to the recruitment shortage of men, which has become increasingly dire, the Equal Employment Opportunity Law of 1986 served as the next significant integrative impulse. As an arm of the Japanese government, the SDF were to comply with laws that concerned equal opportunities for women in all areas of employment. Subsequently, between 1986 (when the Ground Self-Defense Force began admitting women) and 1993 (when the Maritime Self-Defense Force and Air Self-Defense Force did so), almost all branches of the SDF opened their doors to female recruits. In 1992 the National Defense Academy (Bōei Daigaku) admitted the first thirty-nine female cadets. When the SDF began to participate in a long-term peacekeeping operation in the Golan Heights in January 1996, the first female service members from the Ground Self-Defense Force became members of the forty-five-person transport contingent.

By the year 2000, all restrictions for women had been lifted. In 2002, several female service members participated in the peacekeeping mission to East Timor and in the 2003 humanitarian aid mission to Iraq, the SDF's first deployment to a combat zone since their establishment in 1954. They were also part of the largest SDF mission to date: the disaster relief operation in northeastern Japan after the Great East Japan Earthquake on March 11, 2011.[3] This gradual shift has allowed the SDF to present themselves as in step with, if not ahead of, other governmental institutions that established anti-discrimination policies.

Subsequently, the SDF have employed a combined strategy of adaptation and mutation, as an apparent flaw (the erosion of an overwhelmingly male military culture) has been parlayed into a further modernization of the SDF as an institution that provides greater gender equality than some segments of corporate Japan. The relentless overrepresentation of female service members in public relations materials, ranging from recruitment posters to white papers, by contrast, has served two public relations goals: to "deepen the understanding and appreciation of the SDF" within the Japanese population and to "mainstream the SDF" (*Jieitai no futsūka*) as a workplace like any other (Frühstück 2007b). To the women who make up the roughly 5 percent of female service members, the SDF's desire to appear modern in the public eye meshes seamlessly with their own desires to embody mobility and modernity, of both social class and gender.

"Choosing My Path Myself": Female Service Members' Perspectives

What draws young women with high-school degrees into the military while their peers take up low-skill jobs? Many of the young women who describe their socioeconomic backgrounds as poor or say that they would not be able to afford a college education, give a broad range of initial motivations for joining the SDF.[4] Generally speaking, female service members articulate their motivations in feminist terms, pitching their expectation of a meritocratic military against a sexist corporate world, and a life of challenges and hope of upward mobility in the military against an uneventful, predictable professional life outside. In other words, their motivations are about class mobility and crossing gender boundaries, not about the defense of the nation.

Female privates and sergeants, in particular, want to be challenged in the same ways that men are, a desire they do not expect to see fulfilled in civilian jobs. Like male privates who cringe at the thought of living a salaryman's life (Frühstück 2007b), female privates perceive the SDF as a workplace where women with a blue-collar family background and a high-school education can avoid tedious clerical work in a corporate office and achieve some measure of social mobility. For many, the dismaying prospect of a subordinated life as an "office lady," who "never gets to do anything but make copies and tea for male coworkers and superiors . . . and is pressured to quit once married and/or pregnant,"[5] is a strong trigger for joining the SDF. Similar to their male peers, young women do not list a strong sense of patriotism in their reasons for joining the SDF.

Officers' perspectives differ somewhat but are also centered on professional and social mobility rather than contributing to the national defense. Mobility is a defining theme of their professional lives, as it is for enlisted women. For example, Lieutenant Colonel Kuroyanagi Hiroko, close to the end of her career, remembered how difficult it was in the 1970s for a female university graduate to find a good job. When she joined the SDF in 1977, the tenuous job security of the public sector also attracted her to the military (Mineo 1998: 232). Likewise, a college graduate from Kanagawa prefecture who worked for a trading company for two years before she decided that she "wanted to do something different" imagined that by entering the closed world of the SDF she "would find [her] own strength" (Bandō 1990: 284).

Female officers hope that the officer's career path will allow them to rise in the military hierarchy to a level they would be unlikely to achieve in a civilian environment. Major Matsubara Yukue, for instance, had wanted to become a diplomat but failed the exam for the Ministry of Foreign Affairs. Discouraged, she consulted one of her college teachers and eventually decided to join the SDF, in the hope that her career as an officer would someday resemble that of a diplomat.[6] Similarly, when Sekizaki Yōko considered taking the entrance exam at the National Defense Academy, she also had been attracted by the idea of becoming "a kind of diplomat" and had thought she had found her ideal university:

> Before I graduated from high school . . . I surprised my teacher by entering "National Defense Academy" in the survey about my future plans. He asked me how I wanted to realize my dream of becoming a diplomat. I said that I would join the SDF, become an officer, and then go into the Ministry of Foreign Affairs, hoping that I would be posted abroad. I knew then that I would not be able to become an ambassador by taking that route, but I could get pretty close to something like that. (Sekizaki 1995)

Some female service members see their profession as a step toward pursuing other careers, most often in medicine, which would otherwise demand a substantial financial investment, or in sports, which requires much training and competition time. As female Private First Class Teruoka Itsuko pointed out, being a service member worked well with her amateur soccer career, which involved a lot of practice and frequent games on weekends. As Elise Edwards explains in this volume, such practical ideas about career choices are similar to those of young women in other jobs. Even female privates without long-term career aspirations believed that a couple of years in the SDF would provide an opportunity to think about what they really wanted to do with their lives while not wasting time on odd jobs. A twenty-seven-year-old woman from Tokyo, for instance, remembered that her mother had imagined that she would acquire all kinds of qualifications and take the public service exam (*kokka shiken*) while working in and receiving a salary from the SDF.

In addition to the challenge young women expect from and seek in a military career, the expectation of gender equality in the workplace also contributes a great deal to the attractiveness of the SDF. SDF recruitment posters aggressively feed expectations of gender equality and beliefs that women can have a "real career" involving skilled labor and a merit-based promotion system. Women who enlist in the SDF imagine that the military hierarchy will override the gender hierarchy they would undoubtedly encounter in the corporate world. Young and low-ranking female service members imagine this to be true because the SDF are governed by stricter rules than those in other workplaces. They believe that gender will matter less than in a civilian job because rank is ostensibly objectively rewarded and notions of superiority and subordination are integral to military discipline. In short, they see opportunities for advancement based on merit that might not be available elsewhere.

While enlisted service members tend to view their time in the military pragmatically, pursuing an officer's career requires considerable independence and gives female officers the sense that they are pioneers in a potentially hostile, masculinist world. Once in the military, the mobility of female service members is subject to more traditional gendered expectations through a combination of assigned tasks and the dynamics of power relations. They cope with these pressures by negotiating the contradiction between soldierhood and womanhood in various ways: by making it known to their peers that they are committed to performing the same tasks as men; by accepting or fighting the trivialization of gender discrimination and sexual harassment; and by selectively rejecting or embracing the rules of conventional femininity.

Female service members like to insist that, in their everyday lives, they first consider themselves to be service members of a certain rank in a specific regiment and unit. When asked about gender differences and instances of discriminatory treatment, Captain Okura, for instance, held tightly to her conviction that the SDF were not ordered in gender terms. Okura saw herself caught in a quandary that is common to female soldiers who trivialize gender discrimination and sexual harassment: if she were to act hurt or annoyed by how she is treated, she would confirm the very discourse that defines her as weak and vulnerable.

Trivializing such incidents, then, is a strategy for preventing the aggressively marginalizing effect of gender discrimination and sexual harassment from fully unfolding. Moreover, if female service members like Okura had a clear understanding of themselves as victims of sexual aggression, they would position themselves within a discourse of victimization. In their eyes, victims are defenseless and vulnerable and have no place in the armed forces, who are the defenders of the weak. Upon further reflection, Okura conceded that if one defined as a feminist a woman who pursues her career "just like a man would," then perhaps she might be one. It is important to note here, however, that Okura and her female peers believed that women who act victimized would not be accepted as equals in the armed forces.

Thus there is an intrinsic contradiction between discourses of women as victims and their participation in the armed forces as full members. The trivialization of gender discrimination and sexual harassment serves as a mechanism for silencing its victims (Sasson-Levy 2003: 93). But that mechanism has recently become more porous, leading to forced retirement or the firing of male perpetrators.

Sexual harassment, however, is only the most visible barrier to female service members' pursuit of mobility via and within the SDF. Female service members also describe how their daily routines are frequently disrupted by the solidly institutionalized belief that women are physically weaker than men and hurt the overall performance of a unit. Arguing against this widespread belief, Tamura Satomi emphasizes the decreasing importance of physical prowess for many military specialties. From her perspective as a Marine Self-Defense Force underwater maintenance specialist, an enormous achievement in the branch of service most notorious for its informal exclusion of women, she said:

> Men think it's a big deal if a woman joins an all-men group, but it isn't really. Once you are in the water, there is no difference between men and women.

Once you dive, it gets dark and you cannot see much. That can be scary and you
have to get used to it. (Nogan 2002: 37–39)

Initially, Tamura had been frustrated by her lack of physical strength, and she
realized that she would have to work much harder than her male peers. Yet at
some point, she recalled, she made the decision to succeed. Her line of work,
she said, required mental in addition to physical strength.

Some female service members felt that they were treated equally or even
better than men. They believed that their commanders were sometimes nicer
to them because they considered them to be "just girls" and thus somewhat less
than full service members. Thus, while the pay scale is the same for men and
women, these hurdles tied to convention slow down female service members'
professional mobility within the SDF. Discriminatory treatment typically was
perceived in positive terms among women who did not plan to have long-term
careers within the SDF. Private Kawasaki Mizue, who had been training in the
artillery corps, by contrast, had mixed feelings about getting a break because
she was a woman:

> Even though I tried to do my work as best as I could, my commanders never
> reprimanded me or pushed me to work harder. It was obvious that they thought
> whatever I am capable of doing would be fine because I am just a girl, after all.
> (uno! 1997: 163)

In addition to being marginalized within the military, female service members feel that their professional and social mobility is impeded by and their
careers measured against social conventions that promote women's main goals
as being wives and mothers. This is evident in remarks parents have made
about their daughters joining the SDF. By and large, female officers' families are
rarely supportive of their daughters' decision to pursue long-term careers in the
military. Two concerns dominate their perspectives. Some parents fear their
daughters would be "totally taken away by the SDF and become entirely different people."[7] Others worry primarily about the dangers of military training and
handling heavy weaponry and machinery. Mothers of female officer candidates
and officers, in particular, worry that their daughters' professions will harm
their chances to start a family, render them less marriageable, or contribute in
other ways to their not having children.

Off base, workingwomen are expected to be attentive mothers and efficient housekeepers, mostly without much help from their male partners. Even
though the national average age for first marriages is increasing in Japan and

more men and women remain childless, parents of many female officers still imagine the bourgeois nuclear family to be the center of a woman's life, as Major Matsubara Eri's experience indicates:

> On top of the really tough basic training and the officer's training thereafter, in addition to all the uncomfortable situations that came about because of my being always the only female officer in the cafeteria, among the troops, in the classroom, and in the field—along with all this, I had to deal with my mother's negative attitude. My mother was against my military career and did not get tired of pushing me to take a year off and try the exam for the Ministry of Foreign Affairs again. I know that, even now that she sees my success, she still is against my officer's career, even though she has stopped saying so. I guess she has resigned herself to the fact that this is my work now. Recently, however, she asked me to at least marry a civilian.

Female service members had differing opinions about whether it is better to marry military or civilian men, but they all agreed that, once inside the SDF, they no longer have many opportunities to meet, let alone date, men on the outside. Some had never had a civilian boyfriend. Most female privates left no doubt that they planned to marry at some point, and those plans also were informed by pragmatic considerations about the kinds of lives they wanted to lead. They imagined that, in addition to a sense of stability and security, marriage would offer an escape from dormitory life on base and provide some individual freedom. They preferred the privacy of an apartment to group life on base, where they share a room with up to five other women.

One female service member said that she wanted to continue working after marriage and that she would remain single until she found a man who accepted her professional aspirations. Others saw their future husbands as enabling them to become stay-at-home mothers and wives. The fact that female service members, especially officers, tend to be in relationships with male service members often causes them to sever their social ties to civilian friends and communities more readily than they think their male peers do.

Major Kajimoto Masako, for instance, recalled that her parents relentlessly pushed her to marry and have children. Even though at that time, she said she had no desire to start a family, she eventually resigned, married a fellow officer, and had two children. Her assessment of that decision was—rather typically for female service members—pragmatic rather than romantically determined: "He is a good enough man, but I would not have married him if my parents had not insisted that they might die soon and that they wanted to see a grandchild before they did so. They are still alive and well. I feel that they robbed me of my career." In Kajimoto's mind, her parents had acted selfishly. Her parents' preoccupation with grandchildren and perhaps Kajimoto's proper social place as a married woman and mother had, in her estimation, put an end to her shot at a real career and the social and class mobility that she had imagined would come with it.

In these ways, pressures from the ranks of SDF superiors and peers match the concerns of parents and the community about the conflict between women's pursuit of a military career and the social expectation that mature womanhood should lead to motherhood. For officers, there is an additional kind of mobility that has a tendency to run counter to achieving mainstream womanhood and motherhood. Every two or three years, officers are transferred all over Japan and occasionally abroad, wherever Japan maintains embassies. As I explain in the next section, the SDF's public relations and recruitment apparatus fully exploits the very paradox made up of individual female service members' modern mobility and the uniformed conformity of the institution for which they labor.

"Please Bring a Big Dream Along":
SDF Recruitment and Public Relations Materials

The public relations and recruitment apparatus of the SDF taps into the desire for professional and social mobility voiced by female soldiers by dramatically over-representing women in their materials. I have described this feature elsewhere as being designed to deemphasize the masculine and potentially violent character of the SDF (Frühstück 2007b: 86–114). Here, I want to make a different point: other contributions to this volume emphasize that flight attendants, tour bus guides, and elevator girls help make new, modern technologies such as planes, tour buses, and department store elevators less frightening to users, both by virtue of their female and ultra-feminine appearance and by taking on the machinelike character of the vehicles on which they work. The women portrayed in SDF materials, by contrast, rarely appear with (war) technologies. Instead, their bodies stand for what cannot be shown: weaponry. The SDF refrains from establishing or exploiting the combined erotic potential of women and guns.

On SDF posters, leaflets, and other advertisements, cute little dogs say, "As for me, I love peace!" (*Boku datte, heiwa ga daisuki!*).[8] Models call out in English, "Peace[ful] People [of] Japan, Come On!" Uniformed office workers suggest, "Please bring a big dream along" (*Ōkina yume o hitotsu motte kite kudasai*). Uniformed mechanics proceed "Step by Step" (in English) in order to become "Shining people at a workplace of which one can be proud" (*Hokoreru shokuba de, kagayaku hito*). Next to a picture of a member of the Air Self-Defense Force, which covers half of the poster, is the slogan "Believe. Turn toward a steady dream" (*Kawaranu yume ni mukatte*). The erotic potential of a female body in uniform is evoked in a twofold manner: by using uniformed women who are not soldiers and by stripping female service members of their uniforms. Almost all of the women depicted are professional models or celebrities (*tarento*). For example, the woman proclaiming "Peace[ful] People [of] Japan, Come On!" is the extremely proper and cheerful-seeming Kamon Yōko (the phrase "come on" of the slogan is a word play on her last name), who is known for her anime theme songs. Dressed in a white T-shirt and wearing a ponytail, Kamon is most likely a nod to a younger, hipper crowd who might enlist but is much more likely to just embrace SDF figurines and paraphernalia, as they would other popular cultural icons. Toying with the uniform—sometimes the model is wearing a uniform, sometimes not—turns the female body into a malleable surface onto which the SDF can inscribe its desire for attracting "normal/ordinary people."[9] Once she is a female service member, then again just a girl in uniform.

Female service members' not quite secured grown-up status within the SDF is further conveyed in recruitment and public relations materials, including a video clip produced for the Maritime Self-Defense Force. The video opens with a group of men in sailor uniforms onboard a ship, dancing in formation to the tune of "Y.M.C.A."[10] The lyrics are as follows:

> We have seamanship, seamanship, seamanship for love!
> We have seamanship, seamanship, seamanship for peace! [in English]
> Japan is beautiful.
> Peace is beautiful.
> The Maritime Self-Defense Force. [in Japanese]
>   —Maritime Self-Defense Force 2005

When they sing "Japan is beautiful" (*"Nihon ga kirei"*), the camera moves away from the uniformed dancing men and zooms in on the face of a girl, perhaps around age thirteen, who, like many female high-school students, is also clad in a sailor uniform. She smiles and salutes (a combination that violates the rules of proper conduct in the SDF) while Japan's national flag fills the entire background. Similar to the frequent depiction of Japan as female and feminine, a phenomenon that Yano's chapter in this volume addresses, Japan is depicted here as a woman, too. Yet in this Maritime Self-Defense Force video clip, Japan is both feminized and infantilized.[11] While the SDF's public relations apparatus extensively and frequently shows female soldiers to promote the image of the armed forces as supporting women, popular media appear distinctly more conflicted regarding women's representation in the military.

"Cannon Ball Beauties":
Female Service Members in the Popular Media

Female service members have not been widely reported on by magazines and other popular media in part because of the SDF's precarious constitutional status. Only rarely have representations of female soldiers appeared since the attempts in the 1970s to enlist women other than nurses in the military. These representations almost always take aesthetic and narrative clues from the casually sexist tabloid depictions of female bodies that are conspicuous in Japan's mass media. Articles on female service members, police women, and women in similar traditionally male-dominated professions emphasize their exceptional choice of workplace. At the same time, however, they quite literally strip them of their exceptionality by visually representing them in sexually provocative poses, thus reintroducing a measure of conventionality into the narrative and containing the transgressive character of these women's career choices.

For instance, an article entitled "Eight female service members of the SDF" (*Jieitai josei taiin hachi-nin*) (*Shūkan gendai* 1990) includes photographs of enlisted service members clad in swimsuits and crawling provocatively on leopard print scarves. Private Satō Terumi, for example, looks longingly up at the reader. Her profile specifies that she is twenty years old, 153 centimeters tall, and has a waist of fifty-seven centimeters. The author acknowledges, as if relieved, that she is an "ordinary" girl who likes to go to Shibuya and Tokyo Disneyland with her boyfriend. In the SDF, she felt she had found the right atmosphere "to test her limits" but was bothered by "the lack of private time." To the question of what she likes to do most, she replied, "doing nothing and going to a spa." One does not learn anything about Satō's unusual work, the supposed reason for this illustrated article (*Shūkan gendai* 1990). The article also includes smaller photographs of women in uniform to illustrate that "nobody would believe that these bodies in swimsuits belong to the same women as those in combat uniforms" (*Shūkan gendai* 1990). Reminiscent of the interwar modern girls, the trivializing and sexualizing of military women are accomplished through clothing—conventional fashion in the first case, a military uniform in the latter.

Other popular weekly and monthly sports and scandal magazines marketed to men also reduce female soldiers to their physical features—height, weight, waist measurement, and age—and their social status. Such media emphasize sexual availability rather than professional qualities. Titles include "95 women to watch: The beauty with real strength—Kawaue Hitomi" (*95-nen kakukai chūmoku no josei: Jitsuryoku no bijo, Kawaue Hitomi, Shūkan hōseki* 1995); "I want to meet the heroines of the sky" (*Sora no hiroin ni aitai, Flash* 2003a); "'Top gun'. . . This is how beautiful Japan's first female instructor is" (*'Toppu gan'. . . Nihon hatsu josei kyōkan wa konna ni bijin, Flash* 2003b); "War and peace of nine beautiful female service members: My case study" (*Bijin Jieikan 9-nin no arasoi to heiwa, watashi no baai, Sapio* 1996); and "Take a 'cannon ball beauty' as a wife" (*Nyōbō ni suru nara 'tetsuwan bijo'! Scholar* 2002).

In "A former female SDF member reveals it all through hair nudes: Sex in the SDF" (*Moto fujin Jieikan ga hea nūdo de kataru: Jieitai no sei*), published in a 1999 issue of *Shūkan gendai*, Private Satō Yūka is shown in two photographs.[12] In one, she is poker-faced and saluting in uniform, and in the other she smiles flirtatiously and is dressed in kimono with her hair artfully done (*Shūkan gendai* 1999). According to her profile, Satō, who belonged to the Ground Self-Defense Force and worked on a base in Kumamoto, is 159 centimeters tall, and weighs fifty-two kilograms. She counts music, flower arrangement, kendo, and calligraphy among her hobbies. Her boyfriend is also a service member.

She says she joined the SDF because she "wanted to challenge herself under difficult conditions" instead of becoming just another clerical worker. When asked whether she was proud of representing a profession whose purpose is "to contribute to Japan's security," she responded that she was not quite sure what that meant. She did, however, appreciate the gratitude that SDF troops encountered during and after disaster relief missions, clearly her only experience and, perhaps, vision of the SDF on a mission (*Shūkan gendai* 1999). When asked by *Shūkan gendai* which weapon she would like to try, Satō responded that she was most interested in driving a tank. However, she could not think of a military role model. All of the other twelve short portraits show female service members between the ages of nineteen and thirty-four.

All of the women are featured in two photographs. Smaller photographs show them dressed in camouflage fatigues and saluting or pointing machine guns at the reader. In larger ones, they pose in bikinis, gym clothes, or mainstream casual clothes.

Female soldiers have been depicted similarly in other print media. The small publishing company Ikarosu has launched efforts to appeal to fans of anime and manga. In 2011, Ikarosu published the first-ever *Female Service Members 2012 Calendar* (*Josei Jieikan 2012 karendā*), a medium otherwise reserved for *tarento* and other women in entertainment, as well as photo books with more aggressively sexualized messages about female service members. Ikarosu publishes the monthly magazine *Hyper Beautiful Girl-Type Military Magazine* (*Haipā bishōjokei miritarī magajin*), along with the book series *Moe yo!* (*Longing!*). These are aggressive attempts to employ the language of anime and the digital world in order to attract a younger audience that can no longer be reached with the kinds of magazine articles I described above.

By the same token, this foray into new markets might be an indicator of the further mainstreaming of female soldiers due to their increased media exposure in connection with recent disaster relief efforts. Volume titles include *Army School* (*Rikuji gakkō*), *Tank School* (*Sensha gakkō*), *Tank School, II* (*Sensha gakkō II*), *Surprise! A Introduction to an Imperial Army Full of Girls* (*Dokki! Shojō darake no Teikoku Rikugun nyūmon*), *First Love Combined Fleet* (*Hatsukoi rengō kantai*), and *Poisonous War* (*Dokusosen*). Each is by a different author and illustrator. The book series combines considerably detailed descriptions of military matters with black-and-white illustrations and glossy color images of girls with guns, tanks, and other military equipment in suggestive poses.

The depicted female service members are cute and scary, big-bosomed, and scantily dressed; they purse their lips and look daringly at the reader; and some invite a peek up their skirts at their underpants. The sexualization and "pornification" of female bodies is ubiquitous in Japanese popular culture (Napier 2005; Allison 2000). Manifestations of what Dick Hebdige (2008: 40) has termed "sado-cute" include the "sub-teen craze for time-travel (especially time reversal), soft-porn, sci-fi, and sorcery animanga [anime and manga] narratives and video games; pedophiliac loli-com (Lolita complex) fashions, model kits, and signage [. . .]." It is important to highlight that this sexualization and pornification has only now begun to embrace the bodies of female service members.

The term "*moe*" in the series title is often used to indicate the affectionate longing for two-dimensional characters, or, more accurately, to refer to an internalized emotional response to something, generally with no hope of reciprocation. In discussions about the cultural significance of anime in Japan, the idea of *moe* is also associated with larger questions about the ways fans relate to virtual characters and worlds, and in turn about the power of media producers

Figure 13 Female service member on the cover of Tamura Naoya and Nogami Takeshi *Moe yo! Rikuji gakkō* (It's *Moe*! The SDF school), 2008, Ikarosu shuppan.

over consumers (Condry 2011). Whose longing is it and for what? Women longing for the power of a gun? Male readers longing for the depicted girls? The SDF
longing for more recruits? All of the above? Or, perhaps the "normalization" of
the SDF via the mainstreaming of their female service members?

Beyond the question of who might be the object of longing, it is important to note that *Moe yo!* and similar publications for male and female readers
mark a departure from the previously rather cold reception by the producers of
popular culture of the SDF and its members. With very few exceptions, the most
prominent of which was the *Godzilla* film series, and in stark contrast to their
response to the military in wartime Japan (Frühstück 2007a), the producers of
postwar popular culture have rarely depicted the Self-Defense Forces, and when
they did, it was hardly ever in a positive light. Hence, *Moe yo!* represents a recent
interest of the Japanese popular cultural industry in the SDF. It is as if the mak-
ers of popular media have suddenly discovered the power of the mix of Japanese
popular culture and Japanese military figures, at least as long as those come in
the shape of what Anne Allison (2006) has referred to as "millennial monsters."

It remains to be seen whether this new aesthetic will result in more young
female recruits or just feed the old impulse to trivialize women who aspire to
pursue social and class mobility, transgress gender boundaries, and explore
new segments of the labor market.

The SDF on the Go

Female service members, especially officers, embody a challenge to conventional notions of womanhood similar to that articulated by some young women
during the early twentieth century. They self-consciously experience the social
obstacles to the pursuit of their careers, ranging from the pressure to marry
and devote themselves to household and family to the underestimation of their
ability to pursue professional careers. Quite in contrast to Silverberg's modern
girl militants, however, female service members do not just embody the challenge to conventional notions of womanhood. They do so within one of Japan's
most conservative institutions, the armed forces. Their militancy is encased in
the military uniforms they wear, which signal alignment with state objectives.

Who are those young women who shunned some of the most persistent
social conventions of contemporary Japan and overcame their families' pronounced objection to their choice to pursue class and professional mobility,
individuality, and gender equality by laboring for an arm of the state that has traditionally suppressed and negated such aspirations? Young female service mem-

bers "on the go" appear determined and conscious of their choice to transgress social norms. They continuously negotiate the tension between their subjectivities as daughters, women, and (potential or actual) mothers and their integration into the armed forces. This tension continuously reconstitutes itself in how they engage the utterances of their parents who fear their "defeminization," their male peers in the SDF who worry about the armed forces' "feminization," the publicly circulating images of the SDF that typically portray them as young women still being formed, and the casually sexualizing and infantilizing representations of themselves in the popular media.

While the *militancy* that permeates these women's careers and personal lives in many ways mirrors that of some of the more determined modern girls of the early twentieth century, their *militarization* sets them apart dramatically. After all, the SDF are employed to "defend Japan," be it on domestic or international missions concerned with community building, disaster relief, or peacekeeping.

Chapter Eight

THE PROMISES
AND POSSIBILITIES
OF THE PITCH

1990s Ladies League Soccer Players
as Fin-de-Siècle Modern Girls

Elise Edwards

When the Japanese women's national soccer team, Nadeshiko Japan, bested the greatly favored U.S. team in the World Cup Final on July 17, 2011, in Frankfurt, Germany, it was one of several "firsts" achieved by the skillful and inspiring team. It was the *first* time Japan had beaten the Americans in twenty-six meetings stretching back over two decades. Even more historically significant, however, was that this World Cup Championship was the first for an Asian soccer team, women's or men's. The level of interest in the match could be gauged by a new Twitter record set by fans within seconds of Kumagai Saki's decisive final kick in the penalty shoot-out—a shot heard around the world in the wee hours of the morning in Tokyo. A flurry of 7,196 tweets per second easily overwhelmed the previous Twitter record.[1]

Even months after the Japanese women's historic victory, "Nadeshiko Fever" showed few signs of subsiding. The semi-professional Nadeshiko League—the newest incarnation of what had been dubbed the "L-League" (short for "Ladies' League") for more than a decade and no more financially secure than its predecessor—experienced a dramatic new wave of interest and record-setting match attendances. A new average League match attendance of over 6,500 fans was more than nine times the figure before the World Cup. With well over 20,000 fans filling the stands at games in which national team players appeared, earlier records were quickly surpassed and easily rivaled the numbers at men's J-League (Japan League) contests. "Nadeshiko Japan" was chosen as the top media buzzword of 2011, as well as the second most important domestic news event, just behind the Great East Japan Earthquake on March 11, 2011, and the subsequent tsunami and nuclear meltdown (Jiyū kokuminsha 2011; *Daily Yomiuri* 2011a).[2]

For most of the players, there was a dramatic shift from obscurity to spotlight, with adulatory attention coming from journalists, advertising agents, and even Japan's prime minister, Naoto Kan. Many of the players—the majority of them veritable unknowns before the quarter-final round of the World Cup three weeks prior—were enthusiastically courted by companies and advertisers to serve as the spokespeople and public faces for a range of products. Several players signed lucrative sponsorship deals, while others pursued second careers as pop stars; the most prominent few appeared regularly on nightly variety shows. Just weeks after the final penalty shot whizzed by the U.S. team's formidable goalkeeper, it was widely reported that the economic vortex set spinning by the team's success had produced a one trillion yen ($13 billion) windfall, a much-needed emotional and financial boost for Japan's beleaguered economy (Brasor and Tsubuku 2011).

The Nadeshiko team's masterful play throughout the 2011 World Cup, with their signature quick passing and impeccable technique, earned them comparisons to Lionel Messi's FC Barcelona squad of the men's game, touted by many as the best soccer team ever assembled (*Times of India* 2011). Their consummate skill and accolades made it difficult to remember that women's soccer participation rates had paled in comparison to those in rival countries, and that before the Nadeshiko team's fourth-place finish at the 2008 Olympic Games in Beijing, the sport and its players existed for several decades in almost total obscurity.[3] In the span of the few weeks of the 2011 World Cup tournament, Nadeshiko Japan's players went from relative unknowns to their country's most celebrated and adored stars; obscurity made way for fame and visibility. Suddenly an image of Japanese femininity—confident, thickly muscled, often short-haired, and undeniably aggressive—overwhelmed the airwaves, introducing the world and the vast majority of Japanese citizens as well to a form of Japanese womanhood previously unseen, let alone imagined.

Owing to the relative invisibility of women's soccer until recently, many journalists both within and outside of Japan treated the Nadeshiko team's World Cup win as more of a Cinderella story than was warranted, and women's soccer as an anomaly that reflected little understanding of the history of women's soccer, or of women's sports more generally. While Nadeshiko Japan's recent successes can be traced to an array of factors, the most significant was the decision by a handful of companies beginning in the late 1980s to aggres-

sively sponsor women's soccer teams and to provide the country's most promising players with employment and places to train. What has become one of
the most powerful soccer development systems in the world for women began
with the coming together of unlikely "teammates": athletic young women and
industry-leading corporations. The story of the rise of women's soccer engages
directly with issues of mobility, modernity, gender, and labor in contemporary
Japanese society, and its telling reveals the multiple axes upon which these ana-
lytic frames intersect and co-constitute each other.

In this chapter, I describe how female soccer players and the businessmen
who sponsored them were captivated and inspired by soccer for reasons that,
on the surface, often looked dissimilar, but that at their core were very much
alike. Both players and corporate managers involved with women's teams conceptualized soccer as a vehicle for mobility—whether in one's personal life or
in corporate markets—and, in turn, imagined that mobility to be intimately
tied to ideas of a reconfigured and more globally focused modern Japan and
a new vision of ideal workers, as well as atypical forms of femininity. For both
the players and their sponsors, mobility was directly and causally linked with
practices and "ways of being" construed as "modern," which I use here in the
spirit of Bruno Latour to designate "a new regime, an acceleration, a rupture, a
revolution in time" (1993: 10).[4]

As Japan stands in the afterglow of the women's national team's unforget-
table victory, and as we revisit some of the history leading up to that achievement in the stories of some of its earliest teams, we can trace the way that
women soccer players came to embody modern notions of change salient in
recessionary Japan, and we can see the effects of this arbitrary yet historically
significant linkage.

Like the modern girls of the 1920s and 1930s who preceded them, Japanese
female soccer players were linked—because of their engagement with particular physical practices and forms of presentation—with a broad range of ideas
and ideals that stretched far beyond the realities or possibilities of their lives.
While image and reality often differed and the progressive experiences afforded
by soccer were often as short-lived as the corporate sponsorships, there was
a period of time in post-bubble-era Japan when women's soccer held a significance that dramatically changed the environment of women's sports in the
country and planted the seeds for further successes that have reshaped domestic and international perceptions of Japanese women in the opening decades of
the twenty-first century.

In the 1990s, the image of the L-Leaguer, as constituted by L-League officials, company executives, and the players themselves, represented personal
dreams, social concerns, and corporate visions that forged new relationships
between modernity, mobility, labor, and gender. L-Leaguers were women on
the move—moving not only across soccer fields but also into new spaces of
labor and leisure not typically thought of as traditional female domains. For the
players, this movement was often personally liberating and life-changing; for
companies, it symbolized visions of progress and greater gender equality, and
therein, new image-making possibilities. An exploration of the perspectives
and motivations of both the players and the companies who employed them,
the points of overlap in their understandings of and investments in the sport
of soccer, as well as the disconnect between images of L-Leaguers as idealized
corporate citizens and the actual realities of players lives, will highlight not only
the centrality of gender in visions of modern change at the turn of the millen-
nium but also the inconsistencies and contradictions of the L-League's modern
project, which remain salient to this day.

The material for this chapter was collected over more than two decades of
steady involvement with the L-League/Nadeshiko League and the larger world
of soccer actors and organizations in which it is embedded. From an array of
positions, including L-League player, coach, and fan, I have conducted field
research with teams, corporate owners, Japan Football Association administrators, and, of course, countless players and coaches. My approach to understanding the world of Japanese soccer is interdisciplinary, drawing from sites
where soccer and soccer players are discursively constructed, including fan
magazines, coaching journals, and corporate and team brochures, as well as
interviews and interactions with company and team managers, coaches, and
players.

Soccer's Modern Image

Although by happenstance, Japan's "soccer boom" (*sakkā būmu*) coincided
with the bursting of the economic bubble and its recessionary aftermath in the
1990s, and soccer was regularly presented in popular media as a product of and
an antidote to economic instability (Edwards 2003). Despite its century-long
history as a pastime and institutionalized sport in Japan, coaches, journalists,
and executives of corporations sponsoring teams reinscribed soccer as something *new*, a cultural space that attracted and cultivated athletes with colorful
and individualistic personalities. Reporters and pundits, soccer's supporters

and detractors, all pronounced it to be a new and unprecedented sporting realm, with players who had dyed hair, piercings, and jewelry, and who engaged in audacious on-field celebrations after goals; it was "everything that the tightly controlled samurai version of baseball [was] not" and possibly even the springboard to a larger "social revolution" (Sterngold 1994: 4; Morris 1995: 82; Takahashi 1994; Kutsuwada 1993).

In the year of the men's J-League's launch, a famous former professional turned J-League coach was memorably quoted as saying that soccer players were the "first professional athletes [in Japan] permitted to display [their] personalities" (*Newsweek* 1994). This ability to "display one's personality," in turn, was seized by coaches and journalists alike as the quality that made soccer the most "un-Japanese" of all popular sports, and also rendered it a critical site for cultivating new abilities and sensibilities for Japanese youth who needed to compete in an increasingly competitive global economy (Katō 1997: 150).

With its premier event, the World Cup, standing as the most internationally inclusive of all sporting events, soccer became metaphorically connected to the challenges of globalization more broadly. Many of the skills that Japanese soccer players would have to acquire to close their "gap with the world" paralleled the "revolution" in business practices and entrepreneurial abilities deemed necessary for Japanese business to regain its competitiveness (Kiriyama 1998; Katō 1997: 78; Gotō 1995). Whereas baseball was cast as the symbol of an older Japan and all that was good about the industriousness and group-oriented mythology of "Japan, Inc.," soccer was posed as the modern sport of the future, providing fields of possibility, literally, to train new subjectivities, sensibilities, and pathways to success (Hashimoto 1998: 292–93; Gotō 1995: 175). In the final decade of the twentieth century, for many people in Japan, soccer represented a break with the past, and for those who liked the sport, this change was optimistically cast as a way out of the economic and social malaise that seemed to have a stranglehold after the bursting of the financial bubble.

Despite its masculine associations, young female players could not help but be attracted to soccer's new and revolutionary image. Unlike many of the other modern girls analyzed in this volume, young girls and women typically did not take up the sport of soccer—as one would a career path as an SDF soldier, stewardess, or even elevator girl—imagining that it would provide mobility in the form of income, world travel, or greater independence, although for the most talented few it eventually could provide some of those things. Mobility of another kind, however, did seem to attract many to the sport: the chance to move through and experience not only a predominantly masculine space but also one that was marked as culturally new, even transgressive.

The youth players and the L-Leaguers I interviewed reaffirmed popular media portrayals that presented soccer as something novel, exciting, and reflective of a freer and more expressive youth culture. Echoing journalists, these players imagined and experienced soccer as unequivocally modern because it marked a rupture with the past and with tradition, which they saw embodied in postwar Japan's celebrated "group ethic," and more specifically the sport of baseball. Soccer fields were spaces where they could be "more free" but also where "individuals were important," and they could "express their individuality a lot more than [in] baseball." For several players I interviewed, the "more free" and "less Japanese" character of soccer was captured in the relative absence of hierarchical "senior-junior" (*senpai-kōhai*) relationships, which were dominant socializing structures in conventional girls' high-school sports, such as volleyball and softball.

Many young women I have met over two decades of involvement with the L-League were self-defined rebels or individuals who claimed to be "different" (*chigau*), "out of the ordinary" (*futsū to chigau*), or "different than ordinary Japanese" (*futsū no Nihonjin to chigau*). For them, soccer provided a space that allowed, accepted, and at times celebrated that difference. More than regimentation and discipline, soccer promised ways to escape hierarchical relationships, to explore more unconventional forms of dress and expression. Many young players had impressive collections of replica jerseys from all of their favorite international teams and loved that soccer provided the opportunity to wear them on their daily train commutes to and from practice. Many L-Leaguers enthusiastically engaged in what I call "soccer style," which mimicked the fashions (oversized jeans worn low on the hips, men's button-up shirts left untucked, brightly colored brand-name tennis shoes, and spikey hairstyles) and relaxed yet self-assured mannerisms of the J-Leaguers as well as international male players whose images were readily available across different media.

Soccer was imagined and experienced by these young players as a space to cultivate one's individuality—to achieve a mobility of selfhood. The image of soccer as a realm of freedom and modernity that broke radically with tradition, which attracted so many of the L-League's early players, also appealed to the company executives who chose to sponsor teams, although the mobility they sought, of course, was quite different.

In the early 1990s, several large companies decided to support L-League teams, inspired by the idea that these young women and their sport would help them recast their corporate identities and link them with leading-edge thinking and progressive change. The iconoclastic and change-embracing image of men's soccer swirling through the media beginning in the late 1980s provided ample symbolic material to which they could tether new corporate campaigns. Company investments in women's soccer, however, were also informed by an image of women's soccer circulating internationally that connected the game with socially progressive and economically dominant first-world modernity.

While "ground zero" for men's soccer in 1990s Japan—from which soccer's greatness emanated—was unquestionably South America, the geographic core of the women's game was positioned solidly in the United States and Northern Europe. Images of fair-haired Norwegians and strong, smiling American players, hoisting trophies over their heads or sliding stomach-first across the grass in a goal celebrations, were seen by many as part and parcel of progressive sociopolitical systems; women striding across soccer fields symbolically suggested that women were making strides in many other areas of society. Many of the companies that sponsored women's teams wanted to cash in on this image to appeal to new Euro-American business clients, and to symbolically signal— in some cases to their own workers, and in others, to domestic customers—that other progressive transformations within their companies were afoot. While players saw soccer as a means of circumventing, at least temporarily, more conventional life courses and gendered expectations, for many of the companies that supported them, the sport held the promise of image-refashioning via its popular associations with femal social mobility.

"Dream" Projects and "Creative Intelligence": Corporate Investments in Women's Soccer

In 1989, the L-League's predecessor, the Japan Ladies Soccer League (JLSL), which then consisted of six teams from the Kantō and Kansai areas, was inaugurated as the nation's premier women's league. A handful of women's club teams, including Shimizu F.C. and Yomiuri Women's Soccer Club, had been established in the early to mid-1980s in soccer-friendly areas, such as Tokyo and Shizuoka Prefecture. These teams formed the core of the JLSL and were joined by new corporate (kigyō) teams, such as Fujita Construction, a firm that already supported men's teams and had the facilities and staff to start up quickly. Over the following two years, executives at several companies, including Nikko

Securities, Shiroki Industries, and the Tasaki Pearl Company, built teams and facilities from scratch, thus growing the JLSL to ten teams by 1991. In 1994 the JLSL was renamed the "L-League" ("L" for "ladies") to form linkages with and to benefit from the boom in fan interest in the men's J-League.

In the JLSL's inaugural year, Nikko Securities executives announced that the Dream Ladies would be the athletic incarnation of the spirit of the company's new bold "corporate welfare" project called the "Nikko Dream," made possible by many years of steady profits. One initial component of the Nikko Dream was the implementation of two-day weekends for all workers, an uncommon practice among large financial firms at the time. The ambitious plan also called for the creation of new dormitories and family housing units for company workers, as well as the acquisition and building of resorts and recreational facilities, including those at golf courses, ski areas, hot springs, and beaches. Other corporations followed suit and cast their L-League teams as the public faces of company-wide "welfare" programs. The Fujita Tendai team, owned by Fujita Construction and headquartered in Tokyo, for instance, was run out of the "For You Division," which, similar to the Nikko Dream project, was focused on quality-of-life issues, such as housing, leisure activities, and other programs for its employees.

Publicity campaigns flaunting "dream projects" to improve conditions both at and away from work for employees were, at least partially, responses to broader labor issues and debates salient at the time. As Japan entered the 1990s, journalists and government officials alike directed increasing attention to improving the well-being of workers, including tackling such problems as excessive overtime work and weeks of unspent vacation time. With topics like "death from overwork" (karōshi) receiving considerable coverage in both the domestic and international press, the Ministry of Health, Labor, and Welfare pressured employers to cut overtime and weekend hours required of workers. They also found ways to guarantee that workers received their legally allotted vacation time. In addition to the external critiques of their white-collar work-places, Japanese corporations faced a shrinking labor market and had to devise schemes to attract top university graduates. For a small number of companies, supporting women's soccer players and creating winning teams emerged as a strategy not only to promote welfare projects but also to promote themselves as employee-friendly enterprises.

In talking to L-League company workers, I quickly realized that many as-sumed that their companies' decisions to sponsor *women's* soccer, rather than men's soccer or another sport, were rooted in simple economics: in general, women's teams and lesser-known sports were cheaper to fund, and quick success was more likely since there was little competition. Top executives' personal passions for soccer were often another important factor in determining the direction of sponsorship. Even so, corporations quickly provided much more carefully articulated and business-savvy rationales for choosing women's soccer. In interviews and press conferences, company spokespeople frequently underscored the logic that made women's soccer a "perfect fit" with the central tenets of their companies. For instance, in a photo-rich article announcing the launch of the Dream Ladies in the September 1989 issue of *Friday*, then one of Japan's most popular weekly scandal and sports magazines aimed at businessmen, the Nikko Securities president was quoted as saying, "Soccer fits our bright, tough, and healthy image perfectly. Men's soccer [in Japan] still has a long way to go, but women's soccer has a real future" (*Friday* 1989). The president's comments seemed to reflect both the prediction that female players were going to fare better than their male counterparts on the international stage (a prediction proven correct at the 2008 Olympics and the 2011 World Cup) and the belief that women's soccer was carving an uncharted path and thus had a "real future."

Nikko Securities' public relations group created a romantic story for the mass media, replete with a sense of fated destiny and forward-looking vision, with the president as its main protagonist. According to this story, the president's decision to start the team came from his realization that women's soccer was the "future." He hoped that those watching both outside and inside the company would conclude that Nikko Securities was forward-thinking due to its support of women's soccer. The company's purported concern for employee welfare was also regularly paraded via images and stories about the team: Nikko Securities was not only providing young women with a wonderful environment in which to pursue their dreams, but was also guaranteeing them jobs upon their retirement from the team at any of their nationwide branch offices. Executives clearly hoped that their employees, as well as their customers, would assume that the same compassionate business practices extended to them.

Several other corporations used images and stories of their L-League teams in promotional campaigns similar to that of Nikko Securities. Shiroki Industries, an automotive parts manufacturer headquartered in Nagoya, stated in their company narrative that women's soccer was "fresh" and "new" and that their L-League team ideally represented the "New Shiroki Movement," a broad-based strategy to increase, among other things, product diversification, internationalization, and employee training. The guiding theme of the movement and new corporate motto was "Creative Intelligence," which sales brochures and other materials defined as capturing the originality and inventiveness that defined the company's efforts. In the first half of 1990, as plans for the new team named Serena got under way, numerous articles echoed Shiroki Industries' press release that the team "perfectly fit" its image as a "fresh" company "looking towards the twenty-first century" (*Nihon Keizai Shinbun* 1990).[5]

Ishimaru Masayuki, the man in charge of creating the Serena team and who was promoted to president of Shiroki Industries soon after, presented the Serena team as representing the company's more general policies and perspectives toward female employees. In an article in the *Mainichi* newspaper, Ishimaru was quoted as saying, "This is the era of women, and [Shiroki Industries] is aiming to fully utilize women's abilities" (*Mainichi Shinbun* 1990). Just weeks later, in a regionally broadcast radio interview, Ishimaru said that Shiroki Industries wanted to create a company where "the active involvement of women will increase the motivation of male workers, and male and female employees will learn together and make each other better" (*Tōkai Nichi-Nichi Shinbun* 1990a). Article headlines furthered the view of Shiroki Industries as a progressive and women-friendly company. For instance, the large type above one article read, "Expecting Great Things from the Strength of Women" (*Tōkai Nichi-Nichi Shinbun* 1990b).

The evolution of the L-League from a club to a corporate team entity, as well as the creation of more teams, coincided with a critical period of public discussion and legal actions relating to women and work in Japan. The year 1985, which marked the inauguration of the "New Shiroki Movement," also saw the passage of the Equal Employment Opportunity Law, which took effect in 1986. Prominent international reportage on sexual harassment cases against Japanese firms produced an unflattering and generic image of Japanese corporations as unfair to women.[6] Shiroki Industries management's explicit presentation of its commitment to women's soccer team as representative of its broader commitment to women's employment that "fully utilizes their abilities" was, in part, a concerted response to discussions of women's rights and labor.

At the same time, Shiroki Industries featured the Serena team in efforts that seemed to ignore or erase gender. Specifically, corporate images posed the players as generic employees who benefited from their policies. For instance, photographs of Serena players were the only actual images of "employees" in the human resources section of the 1998 company profile brochure. The accompanying text begins:

> Shiroki Industries believes that talented employees are our greatest asset. Our hope is that, while our employees make the most of themselves as individuals, they will also be active participants at work and home. In order to achieve these goals, we seek to build a "creative and energetic company" by establishing working environments that emphasize cooperation between management and labor, improving working conditions, and providing ways for employees to utilize their leisure time. (Shiroki Industries 1998: 18)

The text suggests reciprocal obligations between company and workers: in return for Shiroki Industries' paternalistic concern, employees must make the most of themselves and show dedication to their greatest social obligations—work and family. The blurring of team players' images in one of the most prominent photographs suggests vigorous movement and speed and a sense of rapid progress and aggressive action. The blurring also renders the figures

Figure 14 "Talented employees are our greatest asset." Shiroki Corporation (1998) corporate brochure.

anonymous and genderless: they are any and every employee, dressed in the Shiroki Industries uniform, their bodies in matched strides, moving in unison and pursuing the same goal. They are a perfectly coordinated, seemingly automated, corporeal and corporate unit.[7] The image's arguably modernist bracketing of gender is echoed in the text, which presents an equally modern and nontraditional picture of employees' lives: it suggests that "work and home," the public and the private spheres, are not only on equal footing, but also equally the domains of females and males; it also draws leisure into the realm of work, a move it would seem that was meant to break starkly with a more traditional image of Japan, Inc.

While gender may have been downplayed, and soccer privileged in moments by executives and media personnel at Nikko Securities and Shiroki, they always existed in combination, and the female soccer player was thus produced and deployed as iconic of the "future." Replete with linkages to countercultural rebelliousness, Euro-American feminism, and revolutionary female embodiment, L-Leaguers seemed the perfect symbolic vehicle for corporations eager to convince their own employees and international clients that they were on the move, modernizing employment practices and, even more fundamentally, modernizing the nature of work itself. Unfortunately, the image of modern work promoted by these corporations in the 1990s contrasted sharply with the L-Leaguers' actual employment experiences.

Being an L-Leaguer: Image versus Reality

The ability of female players to take advantage of soccer as an alternative space was in many ways enabled by discourses produced by corporations, coaches, the mass media, social scientists, and the L-Leaguers themselves that portrayed interactions with soccer as progressive and different from the average life course for women. The symbolic positioning of soccer on the margins or outside of daily life was reinforced by the concrete actions of coaches and administrators who effectively circumscribed the physical and social movement of players and confined them to limited spaces. Rigorous training and game schedules kept players on soccer fields for a good part of the day, six or seven days per week. Dormitories and training sites were located in outlying areas, and some enforced strict curfews. In addition, an unwritten but strictly followed L-League rule required that all players be unmarried. Those who decided to marry needed to quit their teams. L-Leaguers' "work" was cast as incompatible with wifehood and, by extension, motherhood. The right to work as a soccer player was bound to an implicit agreement that, regardless of her age, an L-Leaguer must remain an adolescent.

To many players, the L-League environment was socially and experientially limiting. To others, however, the denials, prohibitions, and circumscription of movement created new freedoms and safety from unwanted demands and expectations. For most of the players with whom I spoke, the unwritten understanding that they could not marry as long as they played was a welcome respite. Soccer provided a means of quieting anxious parents eager for their daughters to wed. Others told me that they never wanted to get married, and soccer provided a way to postpone potentially difficult conversations with their parents.

L-League coaches and administrators commonly treated players as naive adolescents, a tactic that justified their control over the teams but also allowed them to dismiss seemingly "boyish" behaviors and same-sex romantic interests as fleeting childish fancies. For instance, when I tried to talk to a coach about the signs of a budding romantic relationship between two teammates, he quickly ended the conversation by dismissing what he called "odd behavior of kids" and "immaturity."

Joining an L-League team offered life-changing experiences of social mobility. The dormitory living arrangements placed players in much more monitored environments than they would have experienced living on their own, a fact lamented by many players; yet these accommodations provided new freedoms as well. In some cases, L-League contracts meant the chance to leave a small town with limited employment possibilities. For many, contracts required leaving the family home, a move that normally occurred after marriage for young women from largely working-class backgrounds. L-League participation afforded players opportunities to travel across Japan for matches and training camps. However, except in the case of a handful of the most talented L-League players, the social mobility afforded by soccer was not accompanied by economic mobility. Although sponsoring corporations had deployed women's soccer players as heralding new modern visions of labor and mobility in the form of employment opportunities, no new or revolutionary work opportunities materialized for L-Leaguers; if anything, their job prospects were narrowed by the demands of their sport.

The Shiroki Industries and Nikko Securities players' actual experiences were worlds away from that of the idealized workers exhorted to "be both active participants at work and home" (Shiroki Industries 1998: 18). Regardless of their educational backgrounds, the vast majority of players were relegated to menial jobs on shop floors and in offices. At another L-League team, players were assigned to work as waitresses and caddies at a golf course.

The unwritten rule against marriage and childbirth made contributions to "home," at least in the respects intended by the corporations, impossible. The players' marginalized position in the workplace existed throughout the L-League: players were often rotated from one worksite to another, much in the same way that temporary and provisional employees are used. Companies rarely put time into training them for more skilled jobs, as they might have done for other entry-level employees. According to the team executives I interviewed in the late 1990s, players were compensated according to the pay grade for their work in the factory or office. However, in many cases, players' wages probably were not commensurate with the lowest-paid female workers at their companies. In my interviews with players in the late 1990s and early 2000s, it appeared that, in addition to the provision of room and board in a company dormitory, the best-paid players received an additional 100,000 to 120,000 yen per month, but most received less than half of that.[8]

Possibly because of this treatment, most L-Leaguers were uninterested in the non-soccer aspects of their employment. The primacy put on soccer was not surprising, however, in an environment where coaches emphasized the need to cultivate "professional consciousness," namely an unfaltering, full-time commitment to their development as players, both on and off the field. According to this rationale, if one wanted to be a "professional," all other aspects of life—family, school, and other work—had to come second to athletic training.

In the late 1990s, seemingly in recognition and support of players' exclusive focus on their athletic development, Nikko Securities and other teams began offering players "professional contracts" (*puro keiyaku*). But what on the surface sounded respectable and lucrative was, in fact, a tactic to alleviate the parent company's responsibilities. While "professional contracts" almost never included a salary raise, they eliminated players' work responsibilities off the soccer field. Efforts to get players out of offices and factories so that they could spend more time in the gym and on the soccer field were also convenient ways to relieve companies of the burden of guaranteeing employment after a young woman's soccer career had ended, since they were no longer legally considered full-time regular employees (*seishain*). It was no surprise that players, who were training in environments where they were exhorted to be "professional" while receiving little encouragement for their effort as company workers, eagerly signed these new contracts. The new contracts also made it possible for companies to immediately terminate players' employment when a team folded, which occurred suddenly and unexpectedly for the Nikko Securities Dream Ladies and several other teams in 1999.

The L-Leaguers' marginalized employment positions contrasted sharply with the company publicity materials that depicted them as ideal mainstream employees. At the same time, the players' liminality as model corporate "family" members, as well as the gender-bending nature of their sport, arguably made them perfect representatives for the impossible task of personifying the kind of gender-neutral worker promoted in the Shiroki Industries brochure. Exemplifying neither typical male nor female employees, L-Leaguers embodied an ambivalence to which more exciting possibilities could be attached. Symbolically separated from factory drudgery, actively connected to images of women's empowerment, and firmly detached from any markers of mainstream female domesticity, Serena players and their friends on other teams were avatars of a new corporate ideal of creativity, energy, and "freshness." At the same time, they were icons of latent possibilities and uncharted opportunities for their fellow workers, fans, and other aspiring young female athletes. The realities of these young women's lives, unfortunately, were often very different from these ideals.

Conclusion: From Individuality to Insecurity?

While a handful of journalists argued that soccer represented the dangers of unfettered globalization, many more corporate executives, athletic coaches, players, and fans in 1990s Japan heralded the sport as the perfect model of the more internationally attuned sensibilities required for Japanese citizens to compete in the twenty-first-century economy.

The United States and Northern Europe led the way in creating soccer opportunities for girls and women in the 1970s and 1980s, thus giving the sport a progressive image in terms of gender equality. Japanese corporate executives made the decision to sponsor L-League teams to benefit from soccer's international image, as well as from the publicity generated by female soccer players, whom they believed looked and acted different from other women in the world of sport. They also saw women's soccer as a means for acquiring more business clients worldwide and for countering global mass media reports of a male-dominated and misogynistic Japanese corporate culture.

Like the corporate leaders who sponsored them, L-Leaguers perceived soccer to be progressive and iconoclastic, but they were interested for different reasons: they saw the job of soccer player as a chance for new experiences, mobilities, and life courses. Soccer provided opportunities for self-realization in ways unintended by coaches and administrators. It gave young women a way to challenge, even transcend, the social expectations that they found restrictive, onerous, or simply unfair. As Miriam Silverberg analyzed, the 1920s and 1930s modern girl "stood as a vital symbol of overwhelming 'modern' or non-Japanese change instigated by both women and men during an era of economic crisis and social unrest" (Silverberg 1991b: 263). Arguably, the L-Leaguer was an analogous figure in the 1990s.

Both interwar modern girls and late twentieth-century soccer players showed progress and mobility to be inherently gendered concepts, connecting female bodies to broader ideas of stability and change. Just as modernity has been tied consistently to various ideals of femininity and womanhood (as is highlighted throughout the chapters in this volume), it also typically presupposes socioeconomic mobility. While the L-Leaguers have certainly been young woman on the move, the vast majority of them have not enjoyed the upward economic mobility experienced by so many of the other modern girls in this volume. Their labor as muscular athletes was very modern indeed, but it was not matched by the financial gains or employment opportunities that their corporate sponsors publicly advertised with the aid of their images.

Although modernity is inherently rife with inconsistencies and contradictions, it is the disjuncture between mobility in the form of "freedom of opportunity" and "self-actualization"—iconized in the form of the L-Leaguer beginning in the 1990s—and labor and economic mobility that needs to be addressed while looking at Nadeshiko Japan's recent achievements.

The recent successes of Nadeshiko Japan in the 2008 Olympics and the 2011 World Cup would not have occurred if L-Leaguers had not paved the way for women in the sport thanks to corporate interests in their symbolic potential. Nadeshiko Japan's surprising World Cup victory has brought unprecedented public attention to women's soccer and a level of visibility never before experienced by many Japanese women athletes. The players have found themselves held up as model citizens, global ambassadors, and national heroes lifting the spirit of their country after the trifold disaster brought about by the earthquake on March 11, 2011. Several journalists also raised public awareness of the tenuous financial situations in which many of these players have lived for years while focusing all of their energies on soccer success (Leighton 2011; Yomiuri 2011).

At the time of their World Cup victory, less than 5 percent of the approximately 230 players in the Nadeshiko League were under professional contracts with their teams, and a handful more had part-time employment with other corporate sponsors, who gave them job assignments that allowed them to train at the level required of top athletes (*Daily Yomiuri* 2011b). However, the majority resorted to unsatisfying and low-paying part-time jobs at restaurants, shipping warehouses, pachinko parlors, grocery store stockrooms, and the like, so that they could purchase their own shoes, pay team dues, and hope to make practices pushed to the evening hours to accommodate everyone's work schedules.

While many commentators have emphasized the irony of these players' predicaments and decried the inequities in compensation between Nadeshiko players and their male counterparts, who have not had the same success on the international stage, several others have celebrated these young women specifically because of the adversity they have faced. "Corporate Japan needs soccer women's hungry spirit," wrote *Nikkei Weekly* economic magazine reporter Iguchi Tetsuya just a week after the World Cup (Iguchi 2011). In contrast to male soccer players who are often richly, or at least adequately rewarded for their athletic talents, for almost two decades Japanese female players have weathered meager and inconsistent financial support at best. However, for Iguchi, the Nadeshiko team's "remarkable performance" is a direct product of the "acute worry" brought about by this persistent insecurity. He compares the players' situation to that of Japanese female corporate employees, who have suffered years of discrimination and inequity in male-dominated workspaces; they too, Iguchi argues, serve as consummate models of the character and attitude toward work needed from laborers for Japan to succeed in the future.

More than twenty years after the birth of what has become the Nadeshiko League, female soccer players appear to have reclaimed their status as modern girls of their age, symbols of change in Japan's current moment of crisis and unrest. It also appears likely that they will once again be cast as exemplars of ideal laborers and representatives of Japan's economic and labor environment more broadly. There is a strong possibility, however, that the previous disconnect between players' lived experiences and the corporate narratives to which they were tied may fall away in a neoliberal economy that not only acknowledges, but also finds its productive energy in, insecurity and "acute worry."

PART IV

Modern Girls Go Overseas

Chapter Nine

MISS JAPAN ON
THE GLOBAL STAGE

The Journey of Itō Kinuko

Jan Bardsley

American-style beauty contests—complete with young women in tiaras, sashes, high heels, and swimsuits—became big business in Japan in the 1950s. Pageants were held for all kinds of reasons, such as to attract tourism, promote products, and, through the Miss Japan/Miss Universe contest, to reinstate the defeated nation in the global community. Intellectuals of the day penned essays about girls confidently striding down runways, reading this as evidence of democracy taking hold in Japan (Bardsley 2008). Contest success, particularly at the national level, promised a woman literal and social mobility: travel to international competitions, instant celebrity status, and the potential for a career in modeling and movies. In 1950s Japan, national beauty queens were among the most envied of all "modern girls on the go."

When Miss Japan Itō Kinuko placed third in the Miss Universe contest in 1953, only one year after the end of the Occupation, she was hailed as a national hero.[1] A graduate of a Tokyo high school who had briefly worked as a department store clerk, the twenty-year-old Itō became an internationally recognized beauty queen and a star fashion model in the space of a few months. In the United States, she enjoyed celebrity treatment as a Miss Universe contestant, had a small part in a major Hollywood film, and met Japan's Crown Prince Akihito during his American tour.

Back in Japan after the contest, Itō earned exorbitant sums as the nation's most famous runway model. For many, her victory proved that, even without family status or prestigious education, women in Japan enjoyed new opportunities for advancement, especially if they had a striking figure and the confident postwar attitude to go with it. Yet as Itō's star rose in Japan, negative publicity also ensued. She was criticized for having fallen prey to the dangers of Americanization, a failing often cited in the 1950s to explain Japanese women's alleged new assertiveness and self-satisfaction (Bardsley 2000). By the late 1960s, however, Itō's life took a different turn as her career concluded in the popular press with a "happily ever after" marriage to an elite diplomat.

Understanding why Americanization would be such a negative charge against Miss Japan requires considering the position of Japan itself in 1953, and especially its strained alliance with the United States in the early Cold War era. After its defeat in 1945, Japan was occupied until 1952 by Allied forces, primarily Americans. Among the reforms enacted by the United States were a new Constitution, which transformed the Emperor from a divinity to a symbol of the nation and its people, and expanded civil rights for women. Most controversial at the Occupation's end was the U.S-Japan Security Treaty, signed in 1951, which allowed American bases to remain in Japan and gave forces stationed there the right to intervene in Japan's domestic affairs.

American investment in Japan to bolster its efforts during the Korean War, which concluded in July 1953, had reinvigorated the Japanese economy, winning some favor for an alliance between the two countries. Nevertheless, in 1953, the United States had instigated a variety of cultural projects in Japan to inspire friendship in the wake of anti-American protests over the Security Treaty. The warm reception accorded Miss Japan in the Miss Universe contest, much like the heavily publicized performance of *Madame Butterfly* in Los Angeles that summer by a visiting Japanese opera troupe, functioned well to support the friendship initiatives.

Although many aspects of American popular culture were winning fans in Japan in the early 1950s, debates arose over the wisdom of encouraging what we term today both the soft power of American culture and the hard power of military alliance. Consequently, Miss Japan, as a representative of her nation and of an American-style competition, stood at the center of highly contested ground. The Emperor was divine no longer, and she was the princess-symbol of a nation bent on democratic reform.

By following the major stages of Itō Kinuko's life in the limelight, this chapter takes up the case of a modern girl on the go as representative of her nation in a uniquely postwar, transnational framework. As Japan's representative to the Miss Universe contest, Itō embodied the nation at home and abroad. Yet she was also seen as charting a new kind of citizenship for women. Did her success prove that the intervention of the United States and women's expanded civil rights had set Japan on a positive course? What did it mean to claim these rights as a beauty queen? Similarly, what did her success in two new kinds of American-inspired glamour jobs—runway fashion model and beauty queen— signal about the reemergence of consumer capitalism?

As this chapter argues, by representing Japan in a much publicized international beauty pageant, Itō paved the way for a new role for women in the public sphere that was interlaced with consumerism and beauty work. Inherent in this role were the pleasures and constraints of femininity itself: the postwar beauty had to be modern (as independent, self-confident, and risk-taking as American women were reported to be), but careful to keep her sexuality in check. It was a role that was expansive in some ways and limited in others, one that prized image over voice, and one that promised monetary success yet demanded continual work to keep body and face in top form. By extension, one can also argue that Miss Japan represented Japan to the world as a feminized nation, a compliant helpmate to the United States. The readings below of some of Itō's "image-texts" explicate this idea further.[2]

It is important to acknowledge that Itō Kinuko's emergence as a celebrity was made possible by the proliferation of women's magazines in Japan in the early postwar, which drew attention to technologies of modern beauty. The magazines combined images of Japanese actresses and models in the latest fashions with photos of Anglo beauties such as Hollywood stars and models from Europe and the United States. These layouts enabled the reader to imagine herself as a cosmopolitan sophisticate with knowledge of important fashion markets and the fantasy of access to them. By instructing the reader in beauty techniques, in part through the example of beauty queens and models, the magazines encouraged readers, for better or worse, to participate in reinventing their own looks and to understand such reinvention as a key to success in private and public life.

Reading Itō's imbrication in the visual world of postwar fashion and media culture leads me to use the critical framework developed by Rachel Moseley and Richard Dyer. Moseley (2002) acknowledges that her use of "image-text" incorporates and expands Richard Dyer's (1986) concept of the "star-text" as the sum total of a film star's public persona as created by such varied sources as screen roles, off-screen life, biography, and interviews. Both Moseley and Dyer's concepts are useful in interpreting Itō's celebrity because her story, too, is one pieced together from a fragmented collection of photographs, newspaper reports, occasional interviews, magazine gossip, and brief film appearances. One can easily detect in these fragments a melodramatic story of loss, stardom, failure, and redemption through romantic love. The image-text of Itō Kinuko that takes shape in these accounts is built on a certain amount of fanciful reporting and exaggeration, but it stands as a text understood as true and worthy of debate by many commentators.

Miss Japan in the World

Itō Kinuko's story offers a radically different experience of women and transportation from the others presented in this volume. Rather than becoming part of the routinized service on trains, planes, or elevators, Itō traversed the Pacific as an honored passenger and enjoyed luxury travel in the United States. During the Miss Universe week, a fleet of British cars and drivers chauffeured Itō and other contestants, bringing a hint of English aristocracy to the festivities. A sightseeing boat ferried them around Long Beach Harbor as photographers snapped their pictures. Itō also rode in the Miss Universe Parade, standing in a swimsuit and heels atop her own float.

Although her work was not on full view in the same way as that of stewardesses, elevator girls, and tour bus guides, as Miss Japan, Itō, too, performed a recognizably feminine form of beauty labor. The requirements of the pageant demanded that contestants appear to be ordinary girls, "natural beauties," who were happy to take part in lighthearted events. Despite the real concerns of jet lag, culture clashes, language difficulties, and serious ambitions for victory, contestants had to present charm and a well-groomed appearance. While the contest included frequent photo shoots of the women in swimsuits, the contestants had to avoid any appearance of being risqué or "professional women" in favor of maintaining an unself-conscious ordinariness (that no doubt took some effort to produce consistently). Indeed, as a beauty queen and an "ordinary girl," Itō had to hide the elements of her position that made it seem as if she were working at all.

Uniforms, as we see in almost every example discussed in this volume, code women as included within a highly gendered, organizational hierarchy and marked as performing some sort of feminized service. But in the case of Miss Japan, although every outfit must communicate femininity, signs of service give way to evocations of sport, fashion, and luxury, and even the swimsuit, when worn by a potential beauty queen, must express a kind of demure playfulness.

Photographs of Itō during her beauty queen year capture her in several different new and equally lovely outfits. Each suggests a different mood or fantasy, offering to women viewers the vicarious experience of glamour. During her Miss Universe competition, Itō was up with the times in her Catalina swimsuit, romantically European in her ball gown, and exotically Oriental in her kimono and the harem-girl gear and hula skirt she later wore in Hollywood films. Such varied fashion fantasies coded the postwar feminine as open to continual play and drama, and far from the ordinary. Such a wardrobe must have seemed unusually abundant to Japanese viewing these photos. After all, they had lived through years of wearing serviceable clothing during the war and ill-fitting, hand-me-down outfits in the immediate postwar, and for many, finding sufficient food for themselves and their families was still the central concern of their daily lives in 1953. The sight of a beautifully dressed, healthy Japanese woman gave hope that better times were ahead for the nation and its people. Yet, as Japanese later learned, even Itō had suffered a great deal during and after the war, too.

Looking at the pictures of Itō in all the events of the Miss Universe contest, one would never guess that she had barely escaped starvation in Manchuria in 1944. Her father, a sake brewer, had died when Itō was only four years old. In the final year of the war, Itō's mother had made the disastrous choice to take her four daughters to Manchuria in hopes of finding a safe haven, only to become embroiled in the violent chaos of the war's end (Tamanoi 2009). She and her eldest two daughters starved to death. Only thirteen years old at the time and plagued by lice and malnutrition, Itō somehow managed to return to Japan with her surviving sister. In Tokyo, they had to force their elder half-brother to give them shelter. At this point, the girls wore the uniform of the refugee—torn and dirty clothing (Watanabe Kieko 1961).

As repatriates (*hikiagesha*) from Manchuria, Itō and her sister likely faced discrimination. Once back in Japan, women and girls returning from Manchuria were regarded as unusually assertive, unfeminine, and even arrogant (Watt 2009). Their use of standard Japanese, uninflected by a regional dialect, also made them seem less rooted in Japan. As news spread of the numerous sexual assaults on Japanese women in Manchuria by invading Soviet soldiers at the war's end, the returnees were further stigmatized as unchaste and contaminated, no longer "ordinary Japanese women," and a potential threat to the homeland. Such stories compounded suspicions that Japanese women abroad were involved in unsavory businesses, lived in a frontier climate of lax mores, and were in general sexually available (Watt 2009: 101).

One wonders whether Itō's victory in the Miss Japan contest and her success in Long Beach functioned to welcome *hikiagesha* back into the national fold. On the other hand, this success might have confirmed that the Manchurian repatriates were exactly the kind of more sexually available, confident young women suited for this American-style competitive display of female flesh. Perhaps even the Itō sisters' act of forcing their half-brother to take them in was read as proof of their "argumentative" repatriate nature.

Despite this childhood trauma and possible stigmatization, Itō managed to attend and graduate from high school, and it was during this period that she realized others found her pretty. Following graduation, she completed a typing course and then became a clerk in a department store. Since, the job of department store clerk had long been considered a chic one reserved for beauties (see chapter by Tipton in this volume), this position was Itō's first step on a career in fashion. Itō reportedly enjoyed being surrounded by lovely goods and yearned to be able to afford them herself.

In 1951, Itō's life took another unusual turn when she answered an open call for models announced by the English-language newspaper *Mainichi Daily News*, which was planning a two-day fashion show (Watanabe Kieko 1961). The pay for the two days of work, 10,000 yen, was astonishing given that many jobs for women at the time rarely paid so much for even a full month's work. Women twenty-two years of age employed by major companies in the relatively prestigious field of secretarial labor in 1951 earned on average 9,003 yen per month [Ministry of Health, Labor, and Welfare (Kōsei Rōdō Shō) 1951].

Although not much is written about Itō's early modeling career, we do know that more good fortune was ahead for her. When she competed in the nationwide Miss Japan contest in the spring of 1953, Itō triumphed over two thousand other entrants to claim the crown, becoming Miss Tokyo and then Miss Japan. As Miss Japan, Itō became an instant celebrity. Later that summer, she enjoyed a "rousing sendoff" upon leaving Tokyo's Haneda Airport on July 4 to compete against twenty-two other international candidates in the second annual Miss Universe contest in Long Beach, California (*Nippon Times* 1953a).

Pax Americana and Pageantry in Long Beach

The Miss Universe contest was held every summer in Long Beach, California, from 1952 through 1959 before moving to other venues. The event drew international attention and thousands of spectators to the seaside city. The 1953 Miss Universe contest produced an extravagant display of Cold War Pax Americana, welcoming young women from around the country and the world. Reservists from the local Los Alamitos Naval Air Station served as uniformed escorts, pushing parade floats and dancing with the contestants at the final gala. President Eisenhower reigned over the pageant as a virtual protective father figure. A fluorescent thirty-foot likeness of Eisenhower stood center-stage during the Miss U.S.A. contest for a black-light number in which the American contestants sang "All the world likes Ike" while contestants from abroad clapped in time (Brackenbury 1953).

The Miss Universe beauty queens, often photographed in groups in either swimsuits or native costume, served to bring attention to the pageant sponsors. The sponsorship of three major corporations, the swimsuit manufacturer Catalina, Inc., Universal-International Studios, and Pan American World Airways, was integrated into pageant spectacles to give the sponsors maximum visibility. The celebrity achieved by the American sponsors of the contest stood out as much as any of the young beauty queens. Their sponsorship associated the corporations and the city of Long Beach with connections to exotic cultures, summertime leisure, and international good will. The Miss U.S.A. and Miss Universe contestants wore sleek, one-piece Catalina bathing suits in a grand parade, for newspaper photo shoots, and on stage at the competition's major evening events.

Following the pageant, Universal-International Studios awarded the top contestants walk-on roles in the film *Yankee Pasha* (discussed in more detail below), which featured them as sultry harem girls. Universal's top makeup artist, Bud Westmore, and some of its actors (including Rhonda Fleming and Jeff Chandler, who would later star in *Yankee Pasha*) served as contest judges; and during the contest Universal offered the beauty queens a one-day studio tour complete with a dinner and greetings from stars.

But probably the sponsor who made the most of the opportunity for good publicity was Pan Am. As Christine Yano's chapter describes, the airline had recently opened a trans-Pacific route to Japan. In its role as the official airline of the Miss Universe contest, Pan Am launched the contest with fanfare.

On July 9, Pan Am flew the international contestants from Los Angeles International Airport the short distance to Long Beach Municipal Airport. The plane, a Stratoclipper, had been named *Queen of the Skies*. A thousand people waited, including newsmen from around the world, eager to snap pictures as the contestants disembarked. To add to the excitement, the Long Beach Municipal Band played "Cheesecake from the Skies," a number created for the event, as airport employees guided the giant plane into place. A photo taken that day for publication in the *Long Beach Independent Press-Telegram* (hereafter *Press-Telegram*) captures twenty international contestants, each in native dress, smiling at the camera as they stand in a long line that stretches the length of the plane.

This tableau underscores one of the themes of this volume, that is, the way that women make new technologies of transportation comforting and even alluring. This particular instance accentuates Yano's argument about the sexualization of the postwar stewardess. In a sense, plane, stewardess, and beauty queen all become "Cheesecake from the Skies," promising safe, fantasy travel to exotic lands.

The city of Long Beach, which contributed $35,000 to the contest, an enormous amount in 1953, strived to involve its citizens in the Miss Universe contest on a personal level. The *Press-Telegram* promoted the contest to the community in photographs, reports, and advertisements that communicate a sense of wholesomeness as the world's girls relax in the welcoming environment created by American friendliness and corny humor. Differences among nations are coded as a harmless diversity of tastes, easily overcome by Americans' efforts to create good will. When some citizens grumbled about the cost to taxpayers or about lack of access to parade viewing because the route was too short, the *Press-Telegram* ran positive editorials about the city's part in fostering international good will through the contest.

The *Press-Telegram* also played a major role in portraying the contest as folksy by covering the contestants' personal reactions, highlighting these as almost childlike discoveries in a new land. Despite two references to serious politics (angry protest against the swimsuit competition in Greece and the concerns of a German contestant about her parents' well-being behind the Iron Curtain), the reportage was consistently upbeat, poking fun at the international contestants as feminine competition for American women and teasing American men about whether they meet the international contestants' standards for male attractiveness. International differences were pointed out frequently through discussions of food, such as whether the visitors liked ice-cream cones or hot dogs and how they missed such odd dishes as snails and eggplant. For example, the *Press-Telegram* closely observed Miss Uruguay's introduction to popcorn, reporting that the white concoction so perplexed the beauty queen that she asked, "Do we eat it?" (Zinser 1953). As for Itō's food preferences, the *Press-Telegram* reports that she is "trying local restaurants in search of some good fried chicken in a basket" because, after all, the "stately beauty who is Miss Japan explained through her interpreter that fried chicken is her personal yen" (Lembke 1953).

As a major community and corporate-sponsored event with international reach, the Miss Universe contest produced what Christina Klein (2003) has described as a Cold War global imaginary of integration achieved through sentimental moments that emphasized connections among people that bridged the divides of race, language, and other differences. The goal of feeling connected to others in the world through everyday practices, such as, in this case, hosting luncheons for visiting international beauty queens, became part of American Cold War culture. Pretty girls as representatives of other nations, some of which had recently achieved independence through revolutionary processes of decolonization, made the world seem like a friendly place, one the United States could help reshape as a stable community of integrated resources, markets, and alliances. As Klein points out, the United States' expansion of its political, military, and economic power in Asia from 1945 through 1961 coincided with a marked increase in representations of Asia in American popular culture (Klein 2003: 5).

Similarly, and as alluded to in the introduction to this chapter, Naoko Shibusawa (2006) has discussed the many ways in which Japan in particular was refashioned from wartime enemy to America's "geisha ally" in the early Cold War, a factor, too, in making the indisputably feminine Miss Japan a figure of fascination at this time.

Coverage of the Miss Universe contest, however, focused on the personal experiences of the candidates, allowing Cold War tensions and the unresolved conflicts of World War II to dissolve largely into the background. For example, one photograph in the *Press-Telegram* features Itō standing with Miss Philippines, Christina Pachio. Both are in swimsuits and heels. The headline reads "Far East Pals" and the caption explains that these friends are rivals in the beauty pageant. Intimations of rivalry come across as comic here and are clearly trumped by the girls' easy friendship (*Long Beach Independent Press-Telegram* 1953b). Any suggestion of Japan's aggression in the Philippines or of American colonization, for that matter, is absent. Similarly, one newspaper report describes how, at a dinner in an American home, "friendship between Japan and US was forged" when Miss Colorado used an English-Japanese conversation guide, lent by her older brother who had served in the Pacific as a sailor, to talk with Miss Japan (Iwata 1953).

In this relentlessly cheerful milieu, Itō became one more Cinderella enjoying a personal adventure. As a participant in the second annual Miss Universe contest, Itō was one of sixty-seven contestants. The international contingent came from twenty countries. American representatives hailed from forty-three states (South Carolina had two entrants, the state pageant winner and Miss Myrtle Beach) as well as the territories of Alaska, Hawaiʻi, and Puerto Rico. The young women received royal treatment during their stay in Long Beach. They stayed in top hotels, enjoyed rounds of luncheons, and were the recipients of constant adulation. Photographs of Itō taken during the contest's whirlwind of festivities display her looking every inch the fine young lady whether clad in a tailored sundress and jewelry, swimsuit, or kimono. Despite the pressures of the competition, Itō managed to maintain the beauty queen persona favored in the American press of a good girl just having fun and not one resolved to win.

Along with all the other contestants, Itō took part in a weeklong series of events that ran morning through evening. Local residents were encouraged to participate in most of them. The *Press-Telegram* invited the public to buy tickets to the official welcome banquet for the contestants on Saturday night, to come to the Sunday afternoon parade on Ocean Boulevard, and to attend the four pageant events at the Long Beach Municipal Auditorium. All contestants participated in the major events. The first two evenings were devoted to selecting Miss U.S.A. and the second two nights to choosing Miss Universe. The week concluded with a beach party for the contestants followed by a Coronation Ball. The week's activities included luncheons hosted by downtown Long Beach service groups such as the Kiwanis Club, Lions Club, Optimist Club, Rotary Club, and the Advertising and Insurance Clubs. Some local families held dinner parties in their homes for small groups of American and international contestants. Long Beach women also served as Miss Universe hostesses, who were "required to wear hats and gloves at all times—to distinguish them from the contestants" (Resnik 1953a).

Itō's participation in the Miss Universe contest received particular attention in the Los Angeles newspaper *Rafu shimpo*, which printed separate sections in Japanese and English and served Japanese and Japanese American residents in the area. *Rafu shimpo* ran several pictures of Itō with articles about her and the Miss Universe contest in July, picturing her alternately in a swimsuit, dresses, and her self-designed kimono-like outfit, described below.

At the same time, *Rafu shimpo* featured several stories, usually with accompanying candidate photos, about the continuing events of the Miss Nisei Week Festival Queen competition (a pageant that today is one of the oldest and best known of all Japanese American beauty pageants).[3] One of these photos shows Itō meeting two of the Nisei candidates. *Rafu shimpo* carried no comment about the racial politics operating in the Miss U.S.A. contest, which was clearly limited to Anglo-Americans at this time, or about the way in which the Miss Universe contest allowed a multiracial cast. That Japanese Americans were acutely aware of such politics has been well demonstrated in studies of Japanese American beauty contests by Yano (2006) and Rebecca Chiyoko King-O'Riain (2006). *Rafu shimpo*, however, makes no secret of favoring Miss Japan: Following the final judging on July 17, when Itō placed in the top five, *Rafu shimpo* gave her—not the victor, Miss France—the headline and ran her picture (*Rafu shimpo* 1953b). The newspaper featured Itō more than any other of the Miss Universe candidates. She was the news that made the Miss Universe contest worth reporting at all.

Applause for the Japanese Beauty on the Miss Universe Runway

From the start, Itō was a huge favorite with audiences and reporters. Through the *Press-Telegram* and *Rafu shimpo* reports, readers in Southern California learned that she had graduated from high school in Tokyo, had been modeling since 1951, enjoyed playing the koto, and had no interest in a movie contract (although Itō seems to have changed her mind on this in the wake of her contest success and did pursue a film career for a short time). When asked if she had boyfriends, Itō reportedly answered in all innocence that she had many friends, some boys and some girls.

One American reporter described Itō as "taller (5 feet 4 inches) than the average Japanese girl, but [with] the reserved poise and dignity so characteristic of her race" (Lembke 1953). The *Rafu shimpo* described Itō as "tall and willowy" and a modern 1950s fashion plate: "For the information of the women readers, Miss Nippon accents her 5 feet 4 inch height with 3½ inch spike heels and she paints her toenails a bright red" (*Rafu shimpo* 1953c).

One photograph taken during the contest week captures Itō standing outside in a light-colored kimono and holding a paper parasol to protect herself from the sun. Locals in Los Angeles who saw this picture might have associated Itō with the much-publicized, upcoming gala production that summer of the opera *Madame Butterfly*. A troupe was flying in from Japan to perform the opera in Japanese at the Greek Theater, and many notables were expected to attend, including the mayor of Los Angeles and the governor of California (*Rafu shimpo* 1953d). Although the public may have read Itō's kimono as uniquely representative of Japanese femininity, Itō saw her original design as a modern, rationalized one likely to appeal to Americans.

Figure 15 The beauty queen at a fashion show with three Japanese royal princesses. Photo courtesy of Kyodo News International.

For easier packing and changing, Itō had designed a two-piece kimono-like outfit with separate skirt, belt, and top. She had also chosen white cotton lace rather than "traditional materials of heavier nature" because of the heat; she thought lace was more "logical for summer wear" (*Rafu shimpo* 1953c). Reportedly, she believed her design had the potential to become wildly popular in the United States. Indeed, one reporter wrote that Miss Japan imagines her design "will sweep the nation like the bikini bathing suit—white lace, red belt, and all" (*Rafu shimpo* 1953a). (This report makes no reference to the fact that the French two-piece swimsuit was named after United States' nuclear testing on Bikini Atoll in 1946; the island remained the site of such testing until 1958).

In contrast to the native costume event, the swimsuit competition emphasized uniformity and promoted Catalina swimwear. Unlike the contestants' "native costumes," which evoked nostalgia for Old World charm, the swimsuit competition presented all the women identically as modern and secular, and as if liberated from their "traditional" clothing. In effect, the particularity of native difference gave way to the universal of the global runway. This exuberant embrace of young womanhood and natural beauty across race and nation, however, turned out to be the most constraining feature of the pageant, for the contestants were all held to the same arbitrary, narrow standard of physical perfection. The swimsuit called attention, often in unflattering ways, to the slightest differences among physiques and deviations from the ideal. On stage with other contestants, each woman was challenged to fit in, yet stand out as unique at the same time. She had to be confident, poised, and modest in her skimpy wear. The press described Itō's qualifications: "The 21-year old Miss Ito is a Tokyo fashion model standing 5 feet 4 inches tall, 115 pounds, and has a 34-inch bust, 22-inch waist, and 36-inch hips" (*Rafu shimpo* 1953b).

Guidelines in the 1950s for judging women's bodies in the Miss Universe pageant were both quasi-scientific in their specificity and vague in their assessment of "poise," which was defined as "grace and charm." According to the *Press-Telegram*, (unspecified) contest sponsors state that judges should assess contestants on "natural beauty alone, as found the world over." The *Press-Telegram* printed the judges' guidelines, which called for nearly thirty separate measures (*Long Beach Independent Press-Telegram* 1953a). Ideals included, "An imaginary line though the center of the head must pass through the center of the neck and torso, dividing the legs. The projection of this line must pass between the two heels." And, "The neck must be graceful enough to act as a pedestal to the head," while "Legs must fuse at the hips, knees and calves" (*Long Beach Independent Press-Telegram* 1953a). In this assessment, women of all ethnicities were expected to measure up to a universal standard.

Both women and men served on the international panel of ten judges, including Alberto Vargas, who was famous for creating the "Varga Girl" in pin-up portraits of beauties that appeared first in *Esquire* men's magazine and then on the nose of World War II American fighter planes. The head judge was Vincent Trotta, former Paramount Pictures art director, who had judged the Miss America contest for sixteen years before an apparent falling out with that pageant. There is no evidence of any kind of problematization of the swimsuit competition other than the question raised by Myrna Hansen, Miss Chicago/Miss Illinois, and ultimately, Miss U.S.A., who reportedly "can't understand how the judges are going to compare the beauty of the Oriental features with that of the Scandinavian features" (Resnik 1953b).

Since the late 1960s, feminists in Japan and the United States have been vocally and visibly critical of the objectifying gaze of swimsuit competitions

(Banet-Weiser 1999; Cohen, Ballerino, and Wilk 1996; Inoue 1997; Watson and Martin 2004). In Itō's case in 1953, however, it was her ability to compete in such bodily display that won her the most admiration at home. Fans in Japan did not want to mirror her personality; they wanted her height and curves.

According to one *Press-Telegram* reporter, Itō excelled in both the gown and swimsuit competitions, and responded to her fans with poise: "The 20-year-old representative from Japan was far and away the crowd favorite. The 3,000 spectators gave her a tremendous ovation when she walked down the runway in a flowered evening gown, and again applauded thunderously when she appeared for judging in a swimsuit. Miss Ito, who has difficulty in understanding the English language, smiled graciously" (*Long Beach Independent Press-Telegram* 1953c). Of Itō's success in the ball gown competition, *Nippon Times* reported, "Miss Japan, Kinuko Ito, appeared to be the audience favorite. She drew whistles and cheers at each appearance. She wore a handpainted gown fashioned by Shimamura" (*Nippon Times* 1953b). Associated Press reporter Bill Becker was effusive about Itō's ball gown moment, writing: "Perhaps the biggest single hit of the evening [on July 16 at the evening's international competition] was Miss Japan's appearance in a white evening gown with hand-painted red roses on the skirt" (Becker 1953). (There is no comment on the similarity of the white ball gown with its accents of red, or the white lace kimono with its red belt, to the colors of the Japanese flag, although many in the audience must have made such associations.)

All reports describe Miss Japan as one of the crowd favorites during Miss Universe week. *Rafu shimpo* reported early on in the competition that observers of the pageant believed Miss Japan was a shoo-in for a spot among the top five, observing how much attention Itō attracted in the initial parade with most on the sidelines calling out "Miss Japan" and "Kinuko" while Japanese Americans yelled "Itō-san" (Iwata 1953).

On July 19, the final evening of judging, according to an Associated Press report, "In the semi-final evening gown competition, the capacity crowd of 3,800 applauded the loudest for Japan's Kinuko Ito" as well as for Miss U.S.A. (who won second place) and Miss Turkey (who, in the end, did not place in the top five) (*Nippon Times* 1953c). Reporting the final results of the pageant, *Rafu shimpo* declared that the judges admitted how close the competition was among the top three women, as Miss U.S.A.'s "superior figure" and "Miss Japan's charm" were major factors (*Rafu shimpo* 1953b).

Reportage on Itō after her success in the Miss Universe contest captures a somewhat more ambitious beauty queen persona, although to what degree reporters manipulate Itō's image-text in their choice of questions and selections of quotes is hard to determine. Itō communicated with the English-speaking reporters with the aid of her interpreter. An INS news wire report published in *Nippon Times* (1953e) describes Itō as "one of the nation's top three fashion models" and further lists her "screen ambitions" as the hope to play opposite Joseph Cotton or Cary Grant in a movie. She is modest about her Miss Universe achievement, commenting that she is satisfied with her film contract, had not expected to win the title, but did want to make "the home folks" proud: "If I hadn't won something I would have been scared to go back to Tokyo." When asked about romance, she "firmly dismissed" the issue, saying "through her interpreter," "No time for boys now. My career comes first" (*Nippon Times* 1953e). It was this single-minded focus on her career and alleged lack of interest in pursuing marriage and motherhood that shaped her image-text back home in Japan, notably leaving her narrative open. Where would this tall, modern girl go next, and had she outgrown Japan and Japanese men?

Democracy's Princess, Harem Girl of the Exotic East

Uniforms, labor, mobility, and beauty work and Cold War politics all come into play, too, in the post-pageant activities that Itō enjoyed. While most other international contestants returned home, Itō remained in the United States until early October to act in two films and to travel. Two major events that occurred during this time—Itō's meeting with the Crown Prince of Japan and having a walk-on role in a full-length Hollywood film—extend her image-text in opposite ways, picturing her on the one hand as a modern girl on the go and on the other as an exotic Oriental beauty. The contrast between the two images shows the range of representations that Miss Japan—and Japan itself—could publicly embody in the United States and back home in this early Cold War moment.

When twenty-year-old Crown Prince Akihito arrived in Los Angeles in late September, Itō was filming *Yankee Pasha* and he was nearing the end of a six-month trip through Europe and North America. Following his investiture as Crown Prince in November 1952, all eyes in Japan were on Akihito, who was "hailed in the press as the 'future hope of Japan'" (Bix 2000: 650). Unlike his father, Emperor Hirohito, who was associated with war, defeat, and divine status, the young prince, with his English-speaking ability and seeming ordinariness, represented modern, democratic royalty. There were high hopes for his first foreign trip, which "was interpreted at the time as bearing tremendous meaning for Japan's re-entry into the international community" (Ruoff 2001: 212).

Figure 16 Crown Prince Akihito Meets Miss Japan at MGM Studios, September 30, 1953. Photo courtesy of Kyodo News International.

A contingent of several reporters and cameramen, representing thirteen Japanese news agencies, recorded his travels. The highlight of the journey occurred when Akihito attended Queen Elizabeth's June 2 coronation, which was intended to communicate "a message of close friendship" to Britain (Bix 2000: 650). Crown Prince Akihito's trip also coincided with the United States' cultural diplomacy to strengthen ties with Japan in 1953 through centennial celebrations of Commodore Perry's opening of Japan. As Chizuru Saeki (2005) explains, such diplomacy was part of a larger American project to encourage Japan's rearmament and aid in the fight to contain the spread of communism and also to quell protest by the Japanese left against the Mutual Security Treatment Agreement. At a dinner in New York at the Japan-America Society that summer, Akihito and 1,500 Japanese and American guests listened as Secretary of State John Foster Dulles underscored the importance of Japan–United States relations for the containment of communism.

Such weighty diplomatic concerns seem far from the scene when Prince Akihito met Miss Japan at a dazzling luncheon given in his honor at MGM Studios on September 30. The event was crowded with Hollywood luminaries, but Akihito was the star of the day (*Asahi Shinbun* 1953). A photograph taken of the two young Japanese meeting at the luncheon speaks simultaneously to the postwar elevation of the beauty queen's status and the diminution of the position of the Crown Prince. The pair smile at each other and shake hands when they meet, as though completely at home with American-style greetings. Both are dressed elegantly, Akihito in tailored suit and tie, Itō in a Dior-look sundress, which has since become iconic of the early 1950s. She carried a sweater and handbag. Taller than Akihito, especially in her high heels, Itō smiles down at the prince as he looks up at her. Together the two create a tableau of postwar Japanese democracy: no longer divine, but still respected, the prince meets a princess who has gained her crown through open competition in both Japan and the United States.

The photo frames the two as equals. The picture might have been read by Americans as presenting an attractive Japanese pair enjoying the benefits of life in the United States, and by extension, the benefits of having been liberated by the American-led victory and Allied Occupation. For Japanese people, the scene could well have indicated the extent of Japan's postwar Americanization. The image reaffirms Akihito's status as an "ordinary" prince of the people. Being photographed smiling at a beauty queen also links Akihito to romance, emphasizing his own star status as a royal on the cusp of becoming an eligible bachelor. In a sense, when pictured together, these two young people, each a royal created by the United States and their meeting made possible by taking place there, send the message that Japan is a recovered nation, a "modern country on the go" under the protective umbrella of a strong Japan–United States alliance.

Itō's appearance in *Yankee Pasha* could not have been more different or less modern, although her pay ($150 weekly [54,000 yen]) was enviable (*Nippon Times* 1953d). The film displays Itō and other Miss Universe finalists in a radically different way as enticing harem girls available for sale. Set in 1800, *Yankee Pasha* tells the swashbuckling tale of spunky Massachusetts redhead Roxana (Rhonda Fleming), who is captured by Barbary pirates on the high seas, held captive in a sultan's harem in Morocco, and finally rescued by the handsome American frontiersman, Starbuck (Jeff Chandler), who masquerades as a "Yankee Pasha" willing to teach sharp-shooting in order to infiltrate the exotic world and save his sweetheart. The film is quite literally a bodice ripper. Scenes of Roxana in Morocco show her defiant and fearless, refusing to be a slave to any man. Torn further in each scene, Roxana's clothing gives way and exposes ever more of her skin. As if to tame her, the Moroccans costume Roxana as a harem girl, outfitting her in green balloon pants, a headdress, and plenty of glitter. To find his sweetheart, Starbuck must pretend to be in the market for a slave girl, a ruse that leads him into a harem.

When the Yankee Pasha enters the harem, he finds a steamy world of hothouse plants, draped walls, and sultry women swathed in chiffon and lying about the room, who smile as if to catch his attention. A salesman (Lee J. Cobb) in Arab-looking clothing introduces Starbuck to the girls on display. These "Miss Universe beauties," as the film's publicity dubs them, include Miss Japan, Miss France/Miss Universe, and Miss Greece. When the slave master claps all the women climb up some stairs and stand under curtains that make each one look like a jewel. They assume the beauty contest pose and smile silently, but look Starbuck directly in the eye. Miss Japan, described as a "Nestorian star from Cathay," represents Asia. She wears a silver outfit with a white bodice that is tightly cinched at the waist atop gauzy pants. Her short, fashionable bob is concealed beneath a wig of long, softly curled dark hair. The master asks if Starbuck has ever seen anything so exquisite. Although he pauses to admire Itō's beauty, Starbuck remains intent on finding Roxana and exits the harem to continue his search. Thus ends the brief film debut of the Miss Universe beauties.

In contrast to the Miss Universe contest, which generally attempted to present its entrants as modern women, *Yankee Pasha* pulls out every Orientalist stop. Although the film idealizes Roxana and Starbuck's relationship as leading to the American companionate marriage, it also attempts to lure the audience with tantalizing suggestions of the raw sexuality available in Morocco.

As Brian Edwards (2001) has explained, the Arab world proved a popular setting for Hollywood films in the early 1950s. Cast as a timeless, placeless desert outside of Cold War politics, Arab settings allowed the kind of display of sexuality not allowed on television, the new competition for movies. The catch was that films could not appear to condone such sexuality, even if it was presented as legitimate among Arabs, and the enticing women could not be seen as Anglo (Edwards 2001). Ironically, while the film builds respect for Yankee girl Roxana and her bold statements about never resorting to subservience, her family's employment of a young African American woman, whom we see Roxana ordering about earlier in the film, is never problematized or offered as a comparison.

Yankee Pasha constructs the Anglo American as a modern girl on the go largely in contrast to the women of color who easily yield to slavery. Only she is the one who refuses to become a slave. Cast as the Asian harem girl, Itō appears alien and compliant, and hardly the princess of democracy described above. Her other appearance for Universal was also that summer in the 1953 3-D short *Hawaiian Nights*, in which Itō danced a hula.

Miss Japan Comes Home a Hero

Back in Japan in October, Itō found herself the center of media fascination. Far from being perceived as a harem or hula girl, Itō represented Japan's recovery and women's new postwar democratic assertiveness and self-confidence. She was literally and metaphorically standing tall. As the historian of Japanese beauty contests Inoue Shōichi writes, Itō's achievement was seen as balm for a defeated nation, and her triumph in the Miss Universe contest was celebrated as a boost to national pride, on par with Yukawa Hideki's Nobel Prize in physics in 1949 and Furuhashi Hironoshin's world-record-breaking performance in freestyle swimming in Los Angeles, also in 1949 (Inoue 1997: 139).

Although beautiful women in Japan usually won praise for their pretty faces, the attention focused on Itō's body raised standards for female attractiveness in Japan. No longer was a lovely face enough to qualify one as a *bijin* (beauty) (Inoue 1997; Miller 2006). Itō became a public curiosity as the embodiment of *hattōshin*, the perfectly proportioned figure in which the body measures eight times the length of the face. The term soon became a shorthand reference for women with fashionably small faces and tall bodies. Capitalizing on this wave of figure fascination, the Nichigeki, a well-known Tokyo theater, placed a life-size cut-out of Itō's silhouette outside its doors, inviting any woman who thought she had the same figure to prove it by stepping through, and awarding those who were successful a free movie ticket (Inoue 1997: 144). Spurred on by Itō's good looks, a boom of interest in beauty contests and beauty treatments such as facials occurred, and the national radio station (NHK radio) began broadcasting "beauty calisthenics" (Nagahara and Yoneda 1986: 187).

Itō's beauty-contest fame worked wonders for her modeling career. The fashion shows in which she appeared became standing-room-only events. Her pay rose dramatically, from 5,000 to 100,000 yen for one stage performance. At the height of her popularity in 1956, Itō famously received 150,000 yen for one day's work (Watanabe Kieko 1961).

Her beauty regimen became a model for emulation. For example, an early interview with Itō that took place before she went to Long Beach and was published in the August 1953 issue of the women's magazine Ladies Club (Fujin kurabu) promises to reveal her beauty secrets. It describes how she moisturizes her skin, gets enough rest, and has trained herself to wear high heels gracefully. The article also explains how she cares for her sore, swollen feet at night after a busy day in high heels. Itō makes a point of saying that to stay trim and healthy she eats three meals a day at fixed times, has meat and vegetables at every meal, and avoids sweets. She consumes grains such as bread and rice only once a day to keep her calorie count in check and expresses pride in having reduced her waist size over the past year and a half. Given that many Japanese were still struggling to obtain sufficient food in the early 1950s, the beauty queen's American-style meat-and-vegetable diet and concern for avoiding calories must have struck many as the height of lavish living.

Nevertheless, Itō comes across as knowledgeable and disciplined, and as focused as any athlete on caring for her body. Her beauty regimen, although strict and vigilant, is relatively simple. Most remarkable in this description is the attention that Itō devotes to herself, a practice that many busy women must have found luxurious, even self-indulgent. At the same time, as Laura Miller (2006) observes, "beauty work is a socially sanctioned form of self-improvement" in Japan, and many regard "the self-management and discipline required to achieve an appropriate body indicate good character and self control" (Miller 2006: 10, 11). Such concern for the consistent display of oneself as a disciplined, groomed body is not merely essential for the beauty queen, but a requirement of modern femininity. As Banet-Weiser (1999) explains, the beauty pageant underscores "the constant and consistent display of the female body as a matter of being—to be a woman means to be judged, objectified, and fragmented" (Banet-Weiser 1999: 67).

Such celebrity did not translate into respect in all quarters. While in the United States, Itō met and fell in love with the exchange-student son of the owner of a major Kansai-area bus company. Reportedly the two were to be married until word came from the man's family that the idea of welcoming a fashion model into the fold was unthinkable The two were forced to separate. As Inoue points out, this incident proves how the fashion model and beauty contestant were still connected to the realm of *mizushōbai* (the "water trade" in pleasure and sexualized entertainment), especially in the minds of many of the class-conscious members of the older generation. Nevertheless, the man later married Miss Japan 1955, Otani Kyoko, who placed fifth in that year's Miss Universe contest (*Shūkan josei* 1957). Since the family found Otani acceptable, one wonders if Itō's status as a repatriate from Manchuria had been an even more negative factor in her case.

Itō eventually retired from modeling, but not to get married. A few years after her Miss Universe achievement, she was still earning 30,000 yen for one runway show, but her fashion career was plainly on a downward slide (*Shūkan josei* 1957). She briefly opened a clothing store in Tokyo's posh Ginza shopping district in 1958 and then went to Paris to study fashion design for eight months before returning to Japan.

Despite these attempts to establish another career, it was Itō's success in the Miss Universe contest that remained her claim to fame. When another Miss Japan, Kojima Akiko, won the Miss Universe contest in 1959, becoming the first Asian to do so, some media attention turned to former Japanese beauty queens. Without fail, Itō was linked to the popularity of *hattōshin* and a victory that had cheered the nation. Yet in an interview at the time, Itō offered no joy at this thought. On July 27, 1959, three days after Kojima's victory, *Rafu shimpo* ran an article featuring comments from Itō. The headline was, "Ex-Miss Universe runner-up tells Akiko crown not means to end." In an Associated Press interview, Itō congratulated Kojima, but wished to add "a candid word of advice. That is, don't let the title give you illusions of grandeur." The newspaper describes the former beauty queen as still unmarried and operating a dress shop in Tokyo. Itō is further quoted as saying: "Look at me," she continued rather wistfully. "Do you think I am a happy woman after placing high in the contest? I do hope Miss Kojima will stick to her statement of wishing to become a good housewife after returning here." After that, Itō reportedly brushed away any more questions, saying, "as a matter of fact I have no further interest in Miss Universe contests" (*Rafu shimpo* 1959). Six years after her success in Long Beach, the one-time national symbol of modern beauty had become a cautionary tale about how too much ambition can make a woman wealthy and leave her bitter and alone.

In 1961, the women's magazine *Mademoiselle* ran a gossip-filled, melodramatic piece on Itō's life and career. Watanabe Kieko, the author of the article, interviewed Itō and spoke with those who had worked with her. Although Itō describes herself as rather old-fashioned, Watanabe portrays her as a tragic figure whose ambition has also been her downfall. She depicts Itō as having lost sight of what is important in a woman's life as she pours herself into her work rather than concentrating on getting married. She writes, "To the young women of defeated Japan, how much courage, confidence and validation did Kinuko's beauty bring to them? It is hard to measure its power. But ironically that same great success and fame forced Kinuko to lose the sweet happiness of a woman" (Watanabe Kieko 1961: 104).

Watanabe's conclusion presents stardom in the competitive field of beauty contests and fashion modeling as rewarding a superficial, modern kind of femininity while drawing women away from the ordinary but deeper pleasures of marriage and motherhood. In effect, Watanabe constructs the unusual social mobility afforded Miss Japan as fixing her on a risky trajectory that for all its excitement ultimately rendered her unhappily out of a step with a normal lifecourse. It is a path, she suggests, that should be pursued only briefly.

From Wayward Cinderella to Fame in Women's History

The unhappiness and role strain evident in the narrative spun about Itō beg for some resolution. This came years later, in 1969, when Itō finally married. An article on her wedding appeared in the magazine *Young Lady*. The article features a photo of Itō, now sporting a 1960s bouffant hairdo, on the telephone with her husband. The headline announces that she has secretly wed a younger man whom she met in Paris. The two had married in a quiet Christian ceremony in a Roppongi church with only thirty guests in attendance. The European aura of the Christian wedding and the couple's Parisian romance make their union chic.

The reporter feels the need to explain to her readers, whom she assumes are teens, what Itō's achievement was and why it was significant in the early 1950s.

Now, however, the main point is that Itō has achieved a personal "woman's happiness" and another kind of glamour by marrying an elite Japanese man, a career civil servant, who is described as about five years her junior and even taller than she is. Itō asks the magazine to keep her husband's name out of the article so as not to complicate his relations with his co-workers. Apparently the mysterious groom is too highly placed in government circles to appreciate mention in the popular press. Looking ahead to their future, Itō remarks that her husband's parents want grandchildren and divulges her own hope to have a daughter. This turning point in Itō's life places her squarely within mainstream notions of the ideal life for a modern woman at the end of Japan's income-doubling decade in which gendered divisions of labor were seen as an important key to the nation's success. The sense is that, luckily, she has got back on track.

As an older woman, Itō Kinuko faded from view and the media trail of her contemporary image-text appears to end. In 1980 the journal *Bungei shunjū* ran a short article on Itō's Miss Universe experience as recalled by Mochida Naoto, a newspaperman who had originally covered the story. When the journal telephoned Itō, who was by then the mother of a daughter in her third year of elementary school, she refused comment, saying simply, "Let it go" (*Bungei shunjū* 1980).

But Itō's beauty queen story took flight again with the advent of Women's Studies in Japan and a renewed and strongly feminist interest in women's history. Books such as *Women's History of Shōwa* (*Onna no Shōwa-shi* 1986), for example, observe her success in the Miss Universe contest, fascination with her perfect figure, and the attendant fad for "beauty calisthenics" in presenting the culture of women's postwar experience (Nagahara and Yoneda 1986: 187–188).

Against the changes taking place in Japanese women's opportunities in the era of abundance afforded by the bubble economy of the 1980s, the beauty contests of the 1950s seem quaint. Itō's remarkable mobility—her ability to travel to California for pleasure—had become routine by this time for a generation of Japanese women, who could now afford to pay their own way, shop for designer clothing and gourmet food as they pleased, and initiate romantic flings on their travels. They were the new modern girls on the go, representatives of a booming Japanese economy and a nation to be reckoned with.

Even if they were not entering pageants, many of these women felt the need and desire to devote themselves to beauty work. They were also heirs to concerns that such self-centered activities kept one from achieving a "woman's happiness," giving rise to fears about Japan's low birth rate and the incompatibility of motherhood with a career. The unresolved anxieties surrounding Itō Kinuko's rise and fall became their own.

This chapter has discussed the image-text of the postwar beauty queen as a particular form of uniformed, gendered labor by using major events in Itō Kinuko's life as publicized in Japan and the United States. As a beauty queen body famous even now for *hattōshin*, Itō's physique presented a specific version of modernity in 1953 that indexed democracy and gender advancement, and even Japan's healthy recovery from the war. Symbolic of the nation's renewed competiveness on the global stage, Itō's body became the envy of many, but her fame opened her to charges of American-style egotism at a particularly sensitive point in Japan-American relations. As a modern girl on the go, Itō Kinuko stood as tangible proof of the risks and rewards of pursuing new opportunities. At the same time, her nation, too, questioned where its new shape and alliances were leading. Was it possible for a modern girl on the go—and her nation—to go too far?

Chapter Ten

TRAVELING TO LEARN, LEARNING TO LEAD

Japanese Women as American College Students, 1900–1941

Sally A. Hastings

In the summer of 1946, Mishima Sumie (1900–1992), a Japanese woman struggling to survive in the rubble of postwar Tokyo, was surprised when a United States Army car pulled up to her house and an American man came to her door. He explained that he was married to one of Mishima's Wellesley College classmates and that he had spent much of his first full day in Japan as part of the military Occupation searching for her house so that he could deliver a letter from his wife.

For Mishima, her surprise visitor was just one of several reminders that summer that as a member of the Wellesley College class of 1927 she had once felt that she was "a part of America." After graduation, with her good knowledge of English, Mishima was offered several jobs in postwar Japan, and she worked as a translator for the International Military Tribunal for the Far East (Mishima 1953: 75–81). Other Japanese women with American college educations also found that suddenly their English-language skills could bring lucrative employment in postwar Japan.[1]

How was it that Japanese women had traveled so far and stayed so long in the United States? Elite Japanese men, who were educated in middle schools, high schools, and universities that did not admit women, usually studied abroad only after they had graduated from university and secured a job. Mishima had departed for Wellesley College after her graduation from Tsuda College in Tokyo.[2] This essay explores the travels of Japanese women in pursuit of education by examining the experience of graduates of Tsuda College who studied in the United States between 1900, when the school was founded, and 1941, when the Japanese attack on Pearl Harbor transformed students into "enemy aliens." Although the graduates of Tsuda College constituted only a fraction of the Japanese women who traveled to the United States for education, the school provides a useful focus.

From its founding in 1900, Tsuda College looked outward, making study of the English language the cornerstone of its program to cultivate an international outlook for women. In contrast to mission schools, such as Kobe College, that were governed by Americans, it was a Japanese institution, albeit one that benefited from funds raised by American women and networks among Japanese and American women. Further, Tsuda College emphasized preparation for employment. Most important, Tsuda Umeko (1864–1929), the founder of Tsuda College, played a major role in institutionalizing study abroad for Japanese women in a manner that made not only graduates of Tsuda but other Japanese women who studied in the United States as well feel that America was a "second home."[3]

To be sure, Tsuda College was not the first or only Japanese women's institution whose students went to America. Several church-related girls' schools sent students overseas before Tsuda Academy was founded. Beginning in 1887, Kobe College sent one or two girls per year to the United States (Ishii 2010: 13). Because, however, so many women from Tsuda College studied abroad, this institution provides us with a window onto the role that American education played in preparing Japanese women to become the leaders of Japanese institutions.

The elite Japanese women who left Tsuda College for education abroad were women on the go. They crossed the Pacific to acquire college degrees in the United States. They traveled extensively within the United States, and most visited Europe as well.[4] They returned across the Pacific to become teachers and leaders of Japanese women. Moreover, foreign travel was not a once-in-a-lifetime adventure for these women; travel abroad was a means of maintaining their expertise, and several of them returned to the United States for graduate degrees.

Tsuda Umeko and Tsuda College

The story of the Tsuda College graduates who traveled far to become leaders of Japanese women must begin with the story of Tsuda Umeko herself, for in institutionalizing women's study in America, Tsuda drew upon her multiple visits to the United States. Tsuda was one of the five girls included in the government-sponsored Iwakura Mission of 1871 to the United States and Europe, dispatched with the primary purpose of convincing the Western powers to renegotiate the "unequal" treaties that Japan had signed in the 1850s. Approximately half those sent on this mission were students, many of whom remained in the United States and Europe for years afterwards.

The decision that girls should be educated at government expense was made by the Hokkaido Development Bureau. Kuroda Kiyotaka and Mori Arinori, the Japanese statesmen who conceived the idea of educating women in America, believed that in order to create a new type of national subject, Japan needed new mothers, more like the American women who had made a strong impression on the first government delegates to the United States. The five girls selected were the daughters of samurai who had either traveled abroad or worked with Westerners in Japan as part of their duties to the former Tokugawa rulers (Kuno 1993: 49–72; 96–112).[5]

Two of the girls who traveled to the United States in 1871 became ill and returned to Japan the next year, but the other three remained in America for over ten years. They lived with American families—Nagai Shigeko (1861–1928) and Yamakawa Sutematsu (1860–1919) in New Haven, and Tsuda Umeko, the youngest of the three, in Washington, D.C. Nagai returned to Japan in 1881 after three years of music study at Vassar College. Yamakawa became the first Japanese woman to graduate from an American college (Vassar, class of 1882). Because she was younger than the others, Tsuda continued to live in the Washington home of Mr. and Mrs. Charles Lanman and completed her American education at the Archer Institute, returning to Japan in 1882 with Yamakawa (Furuki 1991b: 33; Rose 1992: 22). By the time Yamakawa, Nagai, and Tsuda returned to Japan in the 1880s, the Hokkaido Development Bureau no longer existed, and government leaders took little interest in their expertise. Yamakawa and Nagai were soon married, the former to a general and the latter to an admiral. Tsuda secured a position at the government-sponsored Peeresses' School when it opened in 1885 to educate the daughters of the aristocracy.

Having spoken nothing but English for ten years beginning at the age of seven, Tsuda had native fluency in English, an invaluable asset in late nineteenth-century Japan, but she recognized that her unusual childhood was no substitute for educational credentials. Determined to get a leave from her employment at the Peeresses' School and return to America for further education, Tsuda collected catalogues from Wellesley and Smith colleges and normal (teacher training) schools. Whereas Tsuda's first trip to America was a government venture, her later studies at Bryn Mawr College, which extended her knowledge of the United

States and established new contacts, were facilitated by friendships. Mary Harris Morris (1836–1924) of Philadelphia learned of Tsuda's dream through their mutual friend Clara Whitney, an American resident in Japan. Morris's influence and generosity allowed Tsuda to enter Bryn Mawr in 1889 (Rose 1992: 79–80; Furuki 1991a: 314, 316, 318).

Tsuda's life is of interest for its own sake, but her importance in this story of modern girls on the go is that she established institutions that allowed other Japanese women to enjoy educational opportunities similar to her own. During her stay at Bryn Mawr, Tsuda raised funds for an endowment, the interest from which would support a Japanese young woman for a year of preparatory work and four years of college in Philadelphia. The American Women's Scholarship for Japanese Women (AWSJW) was administered by a committee headed by Mary Morris. The Japanese committee included women who had benefited from American institutions such as Wellesley College and the Women's Medical College of Pennsylvania (Rose 1992: 97).[6] The scholarship was awarded on the basis of merit, and it regularized financial support, replacing appeals to college faculty or individual donors.[7]

In 1900, Tsuda realized her dream of establishing a private academy in which young women could further their education in the English language, and she used her wide circle of friends to make it a place where her students could learn to speak fluently, surrounded by native speakers of English. She was assisted at the opening of her school by an American friend from her first visit to the United States, Alice Bacon (1858–1918), the daughter of the Reverend Leonard Bacon, a Congregational minister, with whom Yamakawa Sutematsu had lived in New Haven.[8] When Bacon left Japan in 1902, she was immediately succeeded at the academy by Anna C. Hartshorne, a friend of Tsuda's from Philadelphia. Hartshorne left Japan six months later but returned in 1904 and continued her service to the school with occasional breaks until 1940 (Furuki 1991b: 139). Hartshorne's services were supplemented by other residential teachers who were native speakers of English, some of whom were recruited from among Bryn Mawr graduates and the daughters of members of the American scholarship committee (Furuki 1991a: 397, 406, 475; Johnson 2005: 315).

Tsuda added well-educated women to the staff of her school by every means possible. Through her contacts among North American women residing in Japan, she recruited well-educated native speakers as part-time teachers. Mary Jane Greene, a graduate of Mount Holyoke and wife of the Congregational missionary Daniel Crosby Greene, taught music for several years.

Greene's daughter Fanny, a Wellesley graduate, joined the staff in 1903 (Furuki 1991b: 124).[9] Caroline Macdonald, a Canadian dispatched by the World Young Women's Christian Association (YWCA) to Japan in 1904, began teaching the history of English literature at Tsuda College in the fall of 1905 (Prang 1995: 41). For a time, Carrie Macadam, a Vassar graduate, taught two or three times a week (Kuno 1993: 199). A photograph of the fourth graduation ceremony in 1906 shows Mary Jane Greene, Fannie Greene, Anna Hartshorne, Caroline Macdonald, and two women from the Episcopal missionary community (Tsuda Juku Daigaku 1960: 71).[10] Tsuda expected those whose travel abroad she had facilitated to contribute to her institution, and many of them did.[11] Demonstrating the flexibility that had helped her to establish her academy with limited resources, she increased the number of Japanese faculty members by welcoming American-educated Japanese women who had obtained their education without the benefit of her scholarship, such as Tsuji (Okonogi) Matsu and Uemura Tamaki, both graduates of Wellesley College.[12]

When Tsuda sent women abroad for study, she was preparing them to work as teachers and leaders of women's institutions. It is a testimony to her foresight that three of the women she sent to the United States (Hoshino Ai, Kasuya Yoshi, and Fujita Taki) later served as president of Tsuda College. (In her personal essay in this volume, Yoko McClain shares her memories of Hoshino, who was president of Tsuda College during World War II.) Although Tsuda eagerly awaited the return of her students to Japan and their service at her institution, she saw travel as a continuous activity. She encouraged her protégés to visit Europe and to return to the West for further study. Although she argued that girls in general should be educated to be "capable mothers and fit companions of men," she boasted that nearly fifty of the eighty women who had graduated from her academy by 1910 had gone into teaching (Rose 1992: 102; Tsuda 1910).

Sending Students to the United States

Education in the United States allowed Japanese women to earn a bachelor's degree, an opportunity not readily available to them in Japan, although from its founding in 1907, Tohoku Imperial University admitted women. Otherwise, the only education that the Japanese government made available to women beyond the six mandatory years of elementary education was teacher training and girls' higher schools, the rough equivalent of men's middle school. Tsuda's academy provided Japanese women with education in written and spoken English, which would allow them to benefit from an American education.

The American Women's Scholarship for Japanese Women provided funding for a limited number of women to study in the United States. Tsuda and her supporters, however, intended that Japanese women should acquire far more in the United States than simply a credential. The noted educator Nitobe Inazō told the young Kawai Michi, shortly after their ship arrived in Vancouver, "We have not brought you to America merely to develop your intellect; if that were your only aim, you could find in Japan more to study than you could absorb in your lifetime. Here your real education will be outside of books and college walls" (Kawai 1939: 65). Memoirs and letters allow us a glimpse of how Tsuda arranged for her students to enter into American life.

Each journey began with a properly chaperoned passage across the Pacific. Kawai Michi (1877–1953) traveled in 1898 with Nitobe and his wife. When Alice Bacon left Japan in April 1902, she served as chaperone for Suzuki Utako, a teacher at the academy, intended for enrollment at Bryn Mawr (Furuki 1991a: 381). Hoshino Ai journeyed from Yokohama to New York with Natsuko, the daughter of the Christian educator Ebara Soroku (1842–1922), who was on her way to New York where her husband Fukui Kikusaburō was taking up a new position with the Mitsui Company (Hoshino 1990: 28). Other students traveled with missionaries or tourists.

Strictly speaking, Kawai Michi was not sent to the United States from Tsuda Academy, for the school took shape only after she was there, but she lived with Tsuda Umeko before her departure, and her account of her travels allows us a glimpse of how Tsuda made arrangements for her protégés studying abroad. She enlisted American friends to ensure the safety of Kawai on her train journey from Vancouver to Philadelphia; when there was a delay, Anna Hartshorne's brother Charles sent a message arranging for Kawai to stay in a hotel. The Committee for the American Women's Scholarship for Japanese Women was vigilant about the train travel of their charges, a lesson they had learned in 1893 when delays caused their first student, Matsuda Michi, to arrive in Philadelphia in the middle of the night with no one to meet her. Kawai was met in Philadelphia by Mrs. Nitobe's brother, Joseph Elkinton (Kawai 1939: 66–68; Araki and Demakis 1987: 21).

Tsuda personally arranged Kawai's preparatory studies at Ivy House, the Germantown school directed by Mary E. Stevens. Tsuda accompanied Kawai from the Elkinton Home to the house of Eliza Adams Lewis, a Bryn Mawr alumna doubly linked to Japan, through her friendship with Tsuda and her college roommate Dogura Masa, later Countess Uchida. Lewis installed Kawai at Ivy House, where she herself had studied; Kawai was Stevens's third Japanese student (Kawai 1939: 68–70).[13]

In October 1900, Kawai entered Bryn Mawr as a member of the freshman class, "the only student from the Far East" (Kawai 1939: 75). For four years she lived in college dormitories, sharing rooms with American students. During vacations, she stayed in the homes of members of the Philadelphia Committee, such as Mary Morris in Overbrook and Margaret Vaux Wistar Haines (1831–1917) and her daughters Mary and Jane of Cheltenham (Kawai 1939: 86–87; Wyck House 2009).[14] In the summer of 1902, Kawai was invited to attend the YWCA conference at Silver Bay on Lake George in New York. Friends in Germantown extended her travels, enabling her to go to Europe in the summer of 1903 (Kawai 1939: 90, 92). She graduated in 1904 with majors in history and economics (Kawai 1939: 79).

Tsuda played a determining role in deciding the employment and travel of Hoshino, the fourth recipient of the Philadelphia scholarship. The daughter of a merchant family that had converted to Christianity, Hoshino came to Tsuda College from Ferris School in Yokohama, one of the oldest mission schools in Japan. After Hoshino's graduation in 1906, Tsuda arranged a teaching position for her at the Shizuoka Eiwa Girls' School, a Canadian Methodist mission school. Hoshino had spent only one term in Shizuoka when she received a letter from Tsuda inviting her to take an examination for a scholarship to Bryn Mawr College. With the encouragement of her older brother, a Christian pastor, Hoshino took the examination and was chosen from among about ten applicants.

Tsuda's guiding hand reached to the United States. Mary Haines of the Philadelphia Committee, who had hosted Kawai, met Hoshino when she arrived in Philadelphia (Hoshino 1990: 24–28). Like Kawai, Hoshino began her preparatory studies for Bryn Mawr at Ivy House in Germantown, but after Mary Stevens's death the school had changed, and after one term her transfer was arranged to the more rigorous Miss Kirk's School in Bryn Mawr, operated by Abby Kirk, a graduate of Bryn Mawr class of 1892 and a friend of Tsuda's. The twenty students were all boarders, most of them aspiring to admission to Bryn Mawr. Demonstrating her personal involvement, Tsuda visited Miss Kirk's School in 1907 when Hoshino was there (Hoshino 1990: 30–31).

Although Hoshino was invited to the homes of Bryn Mawr classmates for many holidays, she also socialized in the United States with friends from Tsuda. Sometimes Okonogi Matsu, who was at Wellesley College, came to stay for a few days in the dormitory at Miss Kirk's. Hoshino and Okonogi traveled through America together. With a third Tsuda friend, Okamoto Shinako, who lived in New York, they went to Washington, D.C., where, because Helen Taft, the daughter of the President, was a classmate of Hoshino's at Bryn Mawr, the three were invited for tea at the White House. Hoshino and Okonogi also visited the Elkinton summer home in the Poconos together (Hoshino 1990: 32).

Tsuda's connections were likewise apparent in the arrangements for Hoshino's summer vacations, for she spent all five summers at "Deep Haven," Alice Bacon's camp at Squam Lake in New Hampshire. The guests at this camp were largely Bacon's friends and acquaintances: writers, professors, and clergy, who came either as individuals or as family groups. In addition, there were about fifteen African Americans each summer from Bacon's work at Hampton Institute in Virginia. As a scholarship student, Hoshino did not have to pay, and she contributed to the camp by meeting the mail boat and then distributing the letters and by caring for Bacon's dogs. She also swam, boated, canoed, and hiked along with the campers. In 1907, Tsuda Umeko and her sister Yonako spent the summer at Deep Haven (Hoshino 1990: 33–38; Furuki 1991a: 402).

Despite the fact that she was slightly older than most regular students, Hoshino was included in the undergraduate life of Bryn Mawr College. In her autobiography she recalled that the most important festivals were May Day and Lantern Night. The May Day festival, which included the selection of a May Queen and a Maypole dance, took place only once every four years. Hoshino experienced it during her second year on campus. On Lantern Night, sophomores passed lanterns to members of the freshman class. Other traditions, such as class color, class ring, and class animal centered on the cohort of students who would graduate together. For Hoshino's class of 1912, the class color was light blue (Hoshino 1990: 44–45).

Fujita Taki's journey to the United States in 1920 followed the pattern Tsuda had set for Kawai and Hoshino. At the end of her lengthy travels to Philadelphia, Fujita was met by Mary Haines and taken to her home in Cheltenham (Fujita 1979: 24, 25, 28, 30). Like Hoshino, Fujita entered Miss Kirk's School (Fujita 1979: 33–34).

Fujita's autobiography provides insight into how the members of the Philadelphia Committee cared for the scholarship students. The leadership of the committee remained with the family of Mary Morris, the first committee chair; she was succeeded by her granddaughter Margaret, the wife of W. Logan MacCoy, a lawyer and president of Provident Trust Company.[15] The twenty-one members of the committee, always made up of equal numbers of Episcopalians, Presbyterians, and Quakers, were divided into three subcommittees. One took care of Fujita's plans for vacations, such as Christmas and summer break. A second subcommittee was charged with monitoring her health. A third provided for her dormitory room, supplying her with things such as a carpet, curtains, and a sofa. In Fujita's case, the summer plans included YWCA camp and summer school at Columbia University. Those in charge of health could be rather intrusive. During Easter vacation, Fujita was visiting a friend in New York when she received a telegram from a committee member, summoning her back to Bryn Mawr for a tonsillectomy (Fujita 1979: 34–35). Hoshino was likewise ordered by telegram to leave her Christmas celebration in Pittsburgh to undergo the same surgery (Hoshino 1990: 40).

Although most recipients of the Philadelphia Committee scholarship attended Bryn Mawr, Tsuda found places for her graduates at other institutions as well. In January 1906, Tsuda dispatched Kawashima Yoshiko, a graduate and also a teacher at the academy, to Simmons College in Boston. When she returned in 1909, Kawashima inaugurated a program on home economics, which was soon abandoned (Furuki 1991a: 437, 439; Tsuda Juku Daigaku 1960: 121). Hirano Chieko, who graduated from Tsuda in 1907, likewise earned a degree from Simmons in 1916 (Haga 1993: 874–875). It is likely that Tsuda facilitated the studies of Yamada Koto, a trusted staff member. Yamada was the first international student at the Madeira School when she arrived from Japan in 1911 (Griffith 2005). She graduated from Vassar College in 1916 and taught at Tsuda from her return to Japan until shortly after her marriage to the widowed philosopher Nishida Kitarō in 1931 (Yusa 2002: 238–240, 251).

The alumni publication of Tsuda College documents the ventures of other graduates beyond the northeast: Tanaka Nobuko from the first graduating class went to Mills College in California; Okada Tsugi from the second class to Cornell College in Mount Vernon, Iowa; and Takeda Ayako to Brenau College in Gainesville, Georgia. It is possible that these arrangements were made through their families or churches rather than through the college.

The procession of students from Tsuda College continued long after Tsuda Umeko retired from active leadership precisely because her protégés and successors continued to facilitate journeys. On her second trip to America, Kawai identified Earlham College in Richmond, Indiana, as a desirable educational institution, and she selected Watanabe Yuri to go there. Kawai prepared Watanabe for American life by taking her to Western homes in Karuizawa for a few days and then entrusted her to the care of an elderly American couple for the trans-Pacific trip (Isshiki 1953: 29). The connections built up between Japan and Bryn Mawr College benefited this student as well; Eliza Adams Lewis, Dogura's roommate at Bryn Mawr and hostess to Kawai in Germantown, had moved to Indianapolis and met Watanabe on her arrival in 1911 (Kawai 1939: 69, 134; Watanabe 1911). During her 1915 trip to America, Kawai visited Earlham and stayed for a few days in Watanabe's dormitory (Isshiki 1953: 36). After graduating from Earlham in 1916, Watanabe worked with Kawai at the YWCA and at Keisen Jogakuen, the school that Kawai founded in 1929.

Opportunities in the New Era

World War I, the war meant to make the world safe for democracy and end all wars, marked a new level of economic prosperity for Japan. Changes in the world as well as at Tsuda College created new patterns of overseas travel. Tsuda submitted a letter of resignation to the board of directors of the institution in early 1919. Over the next decade and a half, two Tsuda College students succeeded Fujita at Bryn Mawr, Ban Kaoruko and Nakamura Shizu, who graduated in 1930 and 1935, respectively. In this era, however, Tsuda students found their way to new destinations, including Wellesley and the University of Michigan.

The growth in the number of Tsuda graduates traveling to Wellesley occurred as the leadership of the academy passed to a Wellesley graduate, Tsuji, the acting president of Tsuda College after Tsuda's resignation. In the 1920s, Kasuya Yoshi (1923), Takizawa Matsuyo (1923), Murayama Yone (1926), and Seo Sumie (1927) all earned Wellesley degrees. Ishida Shizuko, Ono Haruko, and Mori Yoshiko were nondegree students; Mori earned a degree from Simmons in 1930 after studying at Wellesley from 1927 to 1929 (Wellesley College Archives, "Foreign Students").

The increasing number of Tsuda students at Wellesley also reflected new Wellesley initiatives. When Hoshino visited Wellesley during the 1918–1919 academic year, Professor Sophie Chantal Hart of the English Department told her that she would like Tsuda to send a student to Wellesley. During her sabbatical year in 1917–1918, Hart had visited the Philippines, Japan, and China, developing an especially strong interest in Japan. After consultation with other faculty members, Hoshino chose Kasuya to attend Wellesley (Hoshino 1990: 62). Mishima credits Hart with the full scholarship that she received from the college, covering tuition and board (Mishima 1941: 111). Hart probably funded

Kasuya's education as well. Hart's generosity was undoubtedly one contributing factor that enabled the Tsuda President Tsuji to reassure Mishima when
she expressed interest in studying in America, "We will get you a scholarship"
(Mishima 1941: 89).

Women's education in Japan had also changed, expanding greatly and as a
consequence becoming more diverse. In 1918, the Tsuda Academy had about
two hundred students, the maximum for its central Tokyo site (Mishima 1941:
66). By 1933 the campus had been relocated to the suburb of Kodaira, and the
student body had increased to 333 (Kawai 1934: 86). The faculty included male
as well as female instructors, and the students were diverse in age and marital
status. Tsuda encouraged married women to enroll in her school. When she
entered Tsuda in 1918, Mishima found that six or seven of the approximately
sixty students in her class had at some point been married. A professor's wife
had dropped out for a year to have a baby. Another student was the wife of a
physicist who was studying abroad. Two or three of the older students had been
married and divorced (Mishima 1941: 61).

Despite the changes in women's education and the society more broadly,
the increasing number of students going from Tsuda to destinations other than
Bryn Mawr did not represent a sudden break in the rituals for Tsuda students
going abroad. Takizawa traveled to the United States for her studies at Wellesley with Hoshino, who was returning to the United States for a year of study at
Columbia Teachers' College. The two spent some time together at the Elkinton
summer home in the Poconos, providing Takizawa with an experience shared
by her predecessors who went to Bryn Mawr (Hoshino 1990: 59).

Whereas the Philadelphia Committee provided a substantial group of
alumnae and community leaders to oversee the activities of the students from
Japan, at Wellesley the responsibility devolved solely to Hart. In 1930, when
Hart was away from campus, she asked Lilla Weed of the library to assume her
duties temporarily. A letter of October 3, 1930, from college president Ellen F.
Pendleton to Weed summed up the necessary work: "Your responsibility in regard to these students is to see that they are properly cared for, to advise them
in any difficulties that may arise, and to make sure some arrangement is made
for their short vacations" (Wellesley College Archives, "Foreign Students").

Hart had been assuming responsibility for Japanese students for a number
of years. In a letter of recommendation, Hart identified herself as Takizawa's
advisor. Kasuya Yoshi, class of 1923, states that Hart, whom she also considered
to be an advisor, "[helped me to] get into the heart of American life, for she in-

troduced me to many families, far and near the campus. They received me most cordially into their homes and helped me find the essence of American ways of life" (Kasuya 1974: 70). Yasuya also credited Hart with arranging her summers at Aloha Camp, run by the Gulick family, as was the camp on Lake Sebago that Mishima Sumie attended (Mishima 1941: 128).[16]

Despite the administrative differences between Bryn Mawr and Wellesley, the pattern of study abroad remained much the same in the 1920s as it had been two decades earlier. A network of personal connections provided chaperonage on the trans-Pacific trip and a welcome at journey's end. Students lived in the dormitories, sharing rooms with American students and engaging in the traditions of their colleges. Wellesley students handed on hoops from seniors to juniors, rather than lanterns from sophomores to freshmen as at Bryn Mawr, but the principles of inclusion were the same. Short vacations were spent with classmates, and camp was usually the destination for summer vacations.

Beginning in 1922, Tsuda students began attending a different kind of institution, the co-educational, state-sponsored University of Michigan. An act of American generosity, parallel to the beneficence of the Philadelphia women and Hart, paved the way. In 1917, Levi L. Barbour gave the University of Michigan $100,000 (to which he added a further $250,000 in 1920) "for the establishment of scholarships for women coming from oriental countries" (University of Michigan 1922–1923: 123). Impressed by two Chinese women who graduated from the University of Michigan medical school in 1896, Barbour endowed the scholarship in the hope that women from Asia could come for education in their chosen fields and then return to service in their countries of origin (Bentley Historical Library).

Kinai Fumi was the first Tsuda graduate to avail herself of this largess. In 1922, the same year that she graduated from Tsuda, Kinai enrolled at the University of Michigan. Mishima mentions that, because the group of seven young women with whom she crossed the Pacific in 1922 included a student headed for the University of Michigan, the group was met in Seattle by one of the school's alumnae, who drove the Japanese party to the YWCA (1941: 99–100). It is highly likely that the student was Kinai, and this incident is another example of how Tsuda mobilized American allies to ease the transition of its students across the Pacific. Kinai graduated with a bachelor's degree in arts and sciences in 1925 after only three years. She remained at the University of Michigan for the summer session after her graduation; the Tsuda College

alumnae publication reported her address as Oxford, England for the following three years.

Kinai was joined in her second year at Michigan by an older Tsuda graduate,
Shōhara Hide (class of 1915). Like Kinai, Shōhara graduated in three years. At
least four more Tsuda graduates came to Michigan for undergraduate degrees:
Hoshino Hanako and Satō Kikue in 1929 and Ōi Fumi and Saishō Fumiko in
1930. As they did at Bryn Mawr and Wellesley, Japanese women in Ann Arbor
lived in women's residence halls. Their social activities on campus, however,
were co-educational. They all joined the Nippon Club; Shōhara participated in
the Cosmopolitan Club as well.

In contrast to the women intent on earning bachelor's degrees at Michigan
in a relatively short period of time, Motoda Mitsu came as a graduate student.
After her graduation from Tsuda in 1920, she went to Dana Hall, the women's
preparatory school in Wellesley. At Goucher College in Baltimore she earned a
bachelor's degree before enrolling in philosophy at the University of Michigan
in 1926 with the support of a Barbour Scholarship. Like the other Tsuda women,
she stayed in a residence hall (in her case the Martha Cook Building) and joined
the Nippon Club. Several other Japanese women had, like Motoda, earned degrees at American colleges before enrolling in graduate study at Michigan: Jodai
Tano at Wells, Kiuchi Ai at Oberlin College, Mibai Sugi at Mills, and Sakanishi
Shiho at Wheaton College in Massachusetts.

Shōhara stayed at the University of Michigan for graduate study after completing her bachelor's degree in 1926. She earned her doctorate in 1929 with a
thesis on speech physiology. She remained in Ann Arbor, working as a teaching
assistant in various capacities: speech, Latin, and general linguistics. In 1933,
she was promoted to instructor in phonetics. When the United States Army
established a Japanese language school at the University of Michigan during
World War II, Shōhara was appointed to the Division for Emergency Training.
After the end of the war, she joined the Department of Far Eastern Languages
and Literatures. She retired in 1965 as a full professor (University of Michigan
(1963–1966): 891). Shōhara's work is hailed in the history of Tsuda College as
the first of many instances in which Tsuda graduates have taught Japanese as a
foreign language (Tsuda Juku Daigaku 2003: 251).

The students who came to the University of Michigan for undergraduate
degrees that they could complete in three years probably did not gain the same
facility in language as those who remained for six years. They may well have
had less access to American homes than their colleagues at women's colleges

with strong identities. As the case of Shōhara illustrates, however, the public university with its graduate programs that bestowed technical expertise allowed some to take up residence in the United States.

Although the number of Tsuda graduates venturing abroad seems to have dropped with the economic woes of the 1930s, only the bombs of Pearl Harbor halted the procession. On December 7, 1941, there were at least two Tsuda students in the United States. Yamaguchi Michiko, who graduated from Tsuda in 1936, was in her second year of study at the Pennsylvania Women's Horticultural School (Takakuwa 2001: 82). Tsurumi Kazuko, Tsuda class of 1939, had just graduated from Vassar and begun graduate work at Columbia University (Kawamoto 2001: 89).

For those who enrolled in American colleges with the expectation of employment afterwards in women's education, undergraduate education was only the beginning of their travels. For many of the women, their initial trip to the United States involved a brief detour to Europe. Kawai went to Europe one summer. Hoshino returned to Japan in 1906 via England, Belgium, Germany, and Russia, where she boarded the Trans-Siberian Railway (Hoshino 1990: 48–54). Kasuya went to Vienna during the summer after her junior year to attend the conference of the International League for Peace and Freedom (Crane 1955: 290). Tsuda encouraged her protégés to pursue further study, and they did: Kawai at YWCA training camp in New York, Hoshino and Kasuya at Columbia University, and Fujita at Smith College.

Conclusion

The Japanese women who traveled to the United States as students and who returned to Japan as educators were women on their way to work. Although they had no prescribed military-type uniforms, the Western clothing they wore on their return marked them as women who could function in international society. In Japanese fiction of the late nineteenth century, women educated in Western ways appeared as what Indra Levy has termed "Westernesque femmes fatales" (Levy 2010). The American-educated Japanese women were in the vanguard of Japanese girls on the go—moving through space, gainfully employed, and contributing to the nation. They also shared with their twentieth-century successors an objectified image, defined by modern clothing and their role outside the home, characteristics that sometimes made women the objects of sexual fantasies.

Japanese women were able to travel far and stay for long periods because a number of Japanese and American individuals dedicated time and resources to raise the level of women's education in Japan by educating Japanese women in the United States. Certain shorter journeys were prerequisites to the long and distant ones that Tsuda graduates made to American institutions. Their families had allowed them to walk to elementary school. Many had left villages to journey by train to Tokyo. Boarding their America-bound ships in Yokohama was only one step in the pilgrimage that brought many of them back to work in the cloistered halls of Tsuda College or other women's educational institutions. Participation in this pilgrimage required minimally that a woman's family be financially secure enough to get along without her labor during her long years of schooling. Families were expected to provide funds for travel and clothing; most did, although there are many tales of sacrifice. More important than wealth were imagination and connections. Families had to imagine that their daughters could teach rather than marry.

Much scholarly attention has been devoted to Tsuda's foresight in establishing the Philadelphia scholarship that supported eleven women before 1941.[17] The research outlined here shows that Tsuda College launched at least three times that number of students on journeys to America in pursuit of education. These findings resonate with the work of Karen Kelsky on the investment of Japanese women in the "realm of the foreign" and show that Kelsky's informants had even more predecessors than she realized (Kelsky 2001: 2). This pilgrimage had regular stations: chaperoned passage, stay in an American home, time in a preparatory school, four years in a dormitory, summers at camp, other vacations in American homes, and a visit to Europe, all facilitated by a network of friends extending from Tsuda. Tsuda's success was in institutionalizing the pilgrimage and inspiring her successors to maintain and enhance its stations.

The trans-Pacific networks binding American and Japanese women together sustained the American Women's Scholarship for Japanese Women over eight decades until the committee disbanded in 1976; it raised the funds that rebuilt Tsuda College after the Great Kantō earthquake in 1923 and incorporated Japanese women into certain parts of American life (Araki and Demakis 1987: 31). These ties were not, however, symmetrical. American donations flowed to Japan in full confidence that American-style education would raise the status of Japanese women and thus of Japan. Personal relationships as well were affected by the difference in wealth between the two countries. When faced with a medical crisis, Mishima asked Mrs. Huyck, the wealthy woman who had hosted her during school vacations, for money (Mishima 1941: 212). The request could not have gone the other way; it depended on the benefactor's citizenship in a wealthy country.

The Tsuda graduates who made pilgrimages to the United States multiplied the connections in Japanese society that they already had as graduates of Tsuda. For instance, graduates of Wellesley became missionaries or the wives of businessmen, foreign correspondents, and diplomats, and they organized an alumnae organization, incorporating the Japanese graduates. Because not all Japanese graduates of Wellesley had attended Tsuda, these meetings brought together in Tokyo women who would otherwise not have met. One occasion that brought alumnae together was the visit to Japan in 1919 of Ellen Pendleton, president of Wellesley. The ties forged in Wellesley dormitories brought American friends to Japan. Takizawa's Wellesley roommate, Marion Dilts, came twice, staying for extended periods; Dilts later wrote a popular history of Japan (Dilts 1938a).

Trans-Pacific ties also had economic benefits; American friends encouraged Mishima to write in English and provided the introductions that led to the publication of several articles (Mishima 1941: 246). International women's associations reinforced the ties among Japanese graduates of American colleges. The founding board of the Tokyo Association of the YWCA included Japanese graduates of Mount Holyoke (Ibuka Hana), Wellesley (Okada Mitsuko), and Bryn Mawr (Kawai Michi) (Prang 1995: 40). Ninomiya Tei, who graduated from Smith in 1910, took charge of the YWCA club in Yokohama in 1912 (Prang 1995: 94).

As noted at the beginning of this chapter, the linguistic and cultural knowledge that Japanese women acquired during their long pilgrimages improved communications when, at World War II's end, the American military occupied Japan for seven years. Over the long term, the American-educated women from Tsuda performed crucial cultural work. Some of them wrote about their experiences in the United States for Japanese audiences (Fujita 1979; Hoshino 1990) and in autobiographies for English-speaking audiences (Kawai 1939; Mishima 1941, 1953), translated English novels into Japanese and Japanese literature into English, taught Japanese language, wrote language textbooks (Shōhara 1954), and compiled dictionaries (Saisho 1980 [originally published in 1954]). Others, more numerous and less visible, followed Tsuda's example and taught English in Japan. These teachers performed the crucial task of sending their students to far places, keeping Japanese women on the go.

Chapter Eleven

A PERSONAL
JOURNEY ACROSS
THE PACIFIC

My Life in Japan and Oregon

Yoko McClain

EDITORS' NOTE: Yoko McClain, who modestly described herself as an "old gal receding," was a true "modern girl on the go." Granddaughter of Natsume Sōseki, Yoko grew up in prewar Tokyo, where she saw elevator girls and department store shop girls firsthand. She attended Tsuda University during World War II and was one of the first Japanese women to travel to the United States to continue her education. During more than thirty years as a professor, Yoko advanced Japanese language studies in the United States. She wrote books in Japanese to promote understanding of American culture (see, for example, McClain 1989 and 1995) and English guides to Japanese linguistics and manners. Her *Handbook of Modern Japanese Grammar* (1981) was an indispensable resource for students in the 1980s and 1990s. Although Yoko has written extensively about her grandfather, this is her first essay about herself. Here she describes, with humor and grace, her experience of the modern changes analyzed in previous chapters and explains how her life exemplifies themes of gender, mobility, and labor.

Prewar Childhood in a Literary Family

I was born in Tokyo. If there is anything special about that, it was that my mother was the oldest daughter of the novelist Natsume Sōseki (1867–1916), and I was born where Sōseki lived the last nine years of his life and produced many of his masterpieces. My mother, Fudeko, married my father, Matsuoka Yuzuru, one of Sōseki's youngest students, two years after Sōseki died in 1916 at the age of forty-nine, thus creating an even stronger link to the famous author. Since all of my mother's siblings were still very young, Sōseki's widow Kyoko,

Figure 17 Yoko McClain, family portrait, 1920s. Yoko is second from the right, standing next to her father. Photograph courtesy of Yoko McClain and her family.

my grandmother, asked my parents to live with her for a while. She needed a dependable young man in the house.

Even though Sōseki was already a well-known novelist in his lifetime, writers did not make much money in those days. With six children—a seventh was lost at an early age—Sōseki and Kyoko could not even afford to buy a house. After Sōseki's death, however, his publisher started issuing his complete works, which sold so well that my grandmother was able to buy the house she was renting. She saved Sōseki's study, which was called the "Sōseki sanbō," had the rest of the house torn down, and built a big new home. That was where I was born eight years after Sōseki's death. My older siblings were born at a nearby hospital. Because I was born four months after the Great Kantō Earthquake in 1923, which caused most of the hospitals to collapse, my mother had to give birth at home.

My mother could not produce breast milk, and because I could not tolerate cow's milk, my parents hired a wet nurse for me. The poor woman's husband died while she was pregnant, and when her daughter was born she entrusted her mother with the daughter's care. She then came to our house to help support her mother financially. Like other working women discussed in this book, the wet nurse left her home to go out to work.

When my mother's siblings were older, my family moved out of my grandmother's home. At the time, my father, the son of a Buddhist priest, was writing a novel titled *People Who Faithfully Follow the Teachings of the Buddha* (*Hōjō o mamoru hitobito*) (Matsuoka Yuzuru 1923–1926). We moved to Kyoto, where Buddhism exerted a stronger influence and sects were headquartered.

In those days it was almost a tradition for a middle-class Japanese family to let their daughters take a maid with them to their new household when they got married. This was because most middle-class urban women were not taught how to do domestic chores. Most of the students I taught later in my career could not understand how the married couple in Sōseki's *Mon* could afford to have a maid when the husband hesitated to buy even a pair of shoes because of their strained financial situation. Many maids were probably from poor families in the countryside and worked for low pay. Some of them, after finishing secondary school, came to Tokyo and worked in a middle-class family to learn the standard dialect and proper manners before they married. Official feudalism was long gone, but society was still far from being democratic. My mother hired a maid, in addition to a wet nurse, in Kyoto.

We stayed in Kyoto for three years before returning to Tokyo. My wet nurse remained with us for a few more years and then found a responsible man to remarry and left us. She was very loyal, however, and kept in touch with us for a long time. In fact, when I went back to Japan after I moved to Oregon, my mother would invite her to the house so I could see her. A few times I remember my sister offered her lunch, but she always declined. She used to say that she would not be able to eat with her master's family. She was a woman of a historical era in which social classes did not mix. During my childhood, we usually had three or four maids at a time.

I still remember prewar Tokyo and how I enjoyed its new entertainments. As a young girl, escalators fascinated me, and I loved the ice cream that was served in the dining rooms of department stores. One of our maids used to take me to the Mitsukoshi department store and let me ride up and down the escalator as many times as I wanted. Then she would let me have a small dish of ice cream. I would have to say that I was brought up in Japan's "good old days," and I experienced modernity and mobility with the innocence and excitement of a child.

I attended a private kindergarten, as public kindergartens had not yet opened. I am guessing it was a Christian kindergarten, judging from the photographs I still have of the nativity scenes in which I played an angel behind Mary.

After going to a public elementary school, I attended a Catholic high school. In Japan people tend to think that girls learn good manners at Catholic schools, so many parents like to send their daughters there, even if they are not Catholic. Both the current Empress Michiko and Crown Princess Masako went to Catholic schools.

In 1937, when I was still in high school, Japan started a war against China, and the country was becoming more and more nationalistic. In our physical education class, we learned *naginata*, a kind of martial art using long-handled bamboo swords, so that we could defend ourselves against enemy invaders. Even then, I wondered what the school authorities could be thinking. They seemed to be so unrealistic about the situation, and their plans made no sense to me.

Because of the war, our maids left one by one, until finally they were all gone. Then my mother, probably in her early forties, had to do housework for the first time. She told me later that, at the time, she actually did not know how to cook rice or make miso soup, the most basic of Japanese foods. However, since she enjoyed good food, she had gone to a cooking school while the maids were still with us and learned how to prepare French cuisine. When she came home from school, she taught her maids how to prepare the dishes, and she did the important part, the last seasoning. After the maids left, I remember she sometimes cooked French food by herself.

Because I felt bad that my mother had to do all the housework alone, I started helping her. In fact, I was very fortunate, for I avoided becoming an inept woman like those of the older generation. The author Akutagawa Ryūnosuke said that every word has two sides, just like a coin. This also applies to a situation. The war was awful, but, because of it, I became a woman who could handle everyday things with ease. If there had not been a war, I might still be dependent on others and unable to take care of myself like most other prewar upper-middle-class women.

While in high school, I was a big fan of American movies. Before war began with the United States, my sister and I went to see American films every Saturday night. I loved Tyrone Power, who to me was the most handsome actor in film, and I hoped to write a letter to him someday. I did not tell my mother, but that was why I studied English so intensively. And when you study a subject like that, you naturally come to like it. When I told my mother that English was my favorite subject, she suggested I consider going to Tsuda College, which was known as the best school for girls who wanted to study English. In those days, men's universities were closed to women.

Because of the war, I never did have a chance to write to Tyrone Power, but my mother turned out to have had great foresight in advising me to go to Tsuda College because knowledge of even a little English became a very useful asset after the war. My mother used to say that every woman should have a skill in case something unexpected happened to her. I am sure this conviction came from her own experiences during the war. Modern women had to define themselves in new ways.

Wartime at Tsuda College

I entered Tsuda College in April of 1942, just four months after Japan's attack on Pearl Harbor, when Japanese militarism and nationalism were at their peak. After I passed the university entrance examination, some people asked me, "Why are you going to study English when we are fighting America? It is useless to study our enemy's language right now." You can see how narrow-minded and nationalistic many Japanese people were at the time.

Of course not everyone thought that way. I remember my father was quite upset to read the special edition of the news on the day of the bombing of Pearl Harbor and that he remarked how bad it was that Japan attacked the United States without first declaring war. I also remember well that, a couple of days later, a younger brother of Prime Minister Konoe Fumimaro visited my family. He was interested in writing and often brought his work for my father to critique. But that day, he just came to tell my father how worried his older brother was about starting the war. Because Konoe was sending his son to Yale University, he knew of the United States' military might and had tried to convince the Emperor that war against the United States would be disastrous. But the faction centered around Army Minister General Tōjō, or the militarists, had convinced the Emperor otherwise, even though they had no idea what kind of country the United States was.

This anecdote reminds me of the words of my sister, who visited the United States for the first time in 1965. Shortly after she arrived in this country, she said to me in amazement, almost even in dismay, "I can't believe Japan ever fought against this country. The Japanese prewar leaders must have been so very ignorant. If they had known America better, they would never have gone to war with her. I always heard America was big and rich, but never expected it to be *this* large and wealthy. The saying 'seeing is believing' is right. You have to look at the country with your own eyes to believe it."

With so many people feeling this way, it is not surprising at all that Japan lost the war. In contrast, the U.S. government recommended that young people study Japanese precisely *because* it was the enemy's language. Young men who had a good aptitude for language were sent to military language school to study Japanese. And that was how many excellent scholars in Japanese studies emerged later.

When I entered Tsuda College, the name of the school was Tsuda Eigaku Juku (Tsuda English Academy) because, even though the school offered a broad humanities curriculum, the emphasis was on the English language. But a year later the name of the college was changed to Tsuda Senmon Gakko, or Tsuda Technical College, and a science department, offering mathematics and physics, was added. It was a good change because women with scientific minds could also attend the school, but at the time, it was the only way for the school to survive. Once, when a Tsuda student was studying English on the train, she was called a traitor by a fellow passenger. This illustrated why the college probably could not survive by teaching only English. Hoshino Ai, Tsuda's president, told us not to study English in public places after that.

Hoshino was Tsuda's president during what I believe was the college's most difficult time. Japan was fighting a terrible war, and as I said before, nationalism and militarism were at their height. But she was admirable in sticking to what she believed. For example, the government authorities pressured Hoshino to have the Emperor's photograph on the wall of her office, but she refused with the clever excuse that there was a classroom upstairs. If the photograph were hung on her wall, students would, in effect, be stepping on it. She did not believe in idolatry.

Early in 1944, Hoshino was ordered to send her students to work in factories to support the war effort, and she had to decide where students should be employed to make military airplane pistons. She looked at factories off campus, but all of them were in very shabby wooden buildings. She could not bear the thought of her students being killed if bombs landed on them. Therefore, she decided it would be better to set up a factory on campus, where everyone could work together in sturdier buildings. We started working in that factory in March 1944.

Hoshino faced another challenge in the spring of 1945, when a large portion of the school's main building, as well as one dormitory and part of the campus grounds, were occupied by a unit of the army, which fastened its nameplates to the stone pillars flanking the college entrance gate. Many of us thought it was outrageous, but we just had to accept it. Four courageous dormitory students, however, took down the nameplates one night and threw them in the Tama River, which runs next to the campus. The military officers were furious and insisted that they would harshly punish those responsible. Hoshino apologized, saying it was done merely because of the students' love of school, and asked to have the army nameplates only on one side, leaving the college nameplate on the other side. The officers at least listened and entrusted the punishment of the students to Hoshino. As I understand, she only asked them to submit a "written apology" and forbade them from going out for a few weeks. As Sally Hastings discusses in her chapter, most of the faculty, including Hoshino, had graduated from Tsuda College and then had continued their education in the United States. As a result, their thinking was liberal during the war, not narrow-mindedly nationalistic, like that of many people who had never left Japan. I can say that Tsuda students were greatly influenced by their professors' ideals.

During my first two years at Tsuda College, 1942 through 1944, despite the war, I had a normal student experience. But the war situation rapidly deteriorated. Classes were eventually canceled because we had to work in the factory. We worked three shifts: 8:00 to 4:00, 4:00 to 12:00, and 12:00 to 8:00. Those who were not working in the factory tilled a part of the school grounds to make vegetable gardens; since Japan is a tiny country, food disappeared quickly. As time went on, air raids became more frequent, often day and night. When we heard the ominous sound of the sirens, we ran into crude shelters until we no longer heard the drone of Allied airplanes.

At the time, most of the students stayed in dormitories. After working Saturday mornings in the factory, those of us who lived in Tokyo went home for the weekend. When we came back to the dormitory one early Monday morning, a student was missing. We later found out that she had been killed by an air raid over the weekend. In the dormitory, we were told to not let any lights be seen by the enemy airplanes in order to avoid being bombed. We had to cover the windows with blankets; the dorm rooms were dimly lit, so even when we did not have to work, we could not read. We learned to keep all our possessions in neat order so that we could find them in the dark.

We also learned how precious time was, because no matter how much we wanted to study, we could not—we had to work either in the factory or in the vegetable gardens. We took this lesson on the value of time with us after the war. And since we suffered from constant hunger, we also learned not to waste a scrap of food. Most important, the horrors of war made us mentally strong. We felt that nothing could be worse than our wartime experiences, and we came to be able to endure most hardships in the years after. And since we shared the same potential fate during every air raid, we students became very close.

None of us knew what an atomic bomb was before one was dropped on Hiroshima on August 6, 1945. Even right after that, my good friend learned from her father, who was a chemist, that it was a very scary bomb, but we did not know the extent of the damage. A supervisor of the factory asked me, "Do you think Japan will win this war?" I seriously doubted we would, but, at the time, we could not express our true opinions to someone we did not know well. One word to the wrong person could send you to jail—the situation was that bad. So even though this man could have been seriously worried, just as we had been, I remembered just saying, "Yes, I think we'll win." The war made us dishonest because it was too risky to be honest.

I still remember very clearly the day we lost the war. President Hoshino told us to gather in the small courtyard near the dormitory, and we listened to the Emperor over the radio. It was the first time we had ever heard his voice. We understood that Japan had surrendered to the Allied Forces. Being young and impressionable, we all cried, but at the same time, we felt kind of relieved. Later that night we all slept straight through the night for the first time in many months, without having to run into a shelter. Some years later I talked with one of my good friends, who had become active in politics and served as a senator for many years. We thought it was a good thing that a militaristic Japan had lost the war. We felt that if the country had won the world would have become a terrible place to live.

Since my classmates and I experienced so much adversity together, we remained good friends. Even now we hold a class reunion every year. Since my retirement, I have attended these reunions every year to renew our friendship and celebrate our luck in surviving. Akutagawa was right: there are two sides to everything.

Moving Forward to New Adventures

Because we had studied only two years in college instead of four, we were not qualified to graduate, but we were given graduation certificates and told to go home as soon as possible. Japanese armies had behaved atrociously abroad during the war, and the school authorities felt that they could not be responsible for the dangers predicted for young women once the Allied Forces arrived.

After a few days and a long wait in line, I was finally able to purchase a ticket to Nagaoka in Niigata, a prefecture northwest of Tokyo. My family had moved there in 1944 because my siblings were still young and the government had encouraged families with little children to move to the countryside where they were less likely to be bombed. I boarded a very crowded train, on which I could hardly move, and went to rejoin my family.

In the countryside, there were few things for me to do. At my mother's suggestion, I decided to attend classes on how to make kimono that a teacher taught in her home. It was a good chance for me to meet and become acquainted with a few local girls. Making kimono was also good training, and, although I have forgotten how to do it, I still do not think the time was wasted. Even now, I pick up a needle without hesitation whenever I need to do some mending. After a year or so, I decided to take the train a couple of hours north to Niigata City, the capital of the prefecture, to attend a typing school for three months. My plan was to return to Tokyo to work as a typist and English translator.

The Allied Occupation turned out to be more peaceful than we had expected. After spending around two years in Niigata, I returned to Tokyo and found a job at a government office as a translator. My typing skills came in handy. But in those days everything was still scarce, and we could hardly buy any good clothes. I quit working there after a year or so and went to a dressmaking school, where I learned from an excellent teacher who had been trained by a well-known designer in Paris. Many people thought I was crazy to go to a dressmaking school after having attended Tsuda College. In fact, I was the only one there with a college education; all the other girls had just graduated from high school.

I had lots of fun with those younger girls, whom I still see whenever I go back to Tokyo, and the dressmaking training helped me a great deal. Since we could not buy any material in those days, the teacher taught us how to make nice clothing out of our fathers' suits and even out of old kimono. Later, while I was a student at the University of Oregon, I made all my dresses during summer vacation, which saved me a lot of money. In those days our everyday attire was not as informal as it is now. In fact, we were not even allowed to wear pants to school, even in the United States. So we needed several everyday dresses. Plus, I could be stylish without spending much money. At some point many years ago, I stopped making my own clothes, as I became too busy, my eyesight deteriorated, and, of course, I could just buy good clothes. But I still think dressmaking and my various nonacademic experiences in Japan turned out to be very useful.

After two years, I graduated from dressmaking school, and, having learned to make things like lined suits and coats, I went back to work again. At the time, if one knew a little English, one could easily get a job, and I found work with the U.S. military. In that sense, we had it easier than do people, even those well qualified, who are struggling to find work today.

One day, one of my Japanese friends who worked in the same office suggested, "There's an examination, and if you pass it, you can go to a university in America. Why don't we take it?" Because all college graduates were eligible, I agreed and took the test with her. In Tokyo the test was administered at Tokyo University on a Sunday. It was close by, and we did not have to miss work. The scholarship was called GARIOA, short for "Government Aid and Relief in Occupied Areas," and it became known as the Fulbright Fellowship after Japan and the United States signed a peace treaty in September 1951, ending the Occupation in 1952.

I honestly had doubts about passing the exam, because I had only attended classes at Tsuda College for two years and my English was not at all good. But the English of others must have been worse, because a few weeks later I found out that I had passed. Soon after, I passed the physical, as well as the oral exams—that was how I came to the United States. I would have to say that my going to Tsuda College to study English on my mother's advice, as well as my taking the test at my friend's suggestion, were simply fortuitous.

Student Life in the United States

Shortly after I passed the exams, the U.S. Department of State sent me a letter asking me where in America I wanted to study. Not knowing anything about the United States, I asked for advice from a Japanese gentleman I had met through a friend, who had studied there before the war. He suggested I ask for a college on the East Coast, because, if traveling to the United States from Japan, I would then have a chance to see the West, the Midwest, and the East. I agreed. A month or two later, the Department of State wrote to inform me that I was assigned to the University of Oregon. Logically, I thought that Oregon must be a state on the East Coast. To my surprise, however, when I consulted a map, it turned out to be on the West Coast, just north of California.

I left Haneda Airport on July 20, 1952, and flew to Seattle-Tacoma Airport. The flight stopped once in the Aleutian Islands to refuel, since we were still in the age of propeller planes. I vaguely remember it took almost twenty-two hours from Tokyo to Seattle. [See Figure 2 in the chapter by Freedman, Miller, and Yano.] At the University of Washington, I took part in a six-week orientation course together with other international students. On weekdays, we had various classes, including English language and American history and literature. On weekends, we were taken to interesting spots, such as Victoria, British Columbia, Mount Rainier, and Whidbey Island. To us international students, it was a luxurious orientation. Seven years after World War II, the United States had recovered financially, and the American government was very generous. I am sure no student in the group would ever have thought of fighting the United States after being treated so well.

After the orientation, I went to Eugene to attend the University of Oregon. To a girl from Tokyo, Eugene was a rather small town, but it turned out to be a good place. In spite of its size, the presence of the university made it intellectually as well as culturally stimulating, and the residents, as well as the university community, were very open-minded and friendly to international visitors. Many people have asked me if I faced prejudice coming to the United States so soon after the war, but I never did. In fact, I met my closest American friend, Sally Maxwell, my first year here, and, in the years since, she and her relatives have been like family to me. Because her father was a prominent attorney, I had a chance to meet several important people in Eugene and all over Oregon, including the mayor and a Supreme Court Justice. All were kind to me. I maintained friendships with the advisor for foreign students, math professor Kenneth S. Ghent, who guided me after my arrival, and with one of my first professors, Robert Clark, who was later made the president of the University of Oregon, until their deaths a few years ago in their nineties.

Having had a curtailed, rather unacademic college experience in Japan, I enjoyed every minute of student life at the University of Oregon. Since my scholarship was for only one year, I was planning to go home when school ended in June. One of the students I became close to in the dormitory was a graduate student and a representative of the Friends Service Committee, a Quaker organization. She suggested that I see other parts of the United States before I went home, and I thought that was an excellent idea. She told me I should go to a Quaker house in Chicago for college students who wanted to work during the summer. Then I would see other parts of the country, meet students from other schools, and also make a little money. (I still correspond with this friend, even after sixty years.)

An international student driving to New York for the summer kindly offered me a ride. He said he would drop me off in Chicago, and we could share expenses. After driving several days, sleeping in the car to save money, we arrived in Chicago. But when we reached the house, we thought we had the wrong address. It was situated in the middle of a poor, predominantly African American neighborhood, what might have been called a ghetto. I was shocked to see such a dilapidated area, since I knew only Eugene, a middle-class small town, surrounded by green. However, when I knocked on the door of the house, the supervising couple and other students all came and greeted me warmly; from my correspondence with the supervisor, they already knew my name. That evening I was told that all the students were supposed to find a job in a factory, and on some weekends and evenings we were to help the neighborhood kids.

The next day I found a job at a Dr. Scholl's foot-care products factory and started packing footpads in boxes. It was easy but tedious, mindless labor for eight long hours. I had worked in a factory as a college student in Japan, but that work required concentration to avoid injury from huge machines. Packing little things at Dr. Scholl's, in contrast, was nearly unbearable. I soon learned to compose poems or to write essays in my mind, and I wrote them down when I got home. Also, many workers were displaced women from European countries. During the fifteen-minute breaks in the morning and afternoon and the thirty minutes we had for lunch, I tried to sit with the French women in order to practice speaking the elementary French I had studied at the University of Oregon.

I still remember how impressed I was with the American students in the Quaker house. They all worked in factories and then came home to our shabby boarding house, but not once did they complain. Even when exhausted from work, they played with the neighborhood children and enjoyed discussing various topics with each other in the evenings. They sometimes found time to go to the open-air concerts in the park or to go swimming in Lake Michigan. One weekend we were all invited to the family home of one of the students. It was a lovely mansion on the outskirts of Chicago. Although he was from a wealthy family, he had decided to spend his summer doing factory labor and helping poor children. I thought I had found the source of strength of American youth, and I felt ashamed of my own disgust for the factory and its tedious work.

Then one day while I was still in Chicago, I received a letter from a successful Japanese-American doctor, Robert H. Shiomi, whom I had met in Oregon through a friend. He wrote that I would never be able to learn about America in just one year. Dr. Shiomi said he would become my sponsor and encouraged me to stay and continue my studies. This was completely unexpected. As someone of Japanese descent, he had lost his well-established medical practice during the war and had been sent to an internment camp. But he was never bitter about the experience. After the war, Dr. Shiomi went back to Portland and rebuilt his successful practice. He was a very generous man and contributed to many educational and cultural institutions, including the University of Oregon. In those days Japan was so poor that we could not bring a penny—or rather a *sen*—out of the country. The only way we could come to this country was with a U.S. scholarship, as I had, or with a wealthy sponsor to assist us in the event that we became ill or faced any other unforeseen catastrophe. I was delighted and took the doctor up on his offer to sponsor me after my one-year scholarship was over.

When the time came to go home from Chicago, four of us rented a car and traveled west together. One student was from Arizona, and two were from California. I did not know how to drive at the time. When we came to the last person's home near San Francisco, her family was nice enough to let me stay for a couple of days. Then I took a Greyhound bus to Eugene.

During my second year at the University of Oregon, the school gave me a scholarship for tuition, and I only had to pay an incidental fee of twenty-five dollars per term. However, I had to find a job to cover other expenses, like rent and books. I went to see the director of the Museum of Oriental Art, now the Jordan Schnitzer Museum, on campus. The director was an art history professor who had just returned from his sabbatical leave in Kyoto. Fortunately, he had good impressions of Japan and hired me on the spot. Since he had been appointed just that fall, he was very enthusiastic about improving the museum, which I remember was open only a couple of afternoons a week. I was very lucky to be hired as a student receptionist and to be able to help the director from time to time as a translator. I also became more fond of Japanese art. It is true that we can better appreciate things when we have a chance to see them from a distance. This was the beginning of my long relationship with the museum. In fact, I met my husband there because he, too, loved Japanese art.

Because the fifty-five cents an hour I received as a receptionist was not enough to cover my expenses. I worked at the small library in the student union from 7:00 to 10:00 p.m. My main duties were to open and close the museum and the library and to answer questions once in a while. Because few patrons came to either place, I had ample time to study. Even though they paid little, they were good jobs for a student. I also worked at the student union cafeteria, where I learned how to make typical American foods, such as hamburgers, hotdogs, french fries, milkshakes, and ice cream sundaes. This came in very handy later when I had my own home, but now, of course, I am too health conscious to eat any of those things. A perk of working at the cafeteria in evenings were the free meals, which were helpful for a poor student who lived alone in a rented room. During every summer and winter vacation, Dr. Shiomi and his family kindly invited me to stay with them. He even hired me as an office assistant in his medical practice. Because of the free room and board, I could save some money. Therefore, I managed quite well with the small amount of money I made working on campus and at the doctor's office.

My extension contract with the U.S. Department of State was for three years, and I was soon ready to return to Japan. By then, however, I had many good American friends, and when I told them I was going home, they insisted that I stay. They all wrote to the Department of State, urging them to let me stay longer. The American government listened and allowed me to stay, only requesting that I give back my return airplane ticket. Immigration procedures were not as strict then as they are now.

I earned a bachelor's degree in French and married my husband, whom I had met at the museum. Because traveling across the Pacific was difficult, my parents could not come to my wedding. My sponsor Dr. Shiomi served as my father and walked me down the aisle.

Married Life in Germany

In those days there was still military conscription, and my husband was soon drafted. He was sent to Germany, though fortunately it was during peacetime. I joined him and spent a year there, which gave me a chance to visit a few different countries in Europe, as well as to practice German, another language I had learned at the University of Oregon. I also had a chance to read many books, which I could borrow from the base library. I recall that the Red Cross office at the base offered me a secretarial job, probably because I had learned shorthand at the university. I declined because my husband was going to be discharged in a few months. Just before my husband's unit was to be sent back to the United States, he was called in to see his commander. He was told that the unit was going to Georgia, where interracial marriages were still outlawed, and thus he would be discharged from the military as soon as we arrived in New York. We were happy to get out of the service early but very surprised at the reason, since there was no longer any such law in Oregon. (Miscegenation laws varied by state and did not exist in some. For example, the law was repealed in Oregon in 1951, but it took until 1967 in Georgia.)

Before we left Germany, my husband's parents wrote us a letter and suggested that we buy a Volkswagen. They had heard it was an excellent, inexpensive car, and they offered to lend us the money for it. We ordered a VW Karmann Ghia, a car with a Volkswagen engine but a sleek Italian design, and asked the company to ship it to New York. We left the port of Bremerhaven and sailed to New York by military ship. We then picked up the car and drove it back to California, where my in-laws lived. Fortunately, we had made good friends in the service whose families lived just the right distances apart, so we could stay with them along the way and save money by not staying in hotels. After staying with my husband's parents for a couple of weeks, we came back to Eugene in the summer of 1958.

Becoming a Professor

I decided to get certified to teach French at the secondary school level so that, no matter where we lived, I would be able to find a job. I went back to the University of Oregon that fall and again worked part-time at the museum. This time I helped the cataloguer by translating information about Japanese art objects.

After I received the teaching certificate, I was offered a job teaching French and English at a local high school. Because I did not feel I was qualified to teach English, I declined. To be honest, I did not have much confidence that I could teach French either, although I enjoyed the one term of "practice teaching" that was required to obtain my certificate. But this was probably because I got along well with high school students. In fact, they were nice enough to give me a farewell party on the last day of practice teaching.

The director of the museum then asked me to be his full-time secretary. He had been very good to me, despite my poor English, but he was rather particular. I worked for him for a few years but wanted to resign after I became pregnant. He interviewed many applicants for my job but rejected almost all of them. I worked until the day I went into labor. Even though I never went back to work there, I have continued to maintain a close relationship with the museum. I have been a member of the Friends of the Museum for many years. My husband collected Japanese prints for many years, and it seemed natural for me to donate a number of them to the museum.

After my son was born, I stayed home with him for several months. It was the first time outside of the year in Germany that I neither attended school nor held a job. Soon after, I received a phone call from a Japanese literature professor asking me if I would be interested in coming back to the University of Oregon graduate school to be a Japanese teaching assistant. Nowadays, a teaching assistant's job is highly coveted, but in those days there were not many students who wanted to teach Japanese. I decided that it might be interesting to teach Japanese, the language I knew best. And I had an excellent babysitter with whom I could entrust my son.

Since there were no graduate classes in Japanese literature, I registered as a student in comparative literature, specializing in three languages—Japanese, English, and French. For the next few years, I studied, taught, and did domestic chores, while raising a child, but no matter how busy I was, I felt my life was full, and I enjoyed every aspect of it.

After I earned a graduate degree, I got a full-time position teaching Japanese at the University of Oregon. After teaching for a few years, I felt I understood most of the difficulties the students were having, and I started making handouts to address them. One of the brightest students told me that my handouts were so useful that I should compile them into a book. Because of his suggestion, I published the *Handbook of Modern Japanese Grammar*, which was reprinted more than twenty times and has sold not only in the United States and Japan but also in Europe, Russia, and South America—wherever Japanese language has been taught (McClain 1981). To my delight, I received many letters from readers around the world.

From 1984 to 1986 I was the resident director for the Japan Study Abroad Program of the Oregon State System of Higher Education, and I took about fifteen students per year from Oregon to Japanese universities. I had returned to Japan several times after I started teaching, but those two years were my first long stay in Japan after moving to the United States. I was amazed how different the cultures and ways of thinking were between the two countries. After coming back to the United States, I wrote a book in Japanese about these differences, titled *American Common Sense, Japanese Common Sense (Amerika no jōshiki, Nihon no jōshiki)*, which was quite well received (McClain 1989).

After thirty enjoyable years of teaching Japanese language and reading modern Japanese literature in the original with students, I decided to retire. I genuinely loved teaching and felt I could go on teaching forever, but I thought it would be interesting to explore other pursuits. Since my retirement in 1994, I have found the time to travel to all seven continents and to write a few additional books (for example, McClain 1995). I have given talks in Japan, the United States, and several other countries, all of which I have enjoyed tremendously.

To briefly summarize, with one serendipitous turn after another, a one-year scholarship to an American university in 1952 turned into a fifty-nine-year stay in July 2011. When I think about it, the course of my life seems to have been charted not by my own decisions but those of others. I studied English in college on my mother's advice, took a test to come to the United States at my friend's urging, started teaching Japanese at a professor's request, and published my first book at my student's suggestion. Thus many kind people both in Japan and the United States have enriched my life, and I am ever more thankful for their support and encouragement. While I still have Tokyo in my blood and many good friends in Japan, I now feel I am a bona fide American, too, and I sincerely enjoy my life in the United States serving as a cultural bridge between the two countries.

Bibliography

"n.d." indicates that no publication date is given.

Abe Masao [Hisao Jūran]. 1937. "Ōgon tonsōkyoku" (Golden Fugue). *Shinseinen* (New Youth). July–December.

Adinolfi, Francesco. 2008. *Mondo Exotica: Sounds, Visions, Obsessions of the Cocktail Generation.* Edited and translated by Karen Pinkus with Jason Vivrette. Durham, NC: Duke University Press.

Aikawa Kazuyoshi, director. 1989. *Ue ni mairimasu: Watashi wa erebētā gāru* (Going Up: I Am an Elevator Girl). Tokyo: HRC hōmu bideo.

Ajioka, Chiaki, Kuwahara Noriko, and Nishiyama Junko. 2000. *Hanga: Japanese Creative Prints.* Sydney: Art Gallery of New South Wales.

Akhavan-Majid, Roya. 1990. "The press as an elite power group in Japan." *Japan Quarterly* 67, no. 4: 1006–1014.

Allison, Anne. 1994. *Nightwork: Sexuality, Pleasure, and Corporate Masculinity in a Tokyo Hostess Club.* Chicago: University of Chicago Press.

———. 2000. *Permitted and Prohibited Desires: Mothers, Comics and Censorship in Japan.* Berkeley: University of California Press.

———. 2006. *Millennial Monsters: Japanese Toys and the Global Imagination.* Berkeley: University of California Press.

Alston, John P. 2005. *Japanese Business Culture and Practices: A Guide to Twenty-First Century Japanese Business.* Bloomington, IN: iUniverse.

Andō Kōsei. 1983 [1930]. "Ginza jidai" (The Ginza Era). In *Gendai no esupuri—Nihon modanizumu* (The Modern Spirit—Japanese Modernism), no. 188, edited by Minami Hiroshi, pp. 131–134. Tokyo: Shibundo.

Aoyama, Tomoko. 2012. "Girls in *Shinseinen, Shinseinen* for Girls: The Early Comic Novels of Hisao Jūran." *Japanese Studies* 32, no. 1: 39–60.

Appadurai, Arjun. 1996. *Modernity at Large: Cultural Dimensions of Globalization.* Minneapolis: University of Minnesota Press.

Araki, Noriko, and Louise Ward Demakis. 1987. "The Scholarship for Japanese Women: 'A Free Gift from American Women.'" *Japan Christian Quarterly* 53, no. 1: 15–32.

Argus. 1946. "Plenty of beer at 10d a bottle in Japan." January 14, p. 3.

Arima Neriko. 2004. "Arima Neriko kaisōroku" (Arima Neriko memoir). In *Pan Am kaisōroku* (Pan Am Memoirs), p. 17. Tokyo: Pan American Alumni Association.

Asahi News. 2008. "Bus tours soar over seasons of war and peace." *Asahi News,* August 25. Online at http://www.asahi.com/english/Herald-asahi/TKY200808250049.html [accessed September 19, 2008].

Asahi Shinbun. 1953. "Sutā-ren ni kakomarete; Hariuddo no Kōtaishihi-sama" (Surrounded by movie stars, the Crown Prince in Hollywood). *Asahi Shinbun,* October 18.

———. 2001. "Takashimaya de erebētā gāru seifuku shō" (Elevator girl uniform fashion show at Takashimaya). *Asahi Shinbun,* September 2.

———. 2009. "Hato Basu de burari Tokyo kenbutsu" (Casual Tokyo sightseeing by Hato Bus). *Asahi Shinbun,* April 1. Online at http://doraku.asahi.com/earth/burari/090401_02.html [accessed November 23, 2011].

Asahi Shinbunsha. 2000. *Asahi Chronicle/Weekly the Twentieth Century: Nihonjin no hyakunen 1924* (Asahi Chronicle/Weekly the Twentieth Century: One Hundred Years for People in Japan 1924). Tokyo: Asahi Shinbunsha.

———. 2005. *Japan Almanac 2006.* Tokyo: Asahi Shinbunsha.

Asunarosya Company, Ltd. 2012. "Gotochi Kitty" (Local Hello Kitty). Online at http://gotochikitty.com [accessed January 2, 2012].

Atkins, E. Taylor. 2001. *Blue Nippon: Authenticating Jazz in Japan.* Durham, NC: Duke University Press.

Baker, Trudy, and Rachel Jones. 1967. *Coffee, Tea, or Me? The Uninhibited Memoirs of Two Airline Stewardesses.* New York: Bantam Books.

———. 1970. *Coffee Tea or Me Girls' Round-the-World Diary.* New York: Bantam Books.

———. 1972. *The Coffee, Tea or Me Girls Lay It on the Line.* New York: Bantam Books.

———. 1974. *The Coffee, Tea or Me Girls Get Away from It All.* New York: Bantam Books.

Bandō Tomiko. 1990. "Joshi jieitaiin tte donna seikatsu?" (What kind of life do female soldiers live?). *Fujin kōron,* no. 5: 284–289.

Banet-Weiser, Sarah. 1999. *The Most Beautiful Girl in the World: Beauty Pageants and National Identity.* Berkeley: University of California Press.

Barakan, Mayumi Yoshida, and Judith Connor Greer. 1996. *Tokyo New City Guide.* New York: Tuttle Publishing.

Bardsley, Jan. 2000. "What women want: *Fujin kōron* tells all in 1956." *U.S.-Japan Women's Journal English Supplement,* no. 19: 7–48.

———. 2007. *The Bluestockings of Japan: New Women Fiction and Essays from Seitō, 1911–1916.* Ann Arbor, MI: Center for Japanese Studies.

———. 2008. "Girl royalty: The 1959 coronation of Japan's first Miss Universe." *Asian Studies Review* 32: 375–391.

Bardsley, Jan, and Laura Miller, eds. 2011. *Manners and Mischief: Gender, Power, and Etiquette in Japan*. Berkeley: University of California Press.

Barlow, Tani E., ed. 1997. *Formations of Colonial Modernity in East Asia*. Durham, NC: Duke University Press.

———. 2004. *The Question of Women in Chinese Feminism*. Durham, NC: Duke University Press.

Barry, Kathleen M. 2007. *Femininity in Flight: A History of Flight Attendants*. Durham, NC: Duke University Press.

Becker, Bill. 1953. "Miss Universe to be acclaimed tonight, Miss Japan impresses." Associated Press. *Rafu shimpo*, July 17.

Benson, Susan Porter. 1988. *Counter Cultures: Saleswomen, Managers, and Customers in American Department Stores, 1890–1940*. Urbana: University of Illinois Press.

Bentley Historical Library. n.d. "China." Online at http://bentley.umich.edu/research/publications/china/main.php [accessed November 11, 2011].

Bernstein, Gail Lee, ed. 1991. *Recreating Japanese Women, 1600–1945*. Berkeley: University of California Press.

Berryz Kōbō, artist. 2009a. "Seishun basu gaido" (Youth bus guide). Produced and lyrics by Tsunku. Arranged by Hirata Shōichirō. Tokyo: Piccolo Town.

———. 2009b. "Seishun basu gaido" (Youth bus guide). Music Video. Tokyo: Dohhh UP!.

———. 2009c. *Berryz Kōbō suppesharu besto*, vol. 1 (Berryz Kōbō Special Best, vol. 1). Tokyo: Piccolo Town.

Bix, Herbert P. 2000. *Hirohito and the Making of Modern Japan*. New York: HarperCollins.

Bōeichō, ed. 2005. *Bōei hakusho 2005* (Defense of Japan 2005). Tokyo: Bōeichō.

Brackenbury, Don. 1953. "Miss Universe: 'Big time salute.'" *Southland Magazine*, July 5, not paginated.

Brasor, Philip, and Masako Tsubuku. 2011. "Nadeshiko Japan obviously doesn't do it for the money." *The Japan Times Yen for a Living*, July 18. Online at http://blog.japantimes.co.jp/yen-for-living/nadeshiko-japan-obviously-doesnt-do-it-for-the-money/ [accessed July 26, 2011].

Brisbane Courier. 1933. "Bright and cheerful. Young Japan's watchword." *Brisbane Courier*, February 9, p. 7.

Brown, Kendall H. 2001. "Yamamura Kōka (1880–1942): New Carlton Dancers." In *Taishō Chic: Japanese Modernity, Nostalgia, and Deco*, edited by Lorna Price and Letitia O'Connor, p. 32. Honolulu: Academy of Fine Arts.

———. ed. 2012. *Deco Japan, Shaping Art and Culture, 1920–1943*. Washington, DC: Art Services International.

Bungei shunjū. 1980. "Hattōshin bijin Itō Kinuko o unda ittsū no sokutatsu" (The express letter that gave rise to Itō Kinuko as the perfectly proportioned beauty). *Bungei shunjū*, September: 181–183.

Cairns Post. 1928. "A night club. Dancing in Kyoto." *Cairns Post*, November 1, p. 11.

Canberra Times. 1930. "Suicide of sweethearts." *Canberra Times*, June 18, p. 2.

CanCam. 1996. "Uchi no kaisha no kanchigai OL" (The really weird Office Ladies in my company). *CanCam,* no. 174 (June): 419–423.

Carlisle, Lonny. 1996. "Economic development and the evolution of Japanese overseas tourism, 1964–1994." *Tourism Recreation Research* 21, no. 1: 11–18.

Carrier, James G., ed. 1995. *Occidentalism: Images of the West.* Oxford, UK: Oxford University Press.

Chang, Leslie T. 2008. *Factory Girls: From Village to City in a Changing China.* New York: Spiegel & Grau.

Cheng, Anne Anlin. 2001. *The Melancholy of Race: Psychoanalysis, Assimilation, and Hidden Grief.* Oxford, UK: Oxford University Press.

Chiba-shi bijutsukan, ed. 2000. *Nihon no hanga 1921–1930: Toshi to onna to hikari to kage to* (Japanese Prints, 1921–1930: The City and Women and Light and Shadow). Chiba: Chiba-shi bijutsukan.

Chimoto, Akiko. 1995. "The birth of the full-time housewife in the Japanese worker's household as seen through family budget surveys." *U.S.-Japan Women's Journal English Supplement* 8: 37–63.

Cohan, Will, director. 1954. *Hawaiian Nights.* Los Angeles: Universal-International.

Cohen, Colleen Ballerino, Richard R. Wilk, and Beverly Stoeltje, eds. 1996. *Beauty Queens on the Global Stage: Gender, Contests, and Power.* New York: Routledge.

Columbia Rose, artist. 1957. "*Tokyo basu gāru*" (Tokyo bus girl). Lyrics by Oka Toshio. Music by Uehara Gento. Tokyo: Columbia Records.

Condry, Ian. 2011. "Love revolution: anime, masculinity, and the future." In *Recreating Japanese Men,* edited by Sabine Frühstück and Anne Walthall, pp. 262–283. Berkeley: University of California Press.

Copeland, Rebecca, and Ortabasi Melek, eds. 2006. *The Modern Murasaki: Writing by Women of Meiji Japan.* New York: Columbia University Press.

Courier Mail. 1938. "Frivolity suppressed in Japan's emergency." *Courier Mail,* January 25, p. 14.

———. 1946. "Japan is on the road back." *Courier Mail,* August 6, p. 2.

Crane, Esther Merrick. 1955. "Yoshi Kasuya, '23." *Wellesley Alumnae Magazine,* July: 289–290.

Creighton, Millie. 1995. "Creating connected identities among Japanese company employees: Learning to be members of department store work communities." *Culture* 15, no. 2: 47–64.

———. 1996. "Marriage, motherhood, and career management in a Japanese 'counter culture.'" In *Re-Imaging Japanese Women,* edited by Anne E. Imamura, pp. 192–220. Berkeley: University of California Press.

Cressey, Paul G. 1969 [1932]. *The Taxi-Dance Hall: A Sociological Study in Commercialized Recreation and City Life.* Chicago: University Chicago Press.

Cresswell, Tim. 2006. *On the Move: Mobility in the Modern Western World.* New York: Routledge.

Czarnecki, Melanie. 2005. "Bad girls from good families: The degenerate Meiji schoolgirl." In *Bad Girls of Japan*, edited by Laura Miller and Jan Bardsley, pp. 49–64. New York: Palgrave Macmillan.

Dai Mitsukoshi rekishi shashinchō kankōkai. 1932. *Dai Mitsukoshi rekishi shashinchō* (A Photographic History of the Great Mitsukoshi). Tokyo: Dai Mitsukoshi rekishi shashinchō kankōkai.

Daily Yomiuri. 2011a. "2011 top 10 domestic and international news stories: Disasters loom large in '11 news." *Daily Yomiuri*, December 28.

———. 2011b. "From square one: Playing for love, not money." *Daily Yomiuri*, August 3.

Dalby, Liza. 1983. *Geisha*. Berkeley: University of California Press.

Denim. 1993. *"Jieikan, fujin keikan, gādoman: genshoku seifuku bijo zukan"* (Self-Defense Force, police women, guards: Picture book of beautiful women in their working uniforms). *Denim* 6: 83–96.

Dilts, Marion. May. 1938a. *Pageant of Japanese History*. New York: Longmans, Green.

———. 1938b. "Wellesley's Japanese Alumnae." *Wellesley Magazine*, December, p. 72.

Donovan, Frances. 1929. *The Saleslady*. Chicago: University of Chicago Press.

Douglas, Susan J. 1994. *Where the Girls Are: Growing up Female with the Mass Media*. New York: Three Rivers Press.

Dower, John. 2000. *Embracing Defeat: Japan in the Wake of World War II*. New York: W. W. Norton.

Driscoll, Mark. 2010. *Absolute Erotic, Absolute Grotesque: The Living, Dead and Undead in Japan's Imperialism, 1895–1945*. Durham, NC: Duke University Press.

Dyer, Richard. 1986. *Heavenly Bodies: Film Stars and Society*. New York: St. Martin's Press.

Edwards, Brian T. 2001. "Yankee pashas and buried women: Containing abundance in 1950s Hollywood orientalism." *Film & History*, no. 31: 13–24.

Edwards, Elise. 2003. "The Ladies League: Gender Politics, National Identity, and Professional Sports in Japan." Ph.D. dissertation, University of Michigan, Ann Arbor.

Endō, Orie. 2006. *A Cultural History of Women's Language*. Ann Arbor: Center for Japanese Studies, University of Michigan.

Enloe, Cynthia H. 2000. *Maneuvers: The International Politics of Militarizing Women's Lives*. Berkeley: University of California Press.

Ericson, Joan E. 1997. *Be a Woman: Hayashi Fumiko and Modern Japanese Women's Literature*. Honolulu: University of Hawai'i Press.

Examiner. 1929. "In Japan: The modern girl." *Examiner*, December 18, p. 18.

Faison, Elyssa. 2007. *Managing Women: Disciplining Labor in Modern Japan*. Berkeley: University of California Press.

Fanning, Evan. 2011. "Women's World Cup final between USA and Japan sets Twitter record." *The Guardian*, July 18.

FIFA. 2007. *FIFA Magazine* ("Big Count" edition). FIFA. July. Online at http://www.fifa.com/mm/document/fifafacts/bcoffsurv/emaga_9384_10704.pdf [accessed November 24, 2011].

Flash. 2003a. "Sora no hiroin ni aitai" (I want to meet the heroines of the sky). *Flash*, May 13, not paginated.

———. 2003b. "'Toppu gan' . . . Nihon hatsu josei kyōkan wa konna ni bijin" ('Top gun' . . . This is how beautiful Japan's first female instructor is). *Flash*, June 10, pp. 40–41.

Franky, Lily. 2005. *Tōkyō tawā—okan to boku to, tokidoki, oton* (Tokyo Tower: Mum, Me and Sometimes Dad). Tokyo: Fusōsha.

Frederick, Sarah. 2006. *Turning Pages: Reading and Writing Women's Magazines in Interwar Japan*. Honolulu: University of Hawai'i Press.

Freedman, Alisa. 2009. "*Train Man* and the gender politics of Japanese 'otaku' culture: The rise of new media, nerd heroes, and fan communities." *Intersections*, no. 20. Online at http://intersections.anu.edu.au/issue20/freedman.htm [accessed November 12, 2011].

———. 2010. *Tokyo in Transit: Japanese Culture on the Rails and Road*. Stanford, CA: Stanford University Press.

Freedman, Alisa, and Kristina Iwata-Weickgenannt. 2011. "The Japanese television drama *Around 40* and the politics of happiness: Count what you have now." *Asian Studies Review* 35, no. 3: 295–313.

Friday. 1989. "Iwasaki shachō no okoegakari de rainen shigatsu 'kikku ofu'" ("Kick off" next year in April thanks to influence of President Iwasaki). *Friday*, September 22.

Frühstück, Sabine. 2007a. "De la militarisation de la culture impériale du Japon" (Militarizing visual culture in Imperial Japan). In *La Société japonaise devant la Montée du Militarisme* (Japanese Society against the Backdrop of Militarism), edited by Jean-Jacques Tschudin and Claude Hammon, pp. 109–120. Arles, France: Editions Picquier.

———. 2007b. *Uneasy Warriors: Gender, Memory and Popular Culture in the Japanese Army*. Berkeley: University of California Press.

———. 2011. "After heroism: Must real soldiers die?" In *Recreating Japanese Men*, edited by Sabine Frühstück and Anne Walthall, pp. 91–111. Berkeley: University of California Press.

Fuess, Harald. 2004. *Divorce in Japan: Family, Gender, and the State, 1600–2000*. Stanford, CA: Stanford University Press.

Fujin kurabu. 1953. "Misu Nippon no Itō Kinuko-san ni kiku: Utsukushii sutairu no hiketsu koko ni" (Ask Miss Japan, Miss Itō Kinuko: Here are the secrets to beauty). *Fujin kurabu*, August, pp. 336–337.

Fujita Taki. 1979. *Waga michi kokoro no deai* (My Path: Encounters of the Heart). Tokyo: Domesu shuppan.

Furuki, Yoshiko. 1991a. *The Attic Letters: Ume Tsuda's Correspondence to Her American Mother*. New York: Weatherhill.

———. 1991b. *The White Plum: A Biography of Ume Tsuda: Pioneer in the Higher Education of Japanese Women*. New York: Weatherhill.

Fussell, Paul. 2002. *Uniforms and Why We Are What We Wear*. Boston: Houghton Mifflin.

Gabriel, Theodore, and Rabiha Hannan, eds. 2011. *Islam and the Veil: Theoretical and Regional Contexts*. London: Continuum.

Garon, Sheldon. 1997. *Molding Japanese Minds: The State in Everyday Life*. Princeton, NJ: Princeton University Press.

Geijutsu Shinbunsha. 2001. "Round about 20: Yanagi Miwa vs. Wakasa Mako." *Āto akusesu* (Art Access). Online at http://www.jca-online.com/yanagi.html [accessed December 28, 2009].

Goffman, Erving. 1959. *The Presentation of Self in Everyday Life.* Garden City, NY: Doubleday.

Goodman, Bryna. 2011. "Capitalism, politics, and gender: A suicide in Shanghai." *CSWS Annual Review* (October). Online at http://csws.uoregon.edu/?page_id=82 [accessed June 4, 2012].

Gordon, Andrew. 1992. *Labor and Imperial Democracy in Prewar Japan.* Berkeley: University of California Press.

Gotō Takeo. 1995. *Sakkaa no seiki* (Soccer's Century). Tokyo: Bungei shunjū.

Gralla, Cynthia. 2010. *The Demimonde in Japanese Literature: Sexuality and the Literary Karyūkai.* Amherst, MA: Cambria Press.

Greene, Evarts Boutell. 1927. *A New-Englander in Japan: Daniel Crosby Greene.* Boston: Houghton Mifflin.

Greenfeld, Karl Taro. 1995. *Speed Tribes: Days and Nights with Japan's Next Generation.* New York: HarperCollins.

Griffith, Elizabeth. 2005. "Legacies." In *Nota Bene, A Newsletter of the Madeira School,* November, not paginated.

Gross, Daniel. 2009. "Can't robots press the elevator buttons?" *Slate,* June 29. Online at http://www.slate.com/id/2221749 [accessed October 9, 2009].

Gusterson, Hugh. 1999. "Feminist militarism." *PoLAR* 22, no. 2: 17–26.

Haga Noboru. 1993. *Nihon josei jinmei jiten* (Biographical Dictionary of Japanese Women). Tokyo: Nihon toshō sentā.

Hamilton, Annette. 1990. "Fear and desire: Aborigines, Asians and the national imaginary." *Australian Cultural History,* no. 9: 14–35.

Harootunian, Harry. 2000. *Overcome by Modernity: History, Culture, and Community in Interwar Japan.* Princeton, NJ: Princeton University Press.

Harvey, David. 1990. *The Conditions of Postmodernity.* Cambridge, MA: Blackwell.

Hashimoto Nao. 1998. "Sakkā shakai to yakyū shakai" (Soccer society and baseball society). *Chūō kōron* 10: 292–297.

Hashizume Shin'ya. 2006. *Modanizumu no Nippon* (Japan's Modernism). Tokyo: Kadokawagakugei shuppan.

Hato Basu. 1960s. *Tokyo kenbutsu—Mammouth Tokyo.* Hato Basu (Hato Bus). Online at http://60y.hatobus.co.jp/history/movies.html [accessed December 30, 2010].

———. 1984. *Hato Basu sanjūgonen shi* (Thirty-Five-Year History of Hato Bus). Tokyo: Hato Basu.

———. 2011. "Hato Basu kaisha gaiyō" (Hato Bus Corporate Outline). Online at http://www.hatobus.co.jp/outline/index.html [accessed November 23, 2011].

Hebdige, Dick. 2008. "The protocols of sado-cute." In *Murakami,* edited by Paul Schimmel, pp. 40–51. Los Angeles: Museum of Contemporary Art.

Hendry, Joy. 1995. *Wrapping Culture: Politeness, Presentation, and Power in Japan and Other Societies.* Oxford, UK: Oxford University Press.

Hisayama Tatsuichi. 1961. *Isetan nanajūnen no ayumi* (Isetan's Past Seventy Years). Tokyo: Isetan.

Hochschild, Arlie. 1983. *The Managed Heart: Commercialization of Human Feeling.* Berkeley: University of California Press.

Hongō, Mitsuru, director. 1992. *Kureyon Shin-chan 14: Erebētā gāru to issho da zo* (Crayon Shin-chan 14: Hey, I'm with the elevator girl). Tokyo: Shin-Ei Animation Co.

Hood, Christopher P. 2006. *Shinkansen: From Bullet Train to Symbol of Modern Japan.* London: Routledge.

Horibe Keisuke, director. 2009. *Akuma no erebētā* (Elevator Nightmare). Tokyo: Nikkatsu Corporation.

Hoshino Ai. 1990. *Shōden* (Autobiography). Tokyo: Ōzorasha.

Hunter, Janet. 1990. "Women's labour force participation in interwar Japan." *Japan Forum* 2, no. 1: 105–125.

———. 1993. *Japanese Women Working.* London: Routledge.

———. 2003. *Women and the Labour Market in Japan's Industrialising Economy: The Textile Industry before the Pacific War.* London: Routledge.

Ibuse Masuji. 1996. *Okoma-san* (Miss Okoma). In *Ibuse Masuji zenshū* (Collected Works of Ibuse Masuji). Vol. 8. Tokyo: Chikuma shobō.

Ichikawa Kon, director. 1954. *Watashi no subete o* (All of Myself). Tokyo: Tōhō Studios.

Igarashi, Yoshikuni. 2000. *Bodies of Memory: Narratives of War in Postwar Japanese Culture, 1945–1970.* Princeton, NJ: Princeton University Press.

Iguchi Tetsuya. 2011. "Corporate Japan needs soccer women's hungry spirit." *Nikkei Weekly*, July 25.

Ikarosu. 2011. *Josei jieikan 2012 karendā* (Female service members 2012 calendar). Tokyo: Ikarosu.

Imamura, Anne E., ed. 1996. *Re-Imaging Japanese Women.* Berkeley: University of California Press.

Inagaki Yoshihiko and Yoshizawa Norio. 1985. *Shōwa kotobashi rokujūnen* (Sixty Years of Historical Shōwa Words). Tokyo: Kabushiki kaisha kōdansha.

Inoue Shōichi. 1997. *Bijin kontesuto hyakunen-shi: Geigi no jidai kara bishōjo made* (The One Hundred-Year History of Beautiful Women: From the Days of Geisha to Those of Pretty Maidens). Tokyo: Shinchōsha.

———. 2002. *Pantsu ga mieru! Shūchishin no gendaishi* (I Can See Your Underpants! A Modern History of Shame and Embarrassment). Tokyo: Asahi Shinbunsha.

Ishida, Hiroshi. 1993. *Social Mobility in Contemporary Japan.* London: Macmillan Press.

Ishii, Noriko. 2010. "The role of church networks in international exchange: Kobe College graduates as students in the United States, 1887–1939." *Ōtsuma joshi daigaku hikō bunka gakubu kiyō* (Otsuma Journal of Comparative Culture), no. 11: 12–29.

Ishikari Jirō. 2005 [1932]. "Abakareta hyakkaten" (Department stores exposed). In *Modan toshi bunka*, vol. 8: *Depāto* (Modern Urban Culture, vol. 8: The Department Store), edited by Wada Atsuhiko, pp. 347–443. Tokyo: Yumani shobō.

Isshiki Yoshiko. 1953. *Ai no hito Kawai Michiko Sensei* (Beloved Teacher, Kawai Michiko). Tokyo: Shokugensha.

Itō Ruri. 2006. "1920–1930 nendai Okinawa ni okeru 'modan gāru' to iu toi: Shoku-minchiteki kindai to josei no mobiriti o megutte" (A question about the "modern girl" in Okinawa in the 1920s and 1930s: On colonial modernity and women's mobility). *Jendā kenkyū* (Journal of Gender Studies) 9: 1–18.

———. 2008. "The 'modern girl' question in the periphery of empire: Colonial modernity and mobility among Okinawan women in the 1920s and 1930s." In *The Modern Girl: Consumption, Modernity, and Globalization*, edited by the Modern Girl Around the World Research Group, pp. 240–262. Durham, NC: Duke University Press.

Itō Ruri, Sakamoto Hiroko, and Tani Barlow, eds. 2010. *Modan gāru to shokuminchiteki kindai—higashiajia ni okeru teikoku shihon jendā* (The Modern Girl and Colonial Modernity: Empire, Capital, and Gender in East Asia). Tokyo: Iwanami shoten.

Iwata Jack. 1953. "Ninki no mato, Misu Nippon" (Target of popularity, Miss Japan). Kyodo News Service. *Rafu shimpo*, July 13.

Japan Football Association. 2011. "Senshu nendobetsu tōrokusū" (Registered players' numbers by year). Online at http://www.jfa.or.jp/jfa/databox/player/year/index .html [accessed November 28, 2011].

Japan Times. 2009. "Elevator decree takes effect: Fatal '06 accident forces new buildings to use lifts with auxiliary brakes." *Japan Times*, September 29. Online at http:// search.japantimes.co.jp/cgi-bin/nn20090929a4.html [accessed May 5, 2010].

———. 2011. "Only SDF nuke responders to stay on in zone." *Japan Times*, August 18. Online at http://www.japantimes.co.jp/text/nn20110818b1.html [accessed November 27, 2011].

Jiyū kokuminsha. 2008. "*Yūkyan shingo ryūkōgo tashō happyō*." (Announcement of the U-CAN top new words and slang for 2008). Online at http://singo.jiyu.co.jp/ [accessed February 3, 2011].

———. 2011. "*Yūkyan shingo ryūkōgo tashō happyō*." (Announcement of the U-CAN top new words and slang for 2011). Online at http://singo.jiyu.co.jp/ [accessed December 27, 2011].

Johnston, Linda L. 2005. "'Contributing to the most promising peaceful revolution in our time': The American women's scholarship for Japanese women, 1893–1941." In *Women and Philanthropy in Education*, edited by Andrea Walton, pp. 298–319. Bloomington: Indiana University Press.

Kaminishikawara. 2009. "'Cute ambassadors' roam globe to promote Japan's pop culture." *Japan Times*, June 17. Online at http://www.japantimes.co.jp/text/nn20090617f1.html [accessed November 15, 2011].

Kanagawa kenritsu kindai bijutsukan, ed. 2007. *Jidai to bijutsu no tamentai: Kindai no seiritsu ni hikari o atete* (Multiple Facets of Art and the Times: Shedding Light on the Formation of Modernity). Kamakura: Kanagawa kenritsu kindai bijutsukan.

Kasuya, Yoshi. 1974. "A foreign language to me." In *Wellesley After-Images: Reflections on Their College Years by Forty-Five Alumnae*, edited by Betsy Ancker-Johnson, pp. 69–70.

Katō Hisashi. 1997. "*Kosei*" o tabanete katsu: Hitori no shūdan (Compound "Individuality" and Win: The Group of Individuals). Tokyo: Kōdansha.

Kawabata Yasunari. 2000. *Onna de aru koto* (Being a Woman). Tokyo: Shinchōsha.

Kawai, Michi. 1934. *Japanese Women Speak*. Boston: Central Committee on the United Study of Foreign Missions.

———. 1939. *My Lantern*. Tokyo: Kyo Bun Kwan.

Kawamoto Shizuko. 2001. "Tsurumi Kazuko." In *Tsuda Umeko no musumetachi* (Umeko Tsuda's Daughters), edited by Kawamoto Shizuko, Kameda Kinuko, and Takakuwa Yoshiko. Tokyo: Domesu shuppan.

Kawauchi Kazuko. 2004. "Kawauchi Kazuko kaisōroku" (Kawauchi Kazuko memoir). In *Pan Am kaisōroku* (Pan Am Memoirs), p. 74. Tokyo: Pan American Alumni Association.

Kelsky, Karen. 2001. *Women on the Verge: Japanese Women, Western Dreams*. Durham, NC: Duke University Press.

Kijima Arisa. 2008. *Goshimei! Koto no basu gaido* (Number One! Bus Guide to the Old Capital). Tokyo: Media Factory.

Kim Jinsong. 2005. *Sōru ni dansu hōru o: 1930 nendai Chōsen no bunka* (A Dance Hall for Seoul: The Culture of Colonial Korea in the 1930s). Tokyo: Hōsei Daigaku shuppan kyoku.

King-O'Riain, Rebecca Chiyoko. 2006. *Pure Beauty: Judging Race in Japanese American Beauty Pageants*. Minneapolis: University of Minnesota Press.

Kinmonth, Earl. 1981. *The Self-Made Man in Meiji Japanese Thought: From Samurai to Salaryman*. Berkeley: University of California Press.

Kinsella, Sharon. 1995. "Cuties in Japan." In *Women, Media and Consumption in Japan*, edited by Lisa Skov and Brian Moeran, pp. 220–254. Honolulu: University of Hawai'i Press.

Kiriyama Hideki. 1998. *"Motomu 'jikosekinin, jihassei, jiyū na hassō' no jinzai"* (Seeking people with "a sense of individual responsibility, spontaneity, and freedom of thought"). *Purejidento (President)* 36, no. 6: 94–99.

Kitazawa Shūichi. 1925. "Shoppu gāru" (Shop girl). *Kaizō* 7, no. 4: 172–178.

Kitazawa Rakuten. 1925. Untitled cover of *Jiji manga* (Manga Times), no. 234, October.

Klein, Christina. 2003. *Cold War Orientalism: Asia in the Middlebrow Imagination, 1945–1961*. Berkeley: University of California Press.

Kōdansha. 1998. *Shūkan Yearbook—Nichiroku 20 seiki 1929* (Weekly Yearbook: Journal of the Twentieth Century 1929). Tokyo: Kōdansha.

Komatsu Eriko. 1992. *Tōkyō erebētā gāru* (Tokyo Elevator Girl). Tokyo: Kōdansha.

Kon Wajirō. 2001 [1929]. *Shinpan dai-Tōkyō annai* (New Guide to Greater Tokyo) Vol. 1. Tokyo: Chikuma gakugei bunko.

Kon Wajirō and Yoshida Kenkichi, eds. 1931. *Kōgengaku saishu: Moderunorojio* (Modernology Collection). Tokyo: Kensetsusha.

Kondo, Dorinne. 1990. *Crafting Selves: Power, Gender, and Discourses of Identity in a Japanese Workplace*. Chicago: University of Chicago Press.

Kovner, Sarah. 2009. "Base cultures: Sex workers and servicemen in occupied Japan." *Journal of Asian Studies* 68, no. 3 (August): 777–804.

Koyama, Shizuko. 1994. "The 'good wife and wise mother' ideology in post–World War I Japan." *U.S-Japan Women's Journal English Supplement*, no. 7: 31–52.

Kristof, Nicholas. 1995. "Japan's feminine falsetto falls right out of favor." *New York Times*, December 13.

Kubota Satoshi and Tanimura Masaki, directors. 2007. *Tōkyō tawā—okan to boku to, tokidoki, oton* (Tokyo Tower: Me, Mom, and Sometimes Dad). Fuji TV. January 8– March 19.

Kuno, Akiko. 1993. *Unexpected Destinations: The Poignant Story of Japan's First Vassar Graduate*. Translated by Kristen McIvor. Tokyo: Kodansha International.

Kurosaki Sogō memoriaru. 2001. *Kurosaki Sogō memoriaru 1979–2000* (Kurosaki Sogō memorial). Online at http://isisis.cocolog-nifty.com/i/ [accessed May 4, 2010].

Kurotani, Sawa. 2005. *Home Away from Home: Japanese Corporate Wives in the United States*. Durham, NC: Duke University Press.

Kutsuwada Takafumi. 1993. "Kawabuchi Saburo: 'Soryūshi' hissha kara Mr. J-riigu e no ōenka" (Kawabuchi Saburo: A cheer song for Mr. J-League from the writer of "Elementary Particles"). *AERA* 18 (May): 57–61.

Laffin, Christina. 2007. "Travel as sacrifice: Abutsu's poetic journey in *Diary of the Sixteenth Night*." *Review of Japanese Society and Culture* 19: 71–86.

Lancaster, Bill. 1995. *The Department Store: A Social History*. London: Leicester University Press.

Latour, Bruno. 1993. *We Have Never Been Modern*. Cambridge, MA: Harvard University Press.

Leach, William. 1984. "Transformations in a culture of consumption: Women and department stores, 1890–1925." *Journal of American History* 71, no. 2 (Sept.): 319–342.

Lee, Leo Ou-fan. 1999. *Shanghai Modern: The Flowering of a New Urban Culture in China*. Cambridge, MA: Harvard University Press.

Leighton, Tony. "Nadeshiko know the score: Slay the giant and get a watch." *The Independent*, July 17.

Lembke, Bud. 1953. "Australian Beauty to Become 20." *Long Beach Independent Press-Telegram*, July 10.

Levy, Indra. 2010. *The Westernesque Femme Fatale, Translation, and Vernacular Style in Modern Japanese Literature*. New York: Columbia University Press.

Life (Asia Edition). 1967. "Newest stewardess fad: A Japanese in every jet." *Life* (Asia Edition), May 1, pp. 42–46.

Long Beach Independent Press-Telegram. 1953a. "Pick judges for pageant of beauties." *Long Beach Independent Press-Telegram*, July 7.

———. 1953b. "Far East pals." *Long Beach Independent Press-Telegram*, July 12.

———. 1953c. "Winner gets title of 'Miss Universe.'" *Long Beach Independent Press-Telegram*, July 17.

Love and Lady. 2010. *Erebētā gāru kōnā* (Elevator Girl Corner). Online at http://www .san-yu.net/osaka_landl/corner_intro/ci_34.html [accessed April 4, 2010].

Lowry, Dave. 2006. *In the Dojo: A Guide to the Ritual and Etiquette of the Japanese Martial Arts*. Boston: Weatherhill.

Mackie, Vera. 2003. *Feminism in Modern Japan: Citizenship, Embodiment and Sexuality*. Cambridge, UK: Cambridge University Press.

———. 2009. "The taxonomic gaze: Looking at whiteness from East to West." *ACRAWSA e-journal* 5, no. 1: 1–16.

———. 2010a. "Sōshukoku no manazashi: Shikaku bunka ni mirareru modan gāru" (The metropolitan gaze: The modern girl in visual culture). In *Modan gāru to shokuminchiteki kindai: Higashi Ajia ni okeru teikoku, shihon, jendā* (The Modern Girl and Colonial Modernity: Empire, Capital and Gender in East Asia), edited by Itō Ruri, Tani E. Barlow, and Sakamoto Hiroko, pp. 91–116. Translated by Suganuma Katsuhiko. Tokyo: Iwanami.

———. 2010b. "Modernism and colonial modernity in early twentieth century Japan." In *The Oxford Handbook of Modernisms*, edited by Peter Brooker, Andrzej Gasiorek, Deborah Longworth, and Andrew Thacker, pp. 996–1011. Oxford, UK: Oxford University Press.

———. 2012. "The modern girl: Icon of modernity." In *Deco Japan, Shaping Art and Culture, 1920–1943*, edited by Kendall H. Brown. Washington, DC: Art Services International, pp. 53–57.

Maeda Hajime. 1929. *Shokugyō fujin monogatari* (Story of Workingwomen). Tokyo: Tōyō keizai shuppanbu.

Mainichi Shinbun. 1990. "Shiroki kōgyō ga joshi sakkaabu" (Shiroki Corporation forms women's soccer club). *Mainichi Shinbun*, January 19.

Masaki Tomohiko. 1992. *Basu no shashō no jidai* (Age of the Bus Girls). Tokyo: Gendai shokan.

Massey, Doreen. 1994. *Space, Place and Gender*. London: Polity Press.

Matsuda, Hiroko. 2006. "Colonial modernity across the border: Yaeyama, the Ryūkyū Islands and colonial Taiwan." Ph.D. dissertation, Australian National University.

Matsuda Shinzō. 2005 [1931]. "Depātomento sutoa" (Department stores). In *Korekushon: Modan toshi bunka*, vol. 8: *Depāto* (Collection: Modern Urban Culture, vol. 8: Department Stores), edited by Wada Atsuhiko, pp. 1–226. Tokyo: Yumani shobō.

Matsuoka Jōji, director. 2007. *Tōkyō tawā—okan to boku to, tokidoki, oton* (Tokyo Tower: Mum, Me and Sometimes Dad). Shōchiku Company Ltd.

Matsuoka, Yoko. 1952. *Daughter of the Pacific*. New York: Harper & Brothers.

Matsuoka Yuzuru. 1923, 1925, and 1926. *Hōjō o mamoru hitobito—jō, chū, ge* (People who Faithfully Follow the Teachings of the Buddha). Vols. 1, 2, and 3. Tokyo: Daiichi shobō.

Matsuzakaya Nanajū Nenshi Henshū Iinkai. 1981. *Matsuzakaya nanajū nenshi*. (Matsuzakaya Seventy-Year History). Nagoya: Matsuzakaya.

McBride, Theresa. 1978. "A woman's world: Department stores and the evolution of women's employment, 1870–1920." *French Historical Studies* 10, no. 4: 664–683.

McClain, Yoko M. 1981. *Handbook of Modern Japanese Grammar*. Tokyo: Hokuseido Press.

———. 1989. *Amerika no jōshiki, Nihon no jōshiki* (American Common Sense, Japanese Common Sense). Tokyo: Yomiuri Shinbunsha.

———. 1995. *Magomusume kara mita Natsume Sōseki* (Natsume Sōseki: A Granddaughter's View). Tokyo: Shinchōsha.

McVeigh, Brian J. 2000. *Wearing Ideology: State, Schooling and Self-presentation in Japan*. Oxford, UK: Berg.

Mehl, Margaret. 2005. "Dancing at the Rokumeikan: A new role for women?" In *Japanese Women: Emerging from Subservience, 1868–1945*, edited by Hiroko Tomida and Gordon Daniels, pp. 157–77. Folkestone, Kent: Global Oriental.

Member of the Occupation Force. 1946. "Jap dancehalls expensive for occupation troops." *The Mercury*, September 10, p. 3.

Menzies, Jackie, ed. 1998. *Modern Boy Modern Girl: Modernity in Japanese Art 1910–1935*. Sydney: Art Gallery of New South Wales.

Miller, Laura. 1989. "The Japanese language and honorific speech: Is there a Nihongo without keigo?" *Penn Review of Linguistics*, no. 13: 8–46.

———. 1998. "Bad girls: Representations of unsuitable, unfit, and unsatisfactory women in magazines." *U.S.-Japan Women's Journal English Supplement*, no. 15: 31–51.

———. 2004. "You are doing burikko! Censoring/scrutinizing artificers of cute femininity in Japanese." In *Japanese Language, Gender, and Ideology: Cultural Models and Real People*, edited by Shigeko Okamoto and Janet Shibamoto Smith, pp. 146–165. New York: Oxford University Press.

———. 2005. "Bad girl photography." In *Bad Girls of Japan*, edited by Laura Miller and Jan Bardsley, pp. 127–141. New York: Palgrave Macmillan.

———. 2006. *Beauty Up: Exploring Contemporary Japanese Body Aesthetics*. Berkeley: University of California Press.

———. 2010. "Japan's Zoomorphic Urge." *ASIA Network Exchange: A Journal for Asian Studies in the Liberal Arts* 18, no. 1 (Spring): 69–82.

———. 2011a. "Behavior that offends: Comics and other images of incivility." In *Manners and Mischief: Gender, Power, and Etiquette in Japan*, edited by Jan Bardsley and Laura Miller, pp. 219–250. Berkeley: University of California Press.

———. 2011b. "Cute masquerade and the pimping of Japan." *International Journal of Japanese Sociology* 20, no. 1: 18–29.

Miller, Laura, and Jan Bardsley, eds. 2005. *Bad Girls of Japan*. New York: Palgrave Macmillan.

Miller, Laura L. 1998. "Feminism and the exclusion of Army women from combat." *Gender Issues*, no. 16: 3–36.

Mills, Mary Beth. 2001. "Auditioning for the chorus line: Gender, rural youth, and the consumption of modernity in Thailand." In *Gendered Modernities: Ethnographic Perspectives*, edited by Dorothy Hodgson, pp. 27–52. New York: Palgrave Macmillan.

Minami Hiroshi. 1986. "Sōsetsu" (General explanation). In *Kindai shomin seikatsu shi* (A History of Modern Common Peoples' Daily Life), vol. 9: *Ren'ai, kekkon, katei* (Romantic Love, Marriage, Family), edited by Minami Hiroshi, Barbara Hamill Sato, and Ueda Yasuo, pp. 538–542. Tokyo: San'ichi shobō.

Mineo Hisao. 1998. *Jieikan wa kataru, sono hōfu to kunō* (Self-Defense Forces Personnel Tell Their Ambitions and Distress). Tokyo: Bunkyō shuppan.

Mini Moni, artist. 2001a. "*Mini moni. Basu gaido*" (Mini moni bus guide). Music Video. Tokyo: Zetima.

———. 2001b. "*Mini moni. Basu gaido*" (Mini moni bus guide). Song produced and lyrics by Tsunku. Arranged by Konishi Takao. Tokyo: Zetima.

Ministry of Health, Labor, and Welfare (Kōsei Rōdō Shō). 1951. *Shokugyō betsu chingin chōsa kekka hōkoku* (Occupational wage survey). October. Tokyo: Labor Statistics and Research Division, Ministerial Secretariat of Labor Ministry, vol. 1: Table 13.

Mishima, Sumie Seo. 1941. *My Narrow Isle: The Story of a Modern Japanese Woman.* New York: John Day Company.

———. 1953. *The Broader Way: A Woman's Life in New Japan.* New York: John Day Company.

Mitsukoshi hyakkaten. 1927. *Mitsukoshi.* Tokyo: Mitsukoshi hyakkaten.

Mizutani Fūka. 2009. "Ōkami no yūutsu" (Melancholy of the wolf). *Tsubomi,* vol. 2: *Manga Taimu* (Manga Time) *KR Komikkusu,* 219–242. Tokyo: Hōbunsha.

Modern Girl Around the World Research Group. 2005. "The Modern Girl around the World: A research agenda and preliminary findings." *Gender and History* 17, no. 2: 245–294.

———. 2008a. "The Modern Girl as heuristic device: Collaboration, connective comparison, multidirectional citation." In *The Modern Girl Around the World: Consumption, Modernity and Globalization,* by the Modern Girl Around the World Research Group, pp. 1–24. Durham, NC: Duke University Press.

———. 2008b. *The Modern Girl Around the World: Consumption, Modernity, and Globalization.* Durham, NC: Duke University Press.

Momoya-Kawasaki City Museum Collection. 2006. "History of Showa reflected on the Japanese dinner table," "TV ads 1954–1968." Online at http://momoya-kcm-en .blogspot.com/2008/01/momoya-tv-ads054-1968-bus-conductor.html [accessed November 16, 2011].

Moorghen, Jean-Marc. 2004. "Speed Tribes revisited: An hour with Karl Taro Greenfeld." Figure 8 Productions, November 19. Online at http://www.figure8productions .com/speedtribesarticle.html [accessed March 3, 2010].

Morning Bulletin. 1929. "Rules at Japanese dances." *Morning Bulletin,* June 18, p. 8.

Morris, Kathleen. 1995. "How Japan scored." *Financial World* 164: 82–85.

Moseley, Rachel. 2002. *Growing up with Audrey Hepburn: Text, Audience, Resonance.* Manchester, UK: Manchester University Press.

Murakami Nobuko. 1983. *Taishōki no shokugyō fujin* (Professional Working Women in the Taishō Period). Tokyo: Domesu shuppan.

Nagahara Kazuko and Yoneda Sayoko. 1986. *Onna no Shōwa-shi* (Women's History of Shōwa Japan). Tokyo: Yuhikaku.

Nagai Yoshikazu. 2004. "Modan toshi no dansu hōru" (Dancehalls in the modern city). In *Korekushon modan toshi bunka* (The Modern City Culture Anthology), vol. 4: *Dansu hōru* (Dancehalls), edited by Nagai Yoshikazu, pp. 659–679. Tokyo: Yumani shobō.

Nagasaki Shinbun. 1946. "Dansā 200-mei daiboshū" (Seeking 200 dancers). *Nagasaki Shinbun,* January 1.

Nagy, Margit. 1991. "Middle-class working women during the interwar years." In *Recreating Japanese Women, 1600–1945*, edited by Gail Lee Bernstein, pp. 199–216. Berkeley: University of California Press.

Nakagawa, Keiichirō, and Henry Rosovsky. 1963. "The case of the dying kimono: The influence of changing fashions on the development of the Japanese woolen industry." *Business History Review* 37, no. 1–2: 59–80.

Nakagawa Kōichi. 1986. *Basu no bunkashi* (The Cultural History of Buses). Tokyo: Chikuma shobō.

Nakamoto Takako. 1973. *Waga sei wa kunō ni yakarete: Waga wakaki hi no ikigai* (My Life Seared with Pain: An Account of My Life in My Younger Days). Tokyo: Shiraishi shoten.

Nakamura Chitose. 2008. *Nakamura Chitose dijitaru shashinshū mizugi basu gaido hen* (Nakamura Chitose's Digital Photobook: Bus Guide in a Swimsuit Volume). Tokyo: Kabushiki kaisha kurafuko.

Nakayama Chiyo. 1987. *Nihon fujin yōsōshi* (History of Japanese Women's Western Clothing). Tokyo: Yoshikawa kobunkan.

Nakayama Michiko. 1998. "Ronten toshite no 'josei to guntai'" ('Women and military' as point of discussion). In *Sei, bōryoku, nēshon* (Sex, Violence, Nation), edited by Ehara Yumiko, pp. 31–60. Tokyo: Keiso shobō.

Nakayama Yoshigorō. 1995 [1931]. *Modango manga jiten* (Manga Dictionary of Modern Language). *Kindai yōgo no jiten shūsei* 19 (Series of Dictionaries of Modern Terminology. vol. 19). Tokyo: Ōzorasha.

Napier, Susan J. 2005. *Anime from Akira to Howl's Moving Castle*. New York: Palgrave Macmillan.

Naruse Mikio, director. 1941. *Hideko no shashō-san* (Hideko the Bus Conductress). Nano Eiga.

———, director. 1952. *Inazuma* (Lightning). Daiei Motion Picture Company.

Natsume Sōseki. 1956. *Sanshirō. Natsume Sōseki zenshū* (Collected Works of Natsume Sōseki). Vol. 7. Tokyo: Iwanami shoten.

New York Times. 1902. "Boston has elevator girls. Employed in a number of fashionable stores and in philanthropic institutions." *New York Times*, November 17.

Newell, Susan. 1997. "Women primary school teachers and the state." In *Society and the State in Interwar Japan*, edited by Elise K. Tipton, pp. 17–41. London: Routledge.

Newsweek. 1994. "In a league of its own." *Newsweek*, June 13.

Nihon Basu Kyōkai. 2008. *Basu jigyō hayakunenshi: Dai niji sekai taisengo no Nihon basu jigyō* (One Hundred Years of the Japanese Bus Industry: Business after World War II). Tokyo: Nihon Basu Kyōkai.

Nihon Erebētā Kyōkai. 2007. "Myūjiamu" (Museum). Nihon Erebētā Kyōkai (Japanese Elevator Association). Online at http://www.n-elekyo.or.jp/square/elevator_08.html [accessed April 10, 2010].

Nihon Keizai Shinbun. 1990. "Joshi sakkaa chiimu sōsetsu e" (Founding a women's soccer team). *Nihon Keizai Shinbun*, January 19.

Nippon Times. 1953a. "Miss Japan." *Nippon Times*, July 5.

———. 1953b. "Miss Japan well-liked in Miss Universe show." Kyodo-United Press. *Nippon Times*, July 18.

———. 1953c. "Miss France wins crown; Miss Japan places third." *Nippon Times*, July 19.

———. 1953d. "Miss Ito to play in movie: Will get ¥54,000 weekly." *Nippon Times*, July 21.

———. 1953e. "Untitled." International News Service. *Nippon Times*, July 21.

Nishi Nippon Shinbun. 2009. "Nihon hatsu josei basu gaido Beppu kankō shoki tsukaeru Murakami Ayame-san shikyo 98 sai" (Japan's first bus guide, Murakami Ayame, who supported the development of Beppu tourism, dies at age 98). *Nishi Nippon Shinbun*, April 1. Online at http://www.nishinippon.co.jp/nnp/item/86695 [accessed April 1, 2009].

Nishijima Dai, scriptwriter. 1958. *Tokyo no basu gāru* (Tokyo Bus Girl). Tokyo: Nikkatsu Corporation.

Nishitani Hiroshi, director. 2006. *Tōkyō tawā—okan to boku to, tokidoki, oton* (Tokyo Tower: Me, Mom, and Sometimes Dad). Fuji TV, November 18.

Nogan Yasuhiro. 2002. "Jibun no michi wa, jibun de hiraku" (Opening my own path myself). *Securitarian*, no. 2: 37–39.

Nomura, Gail, and Shirley Hune. 2003. *Asian/Pacific Islander American Women: A Historical Anthology*. New York: New York University Press.

Ogasawara, Yuko. 1998. *Office Ladies and Salaried Men: Power, Gender, and Work in Japanese Companies*. Berkeley: University of California Press.

Ogawa Takeshi. 1930. "Erebētā gāru no okashimi" (Elevator girl humor). *Jiji manga* (Manga Times), no. 468, October 5, p. 5.

———. 2008 [1935]. "Randebū no annai, abekku" (A Guide to Rendevous, Avec). In *Kindai shomin seikatsu shi* (A History of Modern Common People's Daily Life), vol. 10: *Kyōraku, sei* (Pleasure, Sex), edited by Minami Hiroshi, pp. 381–439. Tokyo: San'ichi shobō.

Ohara, Yumiko. 2004. "Prosody and gender in workplace interaction: Exploring constraints and resources in the use of Japanese." In *Japanese Language, Gender, and Ideology: Cultural Models and Real People*, edited by Shigeko Okamoto and Janet Shibamoto Smith, pp. 222–239. New York: Oxford University Press.

Ohnuki-Tierney, Emiko. 1984. *Illness and Culture in Contemporary Japan: An Anthropological View*. Cambridge, UK: Cambridge University Press.

Okada Saburō. 1931. "Rabu-hantā nijūyoji" (Twenty-four hour love hunter). *Chūō kōron* (November): 254–256.

Omori Kyoko. 2003. "Detecting Japanese Vernacular Modernism: *Shinseinen* Magazine and the Development of the *Tantei Shōsetsu* Genre, 1920–1931." Ph.D. dissertation, Ohio State University.

Onoda Somu. 2004 [1930]. "Ginzatsū" (Ginza connoisseur). In *Korekushon: Modan toshi bunka, dai 1 kan, Ginza no modanizumu* (Collection: Modern Urban Culture, vol. 1: Ginza Modernism), edited by Wada Hirofumi, pp. 1–168. Tokyo: Yumani shobō.

Ōtsuka, Ryūichi. 2011. "Nadeshiko: eigo ni naru ka mo shirenai nihongo" (Nadeshiko: Japanese that might become English). *Yomiuri Online*, July 19. Online at http://www

.yomiuri.co.jp/job/biz/columnbuzz/20110719-OYT8T00373.htm [accessed December 30, 2011].

Owen, Tony, and Bill Robert, producers. 1958–1966. *The Donna Reed Show*. Culver City, CA: Screen Gems.

Ozu Yasujirō, director. 1953. *Tokyo monogatari* (Tokyo Story). Tokyo: Shōchiku Company Ltd.

Pamonag, Febe D. 2010. "Turn-of-the-century cross-cultural collaborations for Japanese women's higher education." *U.S.-Japan Women's Journal*, no. 37: 33–56.

Parreñas, Rhaçel Salazar. 1998. "'White trash' meets the 'little brown monkeys': The taxi dance hall as a site of interracial and gender alliances between white working class women and Filipino immigrant men and women in the 1920s and 1930s." *Amerasia* 24, no. 2: 115–134.

Percival, Jack. 1945. "Japanese 'ladies' take up Americans." *Sydney Morning Herald*, December 22, p. 9.

Pevney, Joseph, director. 1954. *Yankee Pasha*. Los Angeles: Universal-International.

Pincus, Leslie. 2002. "A salon for the soul: Nakai Masakazu and the Hiroshima culture movement." *positions: east asia cultures critique* 10, no. 1: 173–194.

Point True. 1928. "The social status of Japanese women of today." *Brisbane Courier*, December 29, p. 19.

Prang, Margaret. 1995. *A Heart at Leisure from Itself: Caroline Macdonald of Japan*. Vancouver: University of British Columbia Press.

Pratt, Mary Louise. 1991. "Arts of the contact zone." *Profession*, no. 91: 33–40.

Price, Lorna, and Letitia O'Connor, eds. 2001. *Taishō Chic: Japanese Modernity, Nostalgia and Deco*. Honolulu: Academy of Fine Arts.

Queenslander. 1933. "The new woman in Japan." *Queenslander*, June 29, p. 35.

Rafu shimpo. 1953a. "Gorgeous girls from all over world vie for Miss Universe title." *Rafu shimpo*, July 10.

———. 1953b. "Miss Japan places third in Miss Universe beauty pageant." Associated Press. *Rafu shimpo*, July 18.

———. 1953c. "Miss Nippon hulas in 3-D short." *Rafu shimpo*, August 1.

———. 1953d. "Fujiwara 'Butterfly' troupe here for Greek theatre run." *Rafu shimpo*, August 4.

———. 1959. "Ex-Miss Universe runner-up tells Akiko crown not means to end." *Rafu shimpo*, July 27.

Raz, Aviad E. 1999. *Riding the Black Ship: Japan and Tokyo Disneyland*. Cambridge, MA: Harvard University Press.

Reischauer, Haru Matsukata. 1986. *Samurai and Silk: A Japanese and American Heritage*. Cambridge, MA: Harvard University Press.

Resnik, Bert. 1953a. "No stockings on foreign beauties." *Long Beach Independent Press Telegram*, July 11.

———. 1953b. "Miss France likes all except French dressing." *Long Beach Independent Press Telegram*, July 12.

Robbins, Bruce. 1998. "Introduction, part I: Actually existing cosmopolitanism." In

Cosmopolitics: Thinking and Feeling Beyond the Nation, edited by Bruce Robbins and Pheng Cheah, pp. 1–19. Durham, NC: Duke University Press.

Roberts, Glenda. 1994. *Staying on the Line: Blue-Collar Women in Contemporary Japan*. Honolulu: University of Hawai'i Press.

Robertson, Jennifer. 1998. *Takarazuka: Sexual Politics and Popular Culture in Modern Japan*. Berkeley: University of California Press.

——. 1999. "Dying to tell: Sexuality and suicide in Imperial Japan." *Signs: Journal of Women in Culture and Society* 25, no. 1: 1–35.

——. 2001. "Japan's first cyborg? Miss Nippon, eugenics and wartime technologies of beauty, body and blood." *Body & Society* 7, no.1: 1–34.

Rose, Barbara. 1992. *Tsuda Umeko and Women's Education in Japan*. New Haven, CT: Yale University Press.

Rowley, G. G. 2002. "Prostitutes Against the Prostitution Act of 1956." *U.S.-Japan Women's Journal English Supplement* no. 23: 39–56.

Ruoff, Kenneth James. 2001. *The People's Emperor: Democracy and the Japanese Monarchy, 1945–1995*. Cambridge, MA: Harvard University Asia Center.

Russell, Catherine. 2009. "From women's writing to women's films in 1950s Japan: Hayashi Fumiko and Naruse Mikio." *Asian Journal of Communication* 11, no. 2: 101–120.

Russo, Peter Vasquez. 1938a. "Japan tightens her belt at home." *The Advertiser*, August 29, p. 18.

——. 1938b. "Japan mobilises her resources." *The Mercury*, August 31, p. 6.

Saeki, Chizuru. 2005. "The Perry Centennial Celebration: A case study in U.S.-Japanese cultural diplomacy." *International Social Science Review* 80, no. 3/4: 137–150.

Saga Fusako. March 1924. "Nihon fujin no yōso ni tsuite" (About Japanese women's clothing). *Bunka seikatsu no kiso* (The Foundations of Cultural Life) 4, no. 3: 180–183.

Saigan Ryōhei, 1974–2010. *Always: San-chōme no yūhi* (Always: Sunset on Third Street). Tokyo: Shōgakukan.

Saisho Fumi. 1980. *Kenkyusha's Modern Colloquial English Dictionary, English-Japanese, Japanese-English*. Tokyo: Kenkyusha.

Sand, Jordan. 2003. *House and Home in Modern Japan: Architecture, Domestic Space, and Bourgeois Culture, 1880–1930*. Cambridge, MA: Harvard University Asia Center.

Sapio. 1996. "Bijin Jieikan 9-nin no arasoi to heiwa, watashi no baai" (War and peace for nine Jieikan beauties, in my case). *Sapio*, pp. 128–131.

Sasson-Levy, Orna. 2003. "Frauen als Grenzgängerinnen im israelischen Militär: Identitätsstrategien und -praktiken weiblicher Soldaten in 'männlichen' Rollen" (Women in the Israeli military as pioneers: Identity strategies and practices of female soldiers in 'male' roles). In *Gender und Militär: Internationale Erfahrungen mit Frauen und Männern in Streitkräften* (Gender and Military: International Experiences of Women and Men in the Armed Forces), edited by Christine Eifler and Ruth Seifert, pp. 74–100. Königstein, Germany: Ulrike Helmer Verlag and Heinrich Böll Stiftung.

Sato, Barbara Hamill. 1993. "The moga sensation: Perceptions of the modan gāru in Japanese intellectual circles during the 1920s." *Gender and History* 5, no. 3: 363–381.

———. 2003. *The New Japanese Woman: Modernity, Media, and Women in Interwar Japan*. Durham, NC: Duke University Press.

Satō Fumika. 2000. "Jieitai ni okeru jendā—'Bōei hakusho' to Jieikan boshū posutā no hyōshō bunseki kara" (Gender in the Self-Defense Force: An analysis of the images in the 'Defense white paper' and service member recruitment posters). *Sociology Today*, no. 10: 60–71.

Satō Kumiko. 2004. "Sato Kumiko kaisōroku" (Satō Kumiko memoir). In *Pan Am kaisōroku* (Pan Am Memoirs), p. 102. Tokyo: Pan American Alumni Association.

Sawada Kazuhiko. 2001. "Nihon ni okeru hakkei-Roshia-jin no bunka-teki eikyō" (The cultural influence of White Russians in Japan). In *Ikyō ni ikiru—Rai-Nichi Roshia-jin no sokuseki* (Living in a foreign land: Traces of Russian residents in Japan), edited by Naganawa Mitsuo and Sawada Kazuhiko, pp. 31–46. Yokohama: Seibunsha.

Scholar. 2002. "Nyōbō ni suru nara 'tetsuwan bijo'!" (For a wife take a "cannonball beauty"!). *Scholar* (November): 40–50.

Securitarian. 2001. "PKO de katsuyaku suru josei" (The women who are active in PKO). *Securitarian*, no. 9: 41–45.

Seidensticker, Edward. 1983. *Low City, High City: Tokyo from Edo to the Earthquake*. New York: Knopf.

———. 1990. *Tokyo Rising: The City since the Great Earthquake*. New York: Knopf.

Sekizaki Yōko. 1995. "Onna datera no Bōdai ikkisei shimatsuki" (Reflective writing by female students of the class of the first year at the NDA). *Shinchō*, no. 45: 172–184.

Shibusawa, Naoko. 2006. *America's Geisha Ally: Reimagining the Japanese Enemy*. Cambridge, MA: Harvard University Press.

Shida Aiko and Yuda Yoriko. 1987. "Shufu no tomo" (Housewife's Friend). In *Fujin zasshi kara mita 1930 nendai* (Looking at the 1930s Through Women's Magazines), edited by Watashitachi no rekishi o tsuzuru kai. Tokyo: Dōjidaisha.

Shinmura Miki. 2009. *Hyakkaten gāru* (Department Store Girl). Tokyo: Media Factory.

Shiroki Corporation. 1998. *Shiroki Corporation Company Profile*. Yokohama: Shiroki Corporation.

Shirokiya. 1957. *Shirokiya sanbyaku nenshi* (300-Year History of Shirokiya). Tokyo: Shirokiya.

Shohara, Hide. 1954. *Introduction to Spoken Japanese*. Ann Arbor: University of Michigan Press.

Shūkan bunshun. 1993. "Tennō kōgō ryōheika wa 'Jieikan no seifuku' ga okirai" (His and her majesty the Emperor and the Empress dislike 'Self-Defense Force uniforms'). *Shūkan bunshun*, September 30, pp. 36–39.

Shūkan gendai. 1990. "Jieitai josei taiin hachi-nin" (Eight female service members of the Self-Defense Force). *Shūkan gendai*, November 24.

———. 1999. "Moto fujin Jieikan ga hea nūdo de kataru: Jieitai no sei" (A former female Self-Defense Force member tells it through hair nudes: Sex in the Self-Defense Force). *Shūkan gendai*, September 11, pp. 238–241.

Shūkan hōseki. 1995. "'95-nen kakukai chūmoku no josei—jitsuryoku no bijo, Kawaue Hitomi" ('95 women to pay attention to: The beauty with real strength, Kawaue Hitomi). *Shūkan hōseki*, February 23, pp. 223–225.

Shūkan josei. 1957. "Itō Kinuko wa doko e iku" (Where will Itō Kinuko go?). *Shūkan josei*, August 18.

Silverberg, Miriam. 1991a. "Constructing a new cultural history of Japan." *Boundary 2* 18, no. 3: 61–89.

———. 1991b. "The modern girl as militant." In *Recreating Japanese Women, 1600–1945*, edited by Gail Lee Bernstein, pp. 239–266. Berkeley: University of California Press.

———. 1998. "The café waitress serving modern Japan." In *Mirror of Modernity: Invented Traditions of Modern Japan*, edited by Stephen Vlastos, pp. 208–225. Berkeley: University of California Press.

———. 2007. *Erotic Grotesque Nonsense: The Mass Culture of Japanese Modern Times*. Berkeley: University of California Press.

———. 2008. "After the grand tour: The modern girl, the new woman, and the colonial maiden." In *The Modern Girl Around the World: Consumption, Modernity, and Globalization*, edited by the Modern Girl Around the World Research Group, pp. 354–361. Durham, NC: Duke University Press.

Special Correspondent. 1945. "Women in Japan. Cheaper than cattle. The taxi-dance racket." *The West Australian*, December 29, p. 11.

Stashower, Daniel. 2006. *The Beautiful Cigar Girl: Mary Rogers, Edgar Allan Poe, and the Invention of Murder*. New York: Penguin.

Sterling, Marvin. 2010. *Babylon East: Performance, Dancehall, Roots Reggae and Rastafari in Japan*: Durham, NC: Duke University Press.

Sterngold, James. 1994. "Japan Falls for Soccer, Leaving Baseball in Lurch." *New York Times*, June 6.

Stone, Jonathan, director. 1988. *Big Bird in Japan*. Children's Television Workshop. New York: Public Broadcasting Service.

Sunohara Masahisa, director. 1958. *Tokyo no basu gāru* (Tokyo Bus Girl). Tokyo: Nikkatsu Corporation.

Suzuki Makiko. 2004. "Suzuki Makiko kaisōroku" (Suzuki Makiko memoir). In *Pan Am kaisōroku* (Pan Am Memoirs), p. 110. Tokyo: Pan American Alumni Association.

Tabuchi, Hiroko. 2009 "Japan strives to balance growth and job stability." *New York Times*, September 14.

Tada Michio. 1931. "Dansā to zurōzu" (Dancers and drawers). Reprinted in *Korekushon modan toshi bunka* (The Modern City Culture Anthology), Vol. 4: *Dansu hōru* (Dancehalls), edited by Nagai Yoshikazu. Tokyo: Yumani shobō, 2004.

Tago Kazutani. March 1919. "Fujin honrai no mokuteki to fujin no shokugyō" (The purpose of women's nature and women's work). *Fujin kōron*, pp. 13–22.

Takahashi Fumiko. 1989. *Gaikokujin dansei to tsukiau hō* (How to Date a Foreign Man). Tokyo: Shufu to seikatsusha.

Takahashi Yoshio. 1994. *Sakkaa no shakaigaku* (The Sociology of Soccer). Tokyo: Nihon hōsō shuppan kyōkai.

Takakuwa Yoshiko. 2001. "Yamaguchi Michiko." In *Tsuda Umeko no musumetachi* (Daughters of Umeko Tsuda), edited by Kawamoto Shizuko, Kameda Kinuko, and Takakura Yoshiko, p. 82. Tokyo: Domesu shuppan.

Takashimaya hyakugojū nenshi henshū iinkai. 1982. *Takashimaya hyakugojū nenshi* (150-Year History of Takashimaya). Tokyo: Takashimaya.

Takeuchi Hiroshi. 1995. *Zainichi seiyō jinmei jiten* (Biographical Dictionary of Westerners in Japan). Tokyo: Nichigai Associates.

Tamanoi, Mariko. 2009. *Memory Maps: The State and Manchuria in Postwar Japan*. Honolulu: University of Hawaiʻi Press.

Tamari, Tomoko. 2006. "Rise of the department store and the aestheticization of everyday life in early 20th century Japan." *International Journal of Japanese Sociology*, no. 15: 99–118.

Tamura Naoya and Nogami Takeshi. 2008. *Moe yo! Rikuji gakkō* (It's moe! The SDF School). Tokyo: Ikarosu shuppan.

Tanaka Kenzaburō. 2011. *Hato Basu—Ofisharu book* (Official Book of Hato Bus). Tokyo: Futabasha.

Tanaka, Yuki. 2002. *Japan's Comfort Women: Sexual Slavery and Prostitution During World War II and the U.S. Occupation*. London: Routledge.

Tani Jōji [Hasegawa Kaitarō]. 1927. "*Modan Dekameron*" (Modern Decameron). *Shinseinen* (New Youth). In Tani Jōji. 1969 [1933] *Hitori sannin zenshū* (Three-in-one Anthology). Tokyo.

Tanizaki Jun'ichirō [1925]. *Chijin no ai* (A Fool's Love). Tokyo: Chūō kōronsha.

———. 1986. *Naomi*. Translated by Anthony Chambers. New York: Vintage International.

Taylor, Sandra C. 1984. *Advocate of Understanding: Sidney Gulick and the Search for Peace with Japan*. Kent, Ohio: Kent State University Press.

Times of India. 2011. "All-action Japan women earn Barcelona comparisons." *Times of India*, July 15. Online at http://timesofindia.indiatimes.com/sports/tournaments/Womens World-Cup-All-action-Japan-earn-Barcelona-comparisons/articleshow/9236007.cms [accessed July 26, 2011].

Tipton, Elise K. 2002. "Pink collar work: The café waitress in early twentieth century Japan." *Intersections: Gender, History and Culture in the Asian Context*, vol. 7. Online at http://intersections.anu.edu.au/issue7/tipton.html [accessed November 29, 2009].

———. 2005. "Sex in the city: Chastity vs. free love in interwar Japan." *Intersections: Gender, History and Culture in the Asian Context*, vol. 11. Online at http://intersections.anu.edu.au/issue11/tipton.html [accessed September 28, 2011].

———. 2007. "'Cruising Ginza': Seeking modernity in Tokyo During the 1920s and 1930s." *Literature and Aesthetics* 17, no. 1: 25–40.

———. 2009. "How to manage a household: Creating middle-class housewives in modern Japan." *Japanese Studies* 29, no. 1: 95–110.

———. 2012. "The department store: Producing modernity in interwar Japan." In *Rethinking Japanese Modernism*, edited by Roy Starrs, pp. 428–451. Leiden: Global Oriental.

Tipton, Elise K., and John Clark, eds. 2000. *Being Modern in Japan: Culture and Society from the 1910s to the 1930s*. Sydney: Fine Arts Press and Gordon and Breach International for the Australian Humanities Research Foundation.

Tōkai Nichi-Nichi Shinbun. 1990a. "Kenkasho no kigyōnai joshi sakkaa chiimu" (First prefectural corporate women's soccer team). *Tōkai Nichi-Nichi Shinbun*, January 19.

————. 1990b. "Kono hito hōmon. CBC rajio, gozen 11:30" (A visit with this person. CBC Radio, 11:30 a.m.). *Tōkai Hibi Shinbun*, February 12.

Tokita Shin'ya. 2008. "60 shūnen kinen EXPO mo kinjitsu kaisai!—Ripētā no taenai 'Hato basu' tsuā no miroku" (60th Anniversary Expo to be held soon! The incomparable charm of Hato Bus tours). *Journal My Com*, September. Online at http://jour nal.mycom.co.jp/articles/2008/09/20/hatobus/index.html [accessed January 2, 2012].

Tokubuchi Mariko. 2007. *Shinkansen gāru* (*Shinkansen* Girl). Tokyo: Media Factory.

Tōkyō shakaikyoku, ed. 2003. *Fujin jiritsu no michi* (The Road to Women's Independence). In the series *Kindai fujin mondai meicho senshū zokuhen* (Selected Masterpieces on Modern Women's Problems, Supplementary Volume), vol. 7. Tokyo: Nihon tosho sentā.

Tomytec. 2005. "Tetsudō musume" (Young ladies of the railway). Online at http://tetsudou -musume.net/ [accessed November 23, 2011].

————. 2008. "Basu musume." (Bus girls). Online at http://www.tomytec.co.jp/bus -musume/ [accessed January 21, 2012].

Tosaka Jun. 1983 [1936]. "Ken'etsuka no shisō to fūzoku" (The philosophy of censorship and the entertainment industry). *Gendai no esupuri* (The Contemporary Spirit) 188: 44–47.

Townsville Daily Bulletin. 1938. "Dance halls suppressed by Japanese police." *Townsville Daily Bulletin*, January 26, p. 11.

Tōyō keizai shinpōsha. 1936. *Hyakkaten tai chūko shōgyō mondai* (The Problem of Small and Medium-Sized Stores versus Department Stores). Tokyo: Tōyō keizai shinpōsha.

Trends in Japan. 2003. "Touring Tokyo: Bus tours offer unrivaled access to capital's sights." *Trends in Japan*. Online at http://web-japan.org/trends/lifestyle/lif030418.html [accessed November 15, 2011].

Tsuda Ume. 1910. "The past ten years." *Joshi Eigaku Juku: Kinengō* (Anniversary Issue of the Alumnae Report of the Joshi Eigaku Juku), November 13, pp. 1–4.

Tsuda Juku Daigaku. 1960. *Tsuda juku rokujūnenshi* (Sixty-Year History of Tsuda College). Tokyo: Chūō kōronsha.

————. 2003. *Tsuda juku hyakunenshi* (One Hundred-Year History of Tsuda College). Tokyo: Tsusuda Juku Daigaku.

Tsukamoto Hamako. 1997 [1930]. *Katei seikatsu no gōrika* (The Rationalization of Family Life). In *Kindai josei bunken shiryō sōsho 56* (A Collection of Modern Women's Research Materials 56), *Onna to seikatsu* (Women and Daily Life), vol. 8, edited by Nakajima Kuni. Tokyo: Ōzorasha.

Tsukuba Language Group. 1994. *Situational Functional Japanese*, Vol. 2: *Notes*. 2nd ed. Tokyo: Bonjinsha.

Tsurumi, E. Patricia. 1992. *Factory Girls: Women in the Thread Mills of Meiji Japan*. Princeton, NJ: Princeton University Press.

Uchida Michiko. 2000. "Meari H. Morisu shōgakkin: Nihon no josei ni Umeko no anaji kikai o" (Mary H. Morris's philanthropy: Contributing to Japanese women and to Umeko). In *Tsuda Umeko no sasaeta hitobito* (People Who Supported Umeko Tsuda). Tokyo: Tsuda Juku Daigaku.

Uenoda, Setsuko. 1930. *Japan and Jazz: Sketches and Essays on Japanese City Life*. Tokyo: The Taiheiyosha Press.

University of Michigan. 1843–1927. *General Register*. Ann Arbor: University of Michigan Board of Regents. 1837–2007. Proceedings of the Board of Regents.

uno! 1997. "Sentō shūdan 'Jieitai': Onna ga nozomu subete ga koko ni wa aru" (The battle organization 'Self-Defense Force': Everything women desire is here). *uno!* February 1, pp. 161–165.

Uno, Kathleen. 1993. "The death of 'good wife, wise mother'?" In *Postwar Japan as History*, edited by Andrew Gordon, pp. 293–322. Berkeley: University of California Press.

Uranaka, Taiga. 2001. "Tokyo's Hato Bus tours strive to recapture heyday." August 28. Online at http://www.japantimes.co.jp/text/nn20010828m2.html [accessed November 16, 2011].

Usui Yoshito. 1992. *Kureyon Shin-chan 14: Erebētā gāru to issho da zo* (Crayon Shin-chan 14: Hey, I'm with the elevator girl). Tokyo: Shin-Ei Animation Co.

Van Assche, Annie, ed. 2005. *Fashioning Kimono: Dress and Modernity in Early 20th Century Japan*. Milano: 5 Continents Editions.

Wada Hirofumi and Kan Satoko, eds. 2006. *Korekushun modan toshi bunka 23—Sekushuariti* (Modern Urban Culture Collection 23: Sexuality). Tokyo: Yumani shobō.

Wakeman, Frederic. 1996. *Policing Shanghai, 1927–1937*. Berkeley: University of California Press.

Wang Cheng. 2004. "Kindai Nihon in okeru 'shūyō' gainen no seiritsu" (The formation of the concept of 'self-cultivation' in modern Japan). *Nihon kenkyū*, no. 29: 117–146.

Watanabe, Kazuko. 1997. "Militarism, colonialism, and the trafficking of women: 'Comfort women' forced into sexual labor for Japanese soldiers." In *The Other Japan: Conflict, Compromise, and Resistance Since 1945*, edited by Joe Moore, pp. 305–319. Armonk, NY: M. E. Sharpe.

Watanabe Kieko. 1961. "Tokushū: Saijo no kekkon no jōken" (Special issue: Talented women's marriage conditions). *Madomoazeru* (December): 102–108.

Watanabe, Yuri. 1911. "E.C. & Japan: My Trip." *Earlhamite*, November 18. Online at http://www.earlham.edu/japanesestudies/earlham_history_japan/yuri_watanabe/my_trip.html [accessed June 4, 2009].

Watson, Elwood, and Darcy Martin. 2004. *"There She Is, Miss America": The Politics of Sex, Beauty, and Race in America's Most Famous Pageant*. New York: Palgrave Macmillan.

Watt, Lori. 2009. *When Empire Comes Home: Repatriation and Reintegration in Postwar Japan*. Cambridge, MA: Harvard University Asia Center.

Wellesley College. Wellesley College Archives. Wellesley, MA.

———. 1894."Fanny Bradeley Greene." Alumnae Biographical Files. Wellesley College Archives. Wellesley, MA.

———. n.d. "Foreign Students." Wellesley College Archives. Wellesley, MA.

The West Australian. 1938. "Japanese frivolity. Suppression of dance halls." *The West Australian*, January 25, p. 15.

West, Mark D. 2006. *Secrets, Sex, and Spectacle: The Rules of Scandal in Japan and the United States*. Chicago: University of Chicago Press.

Williams, Rosalind. 1982. *Dream Worlds: Mass Consumption in Late Nineteenth-Century France*. Berkeley: University of California Press.

Windolf, Jim. 2009. "Addicted to Cute." *Vanity Fair*, December. Online at http://www.vanityfair.com/culture/features/2009/12/cuteness-200912 [accessed November 15, 2011].

Wyck House. 2009. "A national historic landmark home and garden." Online at http://www.wyck.org/ [accessed December 31, 2011].

Yamakawa Kikue. 1929. "Gendai shokugyō fujinron" (A discussion of contemporary professional working women). *Chūō kōron* (January): 57–64.

Yamazaki Takashi, director. 2005. *Always: San-chōme no yūhi* (Always: Sunset on Third Street). Tōhō Company, Ltd.

Yamazaki Takashi, director. 2007. *Always zoku: San-chōme no yūhi* (Always: Sunset on Third Street 2). Tōhō Company, Ltd.

Yanagi, Miwa. 2007. *Elevator Girls*. Kyoto: Seigensha Art Publishing.

Yano, Christine R. 2003. *Tears of Longing: Nostalgia and the Nation in Japanese Popular Song*. Cambridge, MA: Harvard University Press.

———. 2006. *Crowning the Nice Girl: Gender, Ethnicity, and Culture in Hawai'i's Cherry Blossom Festival*. Honolulu: University of Hawai'i Press.

———. 2011. *Airborne Dreams: Japanese American Stewardesses and Pan American World Airways*. Durham, NC: Duke University Press.

Yasuki Chiba, director. 1940. *Hideko no ōendanchō* (Hideko the Cheerleader). Nano Eiga.

Yokomitsu Riichi. 2001. *Shanghai: A Novel by Yokomitsu Riichi*. Translated with a postscript by Dennis Washburn. Ann Arbor: Center for Japanese Studies, University of Michigan.

Yomiuri Shinbun. 1909. "Henshūya yori geisha gāru wa ima ya seikai-go" (According to an editorial house, geisha girl is now part of global language). *Yomiuri Shinbun*, November 24, p. 2.

———. 1925. "Ōsaka no Daimaru de joten'in no gāru gaido o tsukuru" (Daimaru in Ōsaka creates girl guide saleswomen). *Yomiuri Shinbun*, December 18, p. 7.

———. 1929a. "'Shōkōki gāru' ga Nihon ni mo dekita" ('We have 'up-down controller girl' in Japan, too). *Yomiuri Shinbun*, April 8, p. 3.

———. 1929b. "Fujin shokugyō no shinshutsu-buri: Erebētā no onna untenshu" (An advance in women's occupations: Woman elevator driver). *Yomiuri Shinbun*, July 15, p. 3.

———. 1934. "Shirokiya kara tobiori jisatsu: Hen no shōkōki-jō" (Jumping suicide from Shirokiya: The strange elevator girl). *Yomiuri Shinbun*, August 15, p. 7.

———. 1941. "Supai ni newareru onna" (Women targeted by spies). *Yomiuri Shinbun*, January 15.

———. 2008. "Pointo wa bidakuon" (Nasalization is key). *Yomiuri Shinbun*, March 14. Online at http://osaka.yomiuri.co.jp/depa/de80314a.htm [accessed September 14, 2009].

Yonekawa Akihiko. 1998. *Yonde ninmari: otoko to onna no hayari kotoba* (Read Them and Smile: Popular Words for Men and Women). Tokyo: Shōgakukan.

Yoshida Akio, Katō Hirotake, Kitagawa Masakazau, directors. 1992. *Tōkyō erebētā gāru* (Tokyo Elevator Girl). Tokyo: Tokyo Broadcasting System.

Young Lady. 1969. "Ano Itō Kinuko-san (hattōshin no sekai-teki bijo) ga nenshita no eriito kanryō to himitsu kekkon shita" (Miss Itō Kinuko [World-class beauty famous for perfect figure] secretly married a younger man, an elite civil servant). *Young Lady*, February, pp. 22–24.

Young, Louise. 1999. "Marketing the modern: Department stores, consumer culture, and the new middle class in interwar Japan." *International Labor and Working-Class History*, no. 55: 52–70.

Yusa, Michiko. 2002. *Zen and Philosophy: An Intellectual Biography of Nishida Kitarō*. Honolulu: University of Hawai'i Press.

Zinser, Ben. 1953. "American men 'cold' but 'awfully nice,' says Miss Uruguay." *Long Beach Independent Press-Telegram*, July 16.

Contributors

Alisa Freedman, Associate Professor of Japanese Literature and Film, University of Oregon, is engaged in several interdisciplinary research projects and literary translations that explore how the modern urban experience has shaped human subjectivity, cultural production, and gender roles. Her major publications include *Tokyo in Transit: Japanese Culture on the Rails and Road* (Stanford University Press, 2010) and an annotated translation of Kawabata Yasunari's *The Scarlet Gang of Asakusa* (University of California Press, 2005). Freedman has published articles on Japanese modernism, youth culture, humor as critique, nerd culture, media discourses on new social groups, and the intersections of literature and digital media. Her current research projects include explorations of changing images of working women on Japanese television and Japanese adaptations of global children's culture.

Laura Miller, Ei'ichi Shibusawa-Seigo Arai Professor of Japanese Studies and Professor of Anthropology, University of Missouri–St. Louis, has published widely on topics such as the wizard boom, girls' slang, and print club photos in Japan. She is the author of *Beauty Up: Exploring Contemporary Japanese Body Aesthetics* (University of California Press, 2006). She is the co-editor, with Jan Bardsley, of *Bad Girls of Japan* (Palgrave, 2005) and *Manners and Mischief: Gender, Power, and Etiquette in Japan* (University of California Press, 2011). She is currently working on a new book, *Japanese Girl Stuff*, which explores creative language, activities, and innovations in girl culture.

Christine Yano, Professor of Anthropology, University of Hawai'i, is a former contributing editor of the Society for East Asian Anthropology section of *Anthropology News*. She is the author of *Tears of Longing: Nostalgia and the Nation in Japanese Popular Song* (Harvard East Asia Center, 2002), *Crowning the Nice Girl: Gender, Ethnicity, and Culture in Hawai'i's Cherry Blossom Festival* (University of Hawai'i Press, 2006), and *Airborne Dreams: Race, Gender, Class, and Globalism in Postwar America* (Duke University Press, 2010).

Jan Bardsley, Associate Professor of Japanese Humanities and Chair of the Department of Asian Studies, University of North Carolina at Chapel Hill, is the author of *The Bluestockings of Japan: New Women Essays and Fiction from Seitô, 1911–1916* (University of Michigan Center for Japanese Studies, 2007) and co-editor, with Laura Miller, of *Bad Girls of Japan* (Palgrave, 2005) and *Manners and Mischief: Gender, Power, and Etiquette in Japanese Conduct Literature* (University of California Press, 2011). She is the recipient of the 2011 Hiratsuka Raichō Prize.

Elise Edwards, Associate Professor, Department of History and Anthropology, Butler University, is completing a book manuscript about soccer, corporate sport, the 1990s recession, and national identity in Japan, which is tentatively titled *Fields for the Future: Soccer and Citizens in Japan at the Turn of the 21st Century*. She also is pursuing a project on the intersections between Japan's "hometown" soccer movement, grassroots activism, volunteerism, and the ever-evolving relationships between public and private entities in contemporary Japan. Edwards both played and coached soccer in the Japanese women's L-League in the mid-1990s and continues to enjoy her "side-job" as a goalkeeping coach with Butler University's women's soccer team.

Sabine Frühstück, Professor of Modern Japanese Cultural Studies, University of California, Santa Barbara, is the author of *Colonizing Sex: Sexology and Social Control in Modern Japan* (University of California Press, 2003) and *Uneasy Warriors: Gender, Memory and Popular Culture in the Japanese Army* (University of California Press, 2007), which was translated into Japanese as *Fuan na heishitachi: Nippon Jieitai Kenkyū* (Akashi shoten, 2008). She is the co-editor, with Anne Walthall, of *Recreating Japanese Men* (University of California Press, 2011). Frühstück is pursuing a transnational, multidisciplinary analysis of varying configurations of infantilism and militarism, roughly between the Russo-Japanese War of 1904–05 and the ongoing war in Iraq, tentatively titled, "Playing War." She is also completing two global history essays: "Sexuality and the Nation State" for a volume to be published by Blackwell and "The Sexual History of World War II" for the *Cambridge History of World War I* to be published by Cambridge University Press.

Sally Hastings, Associate Professor of History, Purdue University, is co-editor of the *U.S.-Japan Women's Journal* and author of *Neighborhood and Nation in Tokyo, 1905–1937* (University of Pittsburgh Press, 1995). Her essays on the history of Japanese women include "Assassins, Madonnas, and Career Women: Reflections on Six Decades of Women's Suffrage in Japan" (*Asian Cultural Studies*, no. 35, 2009), "Empress Nagako and the Family State" (in *Handbook of the Emperors of Modern Japan*, ed. Ben-Ami Shillony; Brill, 2008), "Gender and Sexuality in Modern Japan" (in *A Companion to Japanese History*, ed. William Tsutsui; Blackwell, 2007), and "Hatoyama Haruko: Ambitious Woman"

(*The Human Tradition in Modern Japan*, ed. Anne Walthall; Scholarly Resources, 2002). In 2008 she held a Fulbright Fellowship in Japan to investigate the first generation of women legislators.

Vera Mackie is Australian Research Council (ARC) Future Fellow and Professor of Asian Studies, in the Institute of Social Transformation Research, Faculty of Arts, University of Wollongong. Major publications include *Gurōbaruka to jendā hōyshō* [Globalisation and Representations of Gender] (Ochanomizu Shobō, 2003); *Feminism in Modern Japan: Citizenship, Embodiment and Sexuality* (Cambridge University Press, 2003); *Relationships: Japan and Australia, 1870s–1950s* (University of Melbourne History Monographs and RMIT Publishing, 2001), co-edited with Paul Jones; *Human Rights and Gender Politics: Asia-Pacific Perspectives* (Routledge, 2000), co-edited with Anne Marie Hilsdon, Martha Macintyre, and Maila Stivens; and *Creating Socialist Women in Japan: Gender, Labour and Activism, 1900–1937* (Cambridge University Press, 1997). She was a member of an international collaborative research project "The Modern Girl in East Asia," which published an edited collection *Modan gāru to shokuminchiteki kindai: Higashi Ajia ni okeru teikoku, shihon, jendā* [The Modern Girl and Colonial Modernity: Empire, Capital and Gender in East Asia] (Iwanami, 2010), and she contributed an essay on modernism in Japan to the *Oxford Handbook of Modernisms* (Oxford University Press, 2010).

Yoko McClain, Professor Emerita, University of Oregon, was born Yoko Matsuoka in Tokyo. She came to the United States to attend the University of Oregon in 1952 as a recipient of the GARIOA (Government Aid for Relief in Occupied Areas) grant, predecessor of the current Fulbright Fellowship. She went on to earn a graduate degree and taught Japanese modern language and literature at the University of Oregon from 1964 until her retirement in 1994. McClain published widely on Japanese language, literature, and culture, and about her grandfather, author Natsume Sōseki. Her books include the *Handbook of Modern Japanese Grammar* (Books Nippan, 1992) and *Sōseki's Granddaughter's America* (*Sōseki no mago no Amerika*; Shinchōsha, 1984). McClain passed away in November 2011.

Carol Stabile is Director, Center for the Study of Women in Society, and Professor in the School of Journalism and Communication and the Department of Women's and Gender Studies, University of Oregon. Her interdisciplinary research interests focus on gender, race, class, and sexual orientation in media and popular culture She is the author of *Feminism and the Technological Fix*; editor of *Turning the Century: Essays in Media and Cultural Studies*; co-editor of *Prime Time Animation: Television Animation and American Culture*; and author of *White Victims, Black Villains: Gender, Race, and Crime News in U.S. Culture*. Stabile is finishing a book on women writers and the broadcast blacklist in the 1950s, titled *Black and White and Red All Over: Women Writers and the Television Blacklist*. In addition, she is conducting ethnographic research for a project that looks at gender-swapping practices in massive multiplayer online games. She is one of the founders of the University of Oregon Digital Scholars and a founding member of Fembot, an online collaboration of scholars conducting research on gender, new media, and technology.

Elise Tipton is Honorary Associate Professor of Japanese Studies, University of Sydney. Tipton's research focuses on the relationship between society and the state during the interwar years, especially regarding attitudes and experiences of modernity in everyday life. She is the author of *Modern Japan: A Social and Political History* ([Routledge 2008) and co-editor, with John Clark, of *Being Modern in Japan: Culture and Society from the 1910s to the 1930s* (University of Hawai'i Press 2000). A recent publication relevant to her chapter in this volume is "The Department Store: Producing Modernity in Interwar Japan," in *Rethinking Japanese Modernism*, ed. Roy Starrs (Global Oriental, 2012).

Notes

Chapter I

1. The taxi dancer and the saleswoman were the subjects of two early ethnographic studies (Cressey 1932; Donovan 1929).

2. Kon Wajirō (1888–1973) was the leader of a team of ethnographers who observed, surveyed, and sketched social practices in the 1920s in order to understand and record what they perceived as a turning point in Japan's capitalist growth. (For a sketch from their 1931 study of sock wrinkles, see Freedman 2010: 192.)

3. Since 1984, the Jiyūkokumin-sha publishing company has sponsored the annual U-Can survey of new media buzzwords.

4. An anonymous reader contributed greatly to this paragraph and the next.

5. The name of the dress might have been adapted from the word "*pa-to*," meaning "very" in Osaka dialect, for its very wide hem.

6. Media Factory is a subsidiary of the human resources company Recruit Co., Ltd., which is active in job matchmaking.

7. The initial impetus for this volume was one of those serendipitous meetings at academic events in which the similarities between people's individual work was too fortuitous to ignore. The idea arose when Alisa Freedman and Christine Yano met at a 2008 conference on Japanese transnational fandoms at the University of Wollongong, New South Wales, Australia, organized by Mark McLelland and Fran Martin. Their conversation expanded in a panel discussion at the 2009 Association for Asian Studies Annual Meeting, which included Laura Miller. The concept for the book was solidified at a conference held at and funded largely by the University of Oregon in 2010. In short, the gestation of this book—from a transnational workshop in Australia to a large interdisciplinary conference, including the relationships forged in the process—is as important to us as the resulting work. This volume represents nothing short of the mobility that guides the field of Japanese studies, across nations, disciplines, and generations.

Chapter 2

I would like to acknowledge Waseda University for providing hospitality and library access for me as an Exchange Researcher. Support from the School of Languages and Cultures at the University of Sydney enabled me to present an early version of this chapter at the Association for Asian Studies conference in Chicago in 2009.

1. The "second wave" of women's liberation arose in the early 1970s.

Chapter 3

I would like to thank Iino Masakazu at Waseda University in Tokyo for his support. I am very grateful to Koide Izumi and Kadokura Yuriko at the Shibusawa Eiichi Memorial Foundation for the help I received using their collection of *shashi* (corporate histories that are self-published by the companies). At Ohio State University, Maureen Donovan and Choi Hyejeong assisted me with their shashi and manga collections. I am grateful to this volume's co-editors, as well as to colleagues Jan Bardsley, Laura Hein, William Tsutsui, and Rebecca Copeland for their feedback and comments. Permission from Kure Rena, Ambai Akiko, Katō Arata, and Katō Nana to use the Media Factory image is greatly appreciated.

1. One copy of the commercial is online at http://www.spike.com/video/japanese-mcdonalds/2809272 [accessed May 28, 2010].

2. The related Japanese dichotomies of front/back (*omote/ura*), inside/outside (*uchi/soto*), and public face/private feelings (*tatemae/honne*) as a way to explain Japanese behavior became basic fare in postwar Japan anthropology, popular business books, and in the "theories about the Japanese" (*Ninhonjin-ron*) camp. Because these are linguistically marked terms, there is a tendency to imagine that the distinction between intimate domains and public performance, a Goffmanesque shift we find in all societies, is somehow uniquely Japanese. Although linguistic markedness suggests a difference in conscious awareness, it does not mean a qualitative difference in interactive importance.

3. An analysis of the elevator girl that goes beyond the scope or intent of this chapter might include examination of the role of the passengers, her relationship to management (including strikes), and changes in salary and working conditions.

4. The sixteen-year-old was getting out of the elevator at his condo with his bicycle when the lift moved upward with the doors still open, wedging him in and causing asphyxiation.

5. Creighton (1995, 1996) has discussed some of this corporate training in her research on department stores.

6. The elevator girl allegedly bows two thousand times or more a day, an assertion purportedly based on a "study," but actually just a floating factoid found in numerous business books and news articles (an example is Alston 2005: 39).

7. Elevator girls also have their own occupational slang. For example, because they are usually assigned to a specific car, they may be known inside the store as "the number-two-car elevator girl" (*nigō ki no erega*).

8. The Matsuzakaya website is at http://www.matsuzakaya.co.jp/corporate/history/honshi/syowa.shtml [accessed January 2, 2010].

Chapter 4

This chapter draws on research conducted for two projects funded by the Australian Research Council, "The Politics of Visual Culture in Modern Japan" and "The Cultural History of the Body in Modern Japan;" and an international collaborative research project, "Colonial Modernity and the Modern Girl in East Asia," funded by the Japan Society for the Promotion of Science, and coordinated by the Institute for Gender Studies, Ochanomizu University, Tokyo. I am indebted to Taylor Atkins, Hugh de Ferranti, Alisa Freedman, Mark McLelland, Laura Miller, Erik Ropers, and Christine Yano for advice and support.

1. See also Onchi Kōshirō's woodblock print "Dancehall" from the series "One Hundred Scenes of New Tokyo" (reproduced in Chiba-shi Bijutsukan 2000: 142).

2. Social dancing had been introduced to Japan in the 1880s, when the new government built the Rokumeikan pavilion and hosted balls for elite international visitors (Mehl 2005: 157–77).

3. The dancers' changing room thus took on the character of a forbidden space. See Tada Michio's imagining of the dancers in their changing room in *Dancers and Drawers*, where he reiterates that he is describing a space that men are not supposed to enter (Tada 1931: 2–3).

4. This is the ballroom depicted in Auguste Renoir's painting "Bal du Moulin de la Galette" (1876).

5. See also the mention of a Filipino band in a Shanghai dancehall in Yokomitsu Riichi's novel *Shanghai* (Yokomitsu 2001: 80).

6. These are also the sites portrayed in modernist fiction (Omori 2003: 18, 53; Gralla 2010: 83–106).

7. In this chapter, I use "dancehall girls" when referring to Japanese sources, which use the term "*dansu-jō*." I reserve the phrase "taxi dancer" for English-language sources. I have not seen the phrase "taxi dancer" in Japanese-language sources, although the system of selling tickets for dances was similar to that used in the United States taxi-dance halls. Needless to say, the use of words and suffixes describing women as "girls" or "daughters" emphasizes femininity and infantilizes these working women.

8. In *Dancers and Drawers*, Tada describes a young woman who chose to work in a dancehall rather than doing office work, because she could then send more money home to support her younger brother's education (1931: 10–12). While this is, of course, a fictional representation, it provides an insight into common understandings of the choices made by women workers at the time.

9. Several other prints of the time depict the fatigue of women in service industries. See Ōta Saburō's 1914 print "Café Waitress," which depicts a woman alone in a café, despondently resting her hands and chin on the back of a bentwood chair. The print is in two tones: black and sandy beige (reproduced, for example, in Ajioka et al. 2000: 47). See also the photograph of lines of dancehall girls waiting for partners, reproduced in Sato (2003: 62).

10. In her memoir about her time in the labor movement of the 1920s and 1930s, Nakamoto Takako (1903–1991) notes that, in roughly same year, a female factory

worker would receive forty to fifty *sen* a day, with the possibility of a bonus depending on productivity. However, twenty or thirty *sen* would be deducted for meals, leaving the factory worker with around twenty *sen* a day (Nakamoto 1973: 14). Andrew Gordon (1992: 134) reports that the daily wage of a young male worker in 1923 was around one hundred and fifty *sen*.

11. Page numbers hereafter refer to Anthony Chambers's English translation (1986).

12. On Yamamura Kōka [Toyonari], see Menzies (1998: 157) and Brown (2001: 32); on the New Carlton Hotel, see Wakeman (1996: 108).

13. See also *Golden Fugue* (*Ōgon tonsōkyoku*), a novel by Abe Masao (1902–1957; also known as Hisao Jūran), which includes a character of mixed Chinese and Japanese parentage who works in a Shanghai dancehall (Abe 1935; cited in Aoyama 2012: 54).

14. It seems, however, that dancehalls were not found in colonial Korea. Kim Jinsong reproduces an open letter from a group of café proprietors, *kisaeng*, waitresses, and actresses in Seoul who requested the colonial police to allow them to open a dancehall there (Kim 2005: 56–60). However, 1937 was probably too late for such a petition, for the suppression of dancehalls on the mainland of Japan was by then well advanced.

15. The Recreation and Amusement Association (RAA) was established by the Japanese government in preparation for the landing of the occupying armies. Most attention has been paid to the brothels that were run by the RAA, which in recent scholarship have been linked with the enforced military prostitution of the wartime period. It seems that the RAA also ran dancehalls in the early months of the Occupation. On the RAA, see Dower (1999: 127–131) and Tanaka (2002: 133–166).

Chapter 5

1. The other airlines listed in the *Life* article included Qantas, BOAC, Scandinavian Air Service, KLM, Air France, Lufthansa, Air India, Northwest, Alitalia, and Cathay Pacific.

2. *Coffee, Tea, or Me* prompted its own series of books, from the first 1967 publication to *The Coffee Tea or Me Girls' Round-the-World Diary* (1970), *The Coffee Tea or Me Girls Lay It on the Line* (1972), and *The Coffee Tea or Me Girls Get Away from It All* (1974).

3. Some men were traveling to South America to establish and maintain business connections through existing Japanese emigrant networks.

4. Note that Harvey uses this descriptor as a condition of postmodernity. However, I argue that this kind of logical outgrowth of modernity of the Jet Age leads to what Harvey categorizes as a post-modern state.

5. Throughout this paper I use the term "stewardess" primarily because this label reflects common usage during the historical period under study. Some stewardesses took pains to remind me that they were stewardesses at the time, not "flight attendants."

6. Pan American's history of race-based (and gendered) hiring is long and includes several significant milestones (see Yano 2011: Appendix B).

7. The *Life* magazine also noted that some airlines (although notably, not Pan Am) paid Japanese stewardesses less than other stewardesses: "Another inducement is that Japanese stewardesses based in Tokyo can work at a lower pay scale" (*Life* 1967: 42). Pan

Am required its stewardesses to relocate to the United States—specifically to Honolulu, the Asian-language base. There, all stewardesses were paid the same wage.

8. In the early years of commercial air travel, stewardesses were recruited from the ranks of nurses, combining their skills as caregivers and medical professionals.

9. Ironically, in the early postwar years, Japanese passengers often felt they received better treatment from Pan Am than they did from Japan Air Lines. According to one person with whom I spoke, in the 1950s, before many Japanese traveled overseas, the Japanese stewardesses on Japan Air Lines looked askance at fellow nationals for their lack of worldliness and treated them accordingly. These same passengers felt they received better service from Pan Am, which treated all passengers more equitably.

10. All names are pseudonyms, except for those who I identify in conjunction with their specific historical contribution. I provide dates of Pan Am employment parenthetically. Many Japanese women's employment ended in 1986, when Pan Am relinquished its Pacific routes to United Airlines.

11. At the time of their initial employment, the airline's rules required women who married to quit their jobs. Even after unions pressured the airlines to eliminate discrimination on the basis of marital status in 1968, several women I interviewed chose to quit upon marrying. In this, they were following not only the former dictate of the company but, more important, the social norms of Japan.

12. The "Pan Am smile" became a derogatory term used in popular psychology, referring to the frozen mask of performed emotion that was a symbol of trained, automatic service that lacked sincerity. Of all the airlines, Pan Am may have been singled out because of its size and dominance, leading to an assumption of arrogance. But it also may have been singled out because of a company ethos that was more distant and formal than, for example, some American domestic carriers. Pan Am's service was not exactly that of United Airlines' "friendly skies." Rather, it offered an upper-class level of service that gave customers the best food and drink, while maintaining a respectful distance.

13. *The Donna Reed Show* was a prime-time family comedy from 1958 to 1966 produced by the American Broadcasting Company (ABC), starring Donna Reed as nurse-turned-housewife Donna Stone, Carl Benz as her pediatrician husband Dr. Alex Stone, and their two children, teenager Mary and younger brother Jeff. Like other American family television comedies from the 1950s and 1960s, such as *Leave It to Beaver, The Adventures of Ozzie and Harriet*, and *Father Knows Best, The Donna Reed Show* depicted an idyllic American nuclear family living in suburbia, with which the 1950s and 1960s has since become identified.

Chapter 6

I would like to thank Junko Kawakami for her help in securing rights to images. Research for this chapter was funded by the following University of Oregon programs: Center for Asian and Pacific Studies, Center for the Study of Women and Society, Oregon Humanities Center, and Department of East Asian Languages and Literatures.

1. Although still few in number and found mostly on charter buses, male guides

are becoming more common, but their images do not circulate widely. For more on bus conductors, see Freedman (2010).

2. Laura Miller discusses a manners book for men that advises against offensive hand gestures and instead recommends indicating objects by using the "tour guide palm" (Miller 2011: 231).

3. "*Orai*" was also used in phrases, including "*mae orai*" (all clear in front), "*ushiro orai*" (all clear behind), and "*hasha orai*" (Okay! Go!) (Nakagawa 1986: 166). "*Orai*" is now commonly used by other male and female workers, such as train conductors and truck drivers.

4. Tours were offered only in Japanese. Hato Bus started Tokyo tours in English in 1952. The peak number of international passengers, approximately 160,000, was in 1960 (Uranaka 2001).

5. For descriptions of the Hato Bus tours from the 1960s through 2010, see Nakano (2010): 18–38. The list of 2011 offerings is found in Tanaka (2011): 98–109.

6. For more on the sixtieth anniversary celebration, see, for example, Nakano (2010): 18-26.

7. An English language example is *Asahi News* 2008.

8. The video can be seen at http://momoya-kcm-en.blogspot.com/2008/01/momoya -tv-ads054-1968-bus-conductor.html. Bus guides have been parodied in global represen- tations of Japan. For example, in the 1989 American television special *Big Bird in Japan*, Big Bird is bullied by a bus guide, who leaves him and his dog Barkley behind because they are late in returning from a scheduled stop in Tokyo.

9. The 1940 film *Hideko the Cheerleader* (*Hideko no ōendanchō*) was also named for Takamine Hideko. Both *Hideko the Cheerleader* and *Hideko the Bus Conductor* were produced by the Nano eiga company.

10. Naruse adapted six stories by Hayashi, who died in 1951 before the films were made. See, for example, Russell (2009). Hayashi was inspired to write *Inazuma* by the life of her own mother and by a reading of the Strindberg play *Thunder* (*Ovader*) she heard while living in Paris (Ericson 1997: 78).

11. There have been three Japanese singers named Columbia Rose. The one who sang "Tokyo Bus Girl" is now referred to as the "First Columbia Rose" (Shodai Koro- mubia Rōzu, born 1933). She was followed by "Columbia Rose, II" (Nidaime Koromubia Rōzu, born 1944) and "Columbia Rose, III" (Sandaime Koromubia Rōzu, born 1982).

12. Two types of double-decker Hato Buses—one navy blue and the other pink— decorated with Hello Kitty inside and out were available in 2008. Passengers did not know which they would ride until the bus arrived. Both buses were staffed with Hato Bus guides in ordinary uniforms. The seats inside both were embossed with Hello Kitty. Her head glowed in the dark on the ceiling.

13. Hello Kitty was made tourism ambassador to Asia by the Japanese government in May 2008 with the idea that she could help erase memories of wartime atrocities and other issues plaguing the relationship between Japan and other Asian nations.

14. Hello Kitty dressed as a 1950s Tokyo bus conductor in 2006 was part of the Local Kitty (Gotochi Kitty) series, which began in 1998 with Lavender Kitty (marketed only in

Hokkaido); the number of offerings increased beginning around 2001. In this extensive array of collectibles and stationery goods, Hello Kitty dresses as local figures and landmarks. She represents every prefecture and various historical moments, unifying the nation through her adorable image and teaching Japanese culture. Examples are pictured on the website http://gotochikitty.com [accessed October 16, 2012]

15. More information and sample images are at http://www.digbook.jp/product_info.php/products_id/10155 [accessed January 22, 2012].

16. One copy of the music video can be seen at http://www.youtube.com/watch?v=pVoGQDh52Hk&feature=fvst [accessed October 16, 2012]

17. One copy of the music video can be seen at http://www.youtube.com/watch?v=VSNe8UwwVIE [accessed October 16, 2012].

18. At KidZania Tokyo, children can also play flight attendant, firefighter, chef, department store worker, and doctor, among other occupations.

Chapter 7

1. Japan's postwar armed forces were founded on July 8, 1950, as the National Police Reserve (Keisatsu Yobitai) in the wake of the U.S. involvement in the Korean War and were renamed and inaugurated as the Self-Defense Forces (SDF) (Jieitai) on July 1, 1954. In 2004, the SDF celebrated their fiftieth anniversary. In the SDF, Japan has a full-fledged military establishment complete with three services (ground, maritime, and air), the latest military technology (tanks, ships, and planes, as well as a variety of state-of-the-art weaponry, albeit no nuclear weaponry), and all of the organizational accompaniments common to armed forces (territorial divisions, brigades, and training methods). The army, or Ground Self-Defense Force, consisted of around 148,000 troops compared to Air Self-Defense Force with 46,000 and the Maritime Self-Defense Force with 44,000 service members. Most of the service members who were consulted and/or interviewed for this chapter are Ground Self-Defense Force members (Bōeichō 2005: 121).

2. This chapter draws from the methods of ethnography and cultural studies, including intensive interviews and participant observation, as well as the analysis of documents, popular texts, and visual materials. I spent approximately nineteen months between the summer of 1998 and the spring of 2004 conducting fieldwork in Japan and returned for more interviews in summer of 2010. Altogether I interviewed about 195 people in and around the SDF. Ten percent of them were women, or about twice the percentage that serve in the armed forces overall. My interviewees included service members of all ranks, typically between eighteen and fifty-two years of age, and almost all professional specializations.

3. The SDF had deployed as many as 107,000 personnel to seven disaster-hit prefectures, including Iwate, Miyagi, and Fukushima. They have been engaged in search and rescue operations and have helped prepare meals for survivors at evacuation centers. The SDF also participated in attempts to cool the crippled reactors at the Fukushima Daiichi nuclear power plant by spraying water from the air and ground (*Japan Times* 2011).

4. All the enlisted service members, male and female, I interviewed mentioned

poverty, the desire to have a secure job, and the opportunities to acquire skills without having to pay for the training as important reasons for joining the SDF.

5. Composite from several interviews the author conducted in 2001.

6. Interview with the author conducted in June 2003.

7. Interview with the author conducted in June 2003.

8. The official website of the Ministry of Defense used to have an "image gallery" that contained dozens of recruitment posters produced since the 1960s. This gallery is no longer available. Some of the posters described in this chapter were published in my book *Uneasy Warriors: Gender, Memory and Popular Culture in the Japanese Army* (2007). Others are included in Satō Fumika (2000).

9. Concerned about their reputation and their legal status, recruitment officers across Japan explicitly pursue "normal/ordinary people" as opposed to extremists.

10. "Y.M.C.A." is a 1978 song by the *Village People* that became a hit in January 1979. Taken at face value, its *lyrics* extol the virtues of the *Young Men's Christian Association* (YMCA). In the gay culture from which the group sprang, the song was implicitly understood as celebrating the YMCA's reputation as a popular *cruising* and *hookup* spot, particularly for the younger gay men to whom it was addressed.

11. "Japan as child" is a trope that has been evoked by a broad range of commentators over the years, ranging from General MacArthur to pop artist cum billionaire Murakami Takashi (Frühstück 2011).

12. *Hea nūdo* (hair nude) is typically a category of nude photography that shows pubic hair, depictions of which were censored in mainstream media until the 1990s. In this case, however, women are shown in bathing suits, not in the nude, while covering parts of their faces and/or shoulders with their long hair.

Chapter 8

1. The tweet record inspired by Nadeshiko Japan also exceeded the pace of tweets at the conclusion of the Brazilian men's shocking loss to Paraguay in the Copa America just fifteen minutes later. For these and other details, see Fanning 2011.

2. The L-League was renamed the "Nadeshiko League" in 2004, the year the official nickname "Nadeshiko Japan" was created by the JFA in an effort to increase the visibility and appeal of the Women's national team. The name "Nadeshiko Japan" was selected through a contest and was chosen from over 2,700 entries submitted by fans across the nation. "*Nadeshiko*" invokes the nostalgic ideal of a Japanese woman who dutifully serves family and state (Pincus 2002: 180–181; Endō 2006: 139). Despite these overtly nationalist and conservatively gendered connotations that were presumably attractive to the male-dominated leadership of the JFA, "*nadeshiko*" has accrued several additional associations—graceful, cute, delicate, persistent, and strong—due to its connection with the women's team and its rather free and uninformed use by both Japanese and international journalists (Ōtsuka 2011). It is ironic to note that the term "*Yamato nadeshiko*" was used during World War II as a euphemism for prostitutes ("comfort women" [*ianfu*] being the most common) who worked in military brothels (Watanabe 1997: 310).

3. In 2010, the JFA registered 25,278 female players, a number that paled in comparison with the men's participation rate, which topped 850,000 (Japan Football Association 2011). Japanese female player numbers are even more severely dwarfed by participation rates in the United States, where over 40 percent of the estimated 24.5 million youths through adults who play the sport are female, and the number of elite players registered with the United States Soccer Federation now exceeds 1.6 million (FIFA 2007).

4. When we conceptualize "modernity" in the twenty-first century, it is also useful to understand modernity as an attempt to "flee history," or to separate from tradition (Harootunian 2000: xxi). Companies working to reinvent themselves at the twilight of the bubble economy and young female players eager to move beyond more traditional forms of femininity were equally invested in soccer owing to their perception of its ability to provide this modern escape.

5. "Serena" was a reformulated and female version of the Italian word "*sereno*" (clear, serene, or calm), which Shiroki Industries staff rather liberally translated as "*sawayaka*" (refreshing, invigorating, and clean) and as "*harebare to shita*" (clear, bright, and cheerful). In media statements, team representatives claimed that "Serena" captured the essence of female youth.

6. The first sexual harassment suit brought by a woman against her employer in Japan was in 1989 (West 2006: 243).

7. This image captures a sense of homogeneity and group precision usually not present in soccer photos.

8. In January 1995, 100,000 yen was roughly equivalent to $990.

Chapter 9

1. I would like to thank Kyodo News Service for permission to use images of Itō Kinuko in this chapter.

2. "Image-text" is Moseley's term for "the centrality of the visual, the image, 'the look' in relation to this particular star" (Moseley 2002: 31).

3. The Miss Nisei Week Festival Queen competition is the longest-running of the Japanese American beauty pageants. The official website is http://www.niseiweek.org/. For more information on this contest, see Nomura and Hune (2003); King-O'Riain (2006); and Yano (2006).

Chapter 10

The research for my article was supported by a 2009 travel grant from the Northeast Asia Council of the Association for Asian Studies. The College of Liberal Arts, Purdue University supported travel to the Wellesley College Archives.

1. Two other women who, like Mishima, wrote about their experiences were Yoko Matsuoka (1916–1979, a different person from Yoko Matsuoka McClain, who wrote the essay that is Chapter 11 in this book) and Haru Matsukata Reischauer (1915–1998). Matsuoka graduated from Swarthmore College in Pennsylvania in 1939 and Reischauer from Principia College in Illinois in 1937 (Matsuoka 1952; Reischauer 1986).

2. For the sake of simplicity, I use "Tsuda College," an English designation of the

institution adopted early on, although the school began as the "Girls English Academy" and changed its name several times before it was recognized as a university after the war.

3. These exact words are used by Yoko Matsuoka (1952: 101).

4. The experiences of the few Japanese women who traveled to Europe for education are beyond the scope of this study.

5. Two biographies of Tsuda Umeko contain additional information about the girls who traveled with the Iwakura Mission (Furuki 1991b; Rose 1992).

6. Takeda Kin studied at Wellesley and Okami Kei at the Women's Medical College of Pennsylvania.

7. The four Japanese women who graduated from Mount Holyoke College in the 1890s were dependent upon ad hoc arrangements.

8. Tsuda had welcomed Bacon to Japan to teach at the Peeresses' School in 1888, and she had visited Bacon at Hampton Institute in Virginia in 1890 (Rose 1992: 79, 96).

9. Mrs. Greene went to the United States in 1908, where she underwent surgery. She returned to Japan in 1909 and died April 18, 1910 (Greene 1927: 335, 338–340). Fanny Greene remained in Japan until her father's death in 1913 (Wellesley College Archives, Alumnae Biographical Files, Fanny Bradley Greene, 1894).

10. Florence Rhodes Pitman Gardiner (1854–1930), who lived near the school, was enlisted to teach three hours a week (Furuki 1991a: 403). Gardiner, who arrived in Japan as a single missionary in 1877, married James MacDonald Gardiner (1857–1925), an Episcopalian missionary in Japan from 1880. "Miss Schereschewsky" was undoubtedly a relative of Samuel Isaac Joseph Schereschewsky (1831–1906), an Episcopalian missionary to China who lived in Tokyo from 1897 until his death in 1906 (Takeuchi 1995: 83, 176–177).

11. Among them were Kawai Michi in 1904, Suzuki Utako in 1906, Kawashima Yoshiko in 1909, Hoshino Ai in 1912, Yamada Koto in 1916, Kasuya Yoshi in 1923, and Fujita Taki in 1925.

12. A student at Tsuda from 1905 to 1907, Tsuji (Okonogi) Matsu went to the United States under the sponsorship of the Education Ministry. She studied for two years at Wellesley College before going to Oxford University. Returning to Japan in August 1910, she taught from April 1911 until her marriage in 1917 at the Tokyo Women's Higher Normal School. Beginning in September 1915, she also taught part-time at Tsuda Academy (Tsuda Juku Daigaku 1960: 141). That same year, Uemura Tamaki, the daughter of a prominent Tokyo clergyman, graduated from Wellesley College and soon thereafter began teaching at Tsuda (Haga 1993: 144).

13. Dogura Masa was educated at Dōshisha in Kyoto. Her study at Bryn Mawr, from which she graduated in 1897, was sponsored by Mary Morris and her husband, Wistar (Kawai 1934: 134).

14. Mary M. Haines (1860–1928) served at one point as a teacher at the Friends' School in Tokyo. She lived with her mother, Margaret Vaux Wistar Haines (1831–1917) and her sister Jane (1860–1937), Bryn Mawr class of 1891, and thus a classmate of Tsuda Umeko's (Wyck House 2009).

15. Because Mary Morris's daughter Holly died young, Mary Morris brought up Holly's children, Margaret and Charles Wood.

16. Camp Wohelo was founded in 1907 by Luther Halsey Gulick (1865–1918) and his wife Charlotte, who together founded Camp Fire Girls in 1910. It is not exactly clear why Mishima attended that particular camp, but the Gulick family had long-standing ties to Japan. Luther Gulick's brother Sidney was a Congregational missionary there from 1888 to 1913. On Sidney Gulick, see Taylor (1984).

17. A list of the recipients of the scholarship and their contributions to women's education can be found in Uchida (2000: 200–201).

Index